MAXED OUT

MAXED OUT

HARD TIMES, EASY CREDIT

JAMES SCURLOCK

4339501003098442772b012

HarperCollins*Publishers*

HarperCollinsPublishers
77–85 Fulham Palace Road,
Hammersmith, London W6 8JB

HarperCollins' website address is: www.harpercollins.co.uk

First published in the USA in 2007 by Scribner
This edition 2007

1 3 5 7 9 10 8 6 4 2

© 2007 James D. Scurlock

James D. Scurlock asserts the moral right to
be identified as the author of this work

Designed by Davina Mock

A catalogue record of this book is
available from the British Library

ISBN-13 978-0-00-724288-7
ISBN-10 0-00-724288-3

Printed and bound in Great Britain by
Clays Ltd, St Ives plc

This book is proudly printed on paper which contains wood
from well-managed forests, certified in accordance with
the rules of the Forest Stewardship Council.
For more information about FSC,
please visit www.fsc.org

Mixed Sources
Product group from well-managed
forests and other controlled sources
www.fsc.org Cert no. SW-COC-1806
© 1996 Forest Stewardship Council

FSC

For Sean, Mitzi, and Yvonne

Acknowledgments

Writing a book about debt was a challenge. Making a film about debt almost proved impossible. On the one hand, debt is an academic topic, mathematical. On the other hand, it is something that pervades most of our lives on a daily basis, personal. These pages contain many of the stories that we couldn't squeeze into ninety minutes of screen time—sometimes because they were too powerful and sometimes because they were too complex to explore without benefit of a narrator. So my deep gratitude to all of those who agreed to tell me their stories, on film and off, to talk openly about a subject that one interviewee aptly called "the last taboo." This book is a testament to their courage. Many have endured pain, humiliation, and even great loss. While I can't imagine what they have suffered, I can hope that these pages do their stories justice.

I also owe an inestimable debt to my mother—my teacher and editor of the last thirty years. And to my father, whose curiosity and remarkable intelligence are inspiring, and to my sister—my oldest friend who has a far more important job than I. Thanks also to Brandon, Fabian, Barbara, Craig, Octavio, and Mark for advice and encouragement. And to Ken, who provided some much needed (and always appreciated) distraction.

On the film side, Lee Thompson did an extraordinary job of finding compelling stories and convincing dozens of people to share them with us. While most of the interviews were conducted, I was privileged to have the companionship of Jon Aaron Aaseng, a fantastic cinematographer and friend whose insights were, as always, invaluable. In editing, I was fortunate to work with Alexis Spraic, a terrific (and unbelievably young) editor who was always challenging, intelligent, and engaged.

Finally, thanks to Melissa Flashman at Trident, who helped convince many publishers that I could write fast enough and well enough, to Claire Roberts for doing the same overseas, and, of course, to Brant Rumble, my very reliable editor, as well as Nan Graham and Susan Moldow at Scribner for providing faith and guidance.

Preface

More Debt Please, We're British

VINCENT: You know what the funniest thing about Europe is?

JULES: What?

VINCENT: It's the little differences. A lotta the same shit we got here, they got there, but there they're a little different.

"I knew it was bad. I just didn't know it was *that* bad." So I've been told countless times now, by those who've seen my film, *Maxed Out*. Usually I smile back in an appropriately patronizing way to confirm that yes, it is that bad; and shame on you for believing it wasn't! Yet for a very long time, I believed that America was as bad as it could possibly get. Why? Because we are the world's most infamous over-consumers, or, as our president patriotically spins it, we are the locomotive of the world's economy. The inspiration for *Maxed Out* was my fellow countrymen and women—who, incidentally, never needed the title explained to them.

But as it turns out, both the film and this book are rooted in a singular misconception. Because as bad as it is in America, it is much worse in the United Kingdom.

How could this be? It remains more than a little baffling. After all, the UK is the land of free healthcare, free education, the land where understatement, restraint and modesty are time-honored virtues. Even the British colonial model was far more responsible—

at least in the purely economic sense—than our own. The British learned to exact taxes from their subjects while we are inclined to borrow from ours—and yours as well, to be honest. And the famous British virtues of rugged individualism and perseverance that we've never quite taken to, the same principles that made going broke an offense punishable by execution up until a couple of hundred years ago as our founding fathers—debtors and speculators themselves—were creating what have become the most liberal bankruptcy laws in the world. True, the British invented both tabloid journalism and reality television, and their fetish for royal gossip seems a tad over-wrought at times, but it is in my hometown of Los Angeles that paparazzi stalk the boutiques of Beverly Hills, broadcasting the latest clothing and accessories chosen by the latest starlets to the shopping masses, who are expected to pay whatever is demanded for a pair of the right jeans and encrust their cellphones with diamonds. How else to explain $1,500 denims and $200 t-shirts?

So my thoughts did not drift across the Atlantic until a year and a half ago, when an esteemed professor I was scheduled to interview abruptly canceled. He was being flown over to London with the Princeton economist Paul Krugman to commemorate a dubious milestone: Britons' accumulation of over £1 trillion in consumer debt, i.e. credit cards, car loans, and virtually every other form of credit one can pile on excluding the home mortgage. The British, I was told, were in a panic. Credit card executives were brought before parliament and grilled; the Queen warned of the consequences; the Financial Services Authority was investigating. Yet, if American history served as any guide, Britons would quickly forget their first trillion. Why? First off, because the number is so huge as to be incomprehensible, and, therefore, forgettable; and second, because there is an inertia about debt that is as futile to resist as it is counter-intuitive. Because the more debt, the fewer consequences—at least in the short term. Debt has a smoothing effect and an air of inevitability. When our national debt passed the trillion dollar mark in the mid 1980s, there was a brief uproar, but then Ronald Reagan blamed the media and everyone seemed to forget about it.

I've been scanning the British press for almost a year now, searching for clues as to how all of this came about in the first place, as well as to glean some idea of what, if anything, the British government intends to do about it. Over the past couple of years, I've found a number of stories which do just that, including the purchase of the most expensive house in the history of mankind (in London), the explosive growth of the collections industry in the UK, the scaling back of government assistance in areas like education and healthcare, including the case of one woman who was denied cancer treatment because of its high cost, a new study showing that the British are learning to rely on their credit cards to buy necessities like gas and groceries, and the ritual berating of financial executives, one of whom, the CEO of Barclays Bank, famously stated that he would not himself use a credit card, which is his bank's most profitable product.

So living in Britain has become increasingly expensive, health services and other public goods are being reduced (which means that their cost is being shifted onto the backs of the working public), and large, trusted financial institutions are peddling products which they know to be so harmful that they themselves won't partake of them. In other words, the UK bears a striking resemblance to the United States—and to a lot of other "wealthy" nations as well. If our own history is any guide—and we've been playing this game a lot longer than you have—things will get quite a bit worse. Bankruptcies will continue to hit records, people will use high-interest credit as a backstop to keep their places in the middle class (including using credit cards to make interest payments on other credit cards), tabloids and Starbucks will proliferate as arbiters of public taste and wise old souls will observe that the society is regressing into a feudal state with only two classes—owners and renters—while politicians wash their hands and say that nothing can be done because the financial industry is too large and too interwoven into the fabric of society to be regulated.

The irony will be so thick that even Alanis Morissette will recognize it. In a period of unparalleled prosperity and stability, more and more people will feel vulnerable and sink into poverty—slowly at first, then with lightning speed. As free-marketers defend the sovereignty of the national currency, the demand for VISA and Mastercard's tender will make the value of the pound sterling less and less relevant. As leaders warn against putting the brakes on a system spiraling wildly out of control, and self-righteously point out that it is up to the consumer alone to inject responsibility into the system, they themselves will pledge the assets of their constituents at an astonishing rate in order to save their wealthiest citizens and corporations from the specter of higher taxes, increasing the burden of the already maxed-out working classes. As this situation deteriorates into unbridled absurdity, you will see inventions such as credit cards specifically issued to pay medical expenses, collection agencies hired to go after soldiers wounded in battle, the sale of personal information from public to private entities and back again, and perhaps even a new bankruptcy scheme which reverts back to the eighteenth century, i.e. a bear trap where lifelong imprisonment is the norm and death the only way for the vast majority to get out from under. All of these scenarios have played out in America and, at one time or another in the very recent past, each has been heralded as solutions to a problem most of us are loathe to admit exists. If this sounds absurd, it is. If it sounds entirely implausible, I urge you to read the rest of this book. Believe it or not, it gets worse.

The good news is that there is nothing inevitable about the American experience. For one, the British press seems to be much more concerned about the issue and much less concerned by sideshows like whether or not Elton John should be allowed to marry his boyfriend or whether or not the plug should be pulled on a woman who has been brain-dead for decades. Secondly, the British government seems to be taking steps to address the worst cases of abuse by the financial industry—reminding those companies and its citizens that they are not, after all, above the law. The Financial Services Authority, for example, recently ruled against banks and financial services companies which have been charging illegal fees in flagrant violation of UK laws. In the United States, such fees were made entirely legal by the Supreme Court less than a decade ago. Still, the fact that financial corporations in the UK are acting so American is more than a little telling.

Is the financial industry shaking in its boots? Probably not. I recall a conversation with a provisional minister in Canada, who observed that, unlike the United States, his country had usury laws (interest rates above 60 percent are prohibited). Still, those laws went unenforced. Why? He seemed to think that the police were too busy with "real" crime to go after a bunch of respectable bankers. But there is another reason. Most of us in America, Canada and the UK cannot live without easy credit; the threat of our plastic being taken away is terrifying not only to politicians who expect the economy to grow year after year, but to us, who have become conditioned to believing that easy credit will always be there. I suspect that the FSA will find itself playing a game of chicken with the credit card companies, who will threaten to remove the punchbowl and bring the party to an abrupt halt if they are not allowed to charge the kinds of fees and interest rates they've become accustomed to. The financial industry recently played this game with the Japanese government, claiming that a cap on fees and stratospheric interest rates would bring the country's economic recovery to a halt. To their great surprise, the Japanese government didn't buy it.

Lord Acton once predicted a climactic showdown between the people and the banks. He may finally be proven right, that is if people cannot stop borrowing and the banks cannot stop enticing them to ruin. As Charles Dickens remarked of the time leading up to the French Revolution, "it was the best of times, it was the worst of times." At the moment, it is the best of times for the owners of capital. But for the rest of us, it is a very different story.

Pre-Production

"I think everyone knows that something just isn't right."
– Dave Ramsey

The Country Music Hall of Fame sits on the edge of downtown Nashville, across Broadway Street from a row of run-down buildings, one of which houses a FedEx Kinko's store. Downtown is, like most midsize American cities, oddly quiet. The busiest spot is a Starbucks tucked into the mezzanine of a mid-rise office building occupied by a bank. At night, retired couples and newlyweds wander past the Hall of Fame and the FedEx Kinko's on their way to a little strip of bars and restaurants, like the Hard Rock Cafe and Sbarro, the pizza place popular with tourists. The only clue that this is Nashville, and not Louisville or Minneapolis, is a young man in a wifebeater and a cowboy hat strumming a guitar on top of a box. He tells the few good folks who pause to listen that he's looking for a record deal, and they seem to appreciate the lonely note of authenticity he's lending their vacation, but it's hard to figure how he's going to end up across the street someday, in that museum. The fans he'll need are being bused from their hotels over to the Grand Ole Opry, a huge entertainment complex near the airport. And the

1

music producers are scattered around the suburbs, working out of small offices and home studios. He'd have better luck perching outside a strip mall Starbucks, waiting for one of them to emerge with a Frappuccino.

But if this cowboy decided to make that short trip, setting out past Vanderbilt University and into the suburbs, he'd discover just how much the world has changed. He'd pass countless pawnshops, check-cashing outlets, bank branches, title loan stores, and financing companies. He'd see that most billboards were advertising loans of one kind or another—and he'd also see plenty of smaller ads, mostly on the sides of the city's buses, for credit repair companies and bankruptcy attorneys. He'd soon learn that Tennesseans have become obsessed with debt: how to get it, get rid of it, or, most commonly, how to "surf it," i.e., how to ride larger and larger waves of debt without wiping out.

Indeed, if the cowboy headed east along the interstate toward Brentwood, the state's plushest suburb and home to many of his idols, he would see several billboards advertising a middle-age man with a bald head and a silver beard, a man who could easily pass for an aging country music legend, a man promising "Freedom." This man, the cowboy would discover, has the number-one radio show in Tennessee, and one of the fastest-growing audiences in the country. This man reaches millions of Americans in over 260 cities who listen to him religiously. He travels the country and commands adoring audiences in the thousands. He has his own reality television show in development. And he can't even sing or play the guitar.

His name is Dave Ramsey. He sells freedom from debt. And he is arguably the most popular recording artist in Tennessee—which, incidentally, has the second highest bankruptcy rate in the nation.*

I first meet Dave at a two-story brick office building that sits

---

*Number one is Utah.

across the street from the state's most expensive shopping mall. The building is home to Dave's radio show as well as "Financial Peace University," Dave's twelve-step program to get out of debt. Dave is of medium height, stocky build, and bald. He could be Dr. Phil's nephew. For the uninitiated, his intensity can read scary. Onstage he prowls and contorts every muscle like the evangelist he is. When Dave starts preaching the word, there is no room for argument. He's been to the mountaintop. And he's come back to save your soul from the demon that is debt.

Before every show Dave huddles with his staff in a prayer circle. A rock song leads in, then a quick anecdote or bad joke, and then Dave starts taking calls. The callers, as ever, are lost. They are trapped. They cannot help themselves. They do not understand their lives. They do not understand the terms of their credit card agreements and car loans. They are afraid. They are good people, however. They are just confused. Their hearts are willing but their minds are weak. Math scares them. They need a leader, someone to lead them out of the valley of the shadow of debt. Dave is the man.

He listens to them. Then he yells at them. He probes. He scolds. He exposes their hypocrisy and their secrets, which they didn't really want to keep anyway. He is the stern parent they never knew but wish they had. He tells them to sell the minivan, to live on "rice and beans and beans and rice," to get out of school and start making money. He tells them to hold garage sales. Lots of them. Then, during the commercial breaks, he urges his listeners to visit a mattress store where they can get "the really good $5,000 mattress sets for only $3,000" and why not stop by the pawnshop that has been a sponsor of his show from the beginning? That's where rich folks shop, he tells them. The plugs are not so much advertisements as they are testimonials, though it seems more than a little absurd that someone drowning in debt would plunk down three grand for a trophy mattress or spring for a bargain Rolex.

In many parts of the country, "Dave told me to sell it" is a perfectly good explanation to the buyer of a used Jet Ski, an SUV, or any other toy. Dave knows his audience and he makes allowances for their weakness. The centerpiece of Financial Peace University is what he calls the "debt snowball," which means paying small bills first, regardless of the interest rate. Of course, this is not such a good idea from a strictly mathematical standpoint (most experts advise paying off the highest-interest debts first). But Dave has succeeded by being a realist, not an academic. He knows that his listeners have short attention spans and Americans aren't so good at math in general. Dave defends the debt snowball by pointing out that it makes people feel as if they are achieving something quickly so they stick with the program longer. In other words, the debt snowball is no different from the crash diets which have become so ingrained in American life. What counts is fast results.

And, like *Stop the Insanity!* Susan Powter, the queen of diet infomercials, Dave can relate. He can tell his flock how, in the mideighties, he built a multimillion-dollar real estate fortune, only to lose it all by being stupid. He had to sell the Jaguar the day before it was going to be repo'd. He lost his house. He almost lost his marriage. He declared bankruptcy. The empire was built on a fantasy—on debt. Debt is evil. Debt is so evil, in fact, that Dave advocates paying cash for everything, with the exception of a mortgage, which should be no longer than fifteen years. When I ask Dave to define *predatory lending*, he responds, "All debt, to a degree, is predatory."

The day after I meet Dave, I decide to visit his bankruptcy attorney, Edgar Rothchild. Edgar is perhaps the most successful bankruptcy attorney in the state—if you define success by sheer volume. Edgar mostly processes Chapter 13s, where debts are not discharged but repackaged into a court-supervised plan. Debtors then make a monthly payment to a bankruptcy trustee, who pays off the creditors. But the vast majority of Chapter 13s that Edgar processes are eventually converted into Chapter 7s, where the debts are discharged, for the simple reason that most debtors can't keep up the payments.

Edgar won't talk about Dave on the record, but the mention of his most famous client brings an immediate smile that says, *I operate in the real world.* When you ask Edgar why so many Americans are declaring bankruptcy—the rate is now ten times that during the Great Depression—he can cite a number of reasons, but they all revolve around a simple truth: Americans' incomes have not kept pace with expenses. And, as far as Tennessee is concerned, the educational system is failing its students. A lot of Edgar's clients are illiterate. They can't get good jobs and they are easy prey for con artists. His wealthier clients have other problems: divorce, medical bills, job losses, children. "Do you have any idea what it takes to feed a teenage boy?" he smiles.

That afternoon, I return to Financial Peace University to ask Dave a few questions. I wonder if his "tough love" approach might be for show—if, off-air, Dave might have more sympathy for his listeners than he demonstrates on-air. If he might have some insights into why debt has become a cultural phenomenon. After all, the notion that millions of Americans woke up one day and willingly ensnared themselves in a trap they could never escape seems a little far-fetched. It also seems to me that the government bears some of the responsibility. After all, didn't President Bush tell Americans, in the wake of September 11, to go to Disney World, to *enjoy America as we want to enjoy it*? Didn't Tom Daschle, then the Democratic leader of the United States Senate, tell us to "go out and buy that suit you've been thinking about"? Hasn't the United States Congress put every American family $80,000 in debt in a single generation, using our full faith and credit to pay for thousand-dollar toilet seats and countless "fact-finding" missions to exotic island nations and ski resorts?

But Dave will have none of these excuses. His listeners change their lives, he tells me, when "they look in the mirror and say, 'You! You're the problem! It's the guy I shave with every day.' If I can change his behavior, I can be rich *and* thin." (Like a number of people I will meet, Dave thinks that obesity and indebtedness are flip sides of the same moral failing.)

"Is it any surprise," he continues, "that people who go into debt elect people who go into debt? I don't think it's the other way around." Finally he adds with a little smirk, "My savior doesn't live in Washington, DC. That's not where he lives."

I leave Financial Peace University contemplating God and debt. And feeling a little like the cowboy with the guitar: that maybe I've missed the boat. After all, I've spent two days in Tennessee and seen dozens of bumper stickers advertising how Jesus saves. I am smack in the middle of the Bible Belt. If the good people of Tennessee were having so many problems with money, surely the first question on their tongues would be "What would Jesus do?"

(Note to cowboy with guitar: Christian music sales are growing much faster than country and western.)

As it turns out, a lot of ministries have started to answer that very question. Earlier that week Jerry Falwell had delivered a sermon from his compound in Lynchburg called "People Who Steal from God." The message? People get into financial trouble because they don't give the church enough money. I've heard about a preacher in North Carolina holding debt revivals, where families cleanse themselves by destroying their credit cards at the altar. There was a pastor at the West Angeles Church in Los Angeles who's developed a ministry called Millionaires in Training. No matter that some of the highest bankruptcy rates are to be found along the Bible Belt. God wants Christians to be debt free.

After trolling the Internet for less than an hour, I find myself with an invitation from an evangelist named Steve Diggs to attend his No Debt, No Sweat! ministry that evening in Antioch, an undergentrified suburb fifteen miles southeast of Nashville whose finest establishment is the obligatory (and cash-only) Waffle House.* Steve is a former advertising man who used to be fat and in debt. With the Lord's help, he and his wife conquered those demons. Now he is trim, debt free, and out of the advertising business—sort of. Steve sells a plan to help Christians get their financial house in order for $36. The No Debt, No Sweat! mission(ary) statement is "to teach you to handle money so you can take off like a bullet with a tailwind." On the phone Steve is a nice guy, full of energy, and he promises a great show, complete with feathered boas, loud Hawaiian shirts, sunglasses, and a female impersonation. I can hardly wait.

The seminar turns out to be quite tame, but then again, I am from L.A., a fact that Steve receives with a look of some consternation or apprehension or both. Later on he will tell his "L.A. story": Steve and his wife win tickets to the Emmys from a local radio contest and go to Hollywood, but the moment they arrive at the red carpet, they find that *their* people are protesting the industry's immoral agenda from the other side of the velvet rope. Steve has a crisis of conscience, realizes he's on the wrong side of the rope, yet he and his wife decide to go to the Emmys anyway. They even go to the after-party to mingle with the hedonists. Steve has had an epiphany not uncommon among the evangelical crowd: It's better to be an insider if you want to effect change. Plus, there's the gift bag . . .

The Antioch audience listens politely (they are in church, after all) as Steve paces the center aisle talking very fast into a Garth Brooks–style headset. When a gray hair complains that Steve needs to slow it down, Steve shocks me by telling the old guy tough luck.

---

*The chain finally began accepting credit cards in February 2005. *Et tu*, Waffle House?

This turns out to be by far the most dramatic moment of the evening.

Steve tries to be funny, but the crowd doesn't laugh much. Maybe he is talking too fast. And maybe they are more confused by the camp antics (feathered boa and otherwise bad drag) than amused by them. He gratuitously mentions his dislike of the "homosexual agenda" to reassure them of his conservative Christian credentials. But no matter. I am here to learn what Jesus would do if he got into debt. And you know what? He wouldn't give up everything he owned. He would hold a garage sale, call his credit card company and renegotiate his interest rate, and probably get rid of the SUV, unless the disciples ponied up some dough for the gas, maybe.

I leave Antioch admiring Steve's spirit but with no more understanding of why Christians, like everyone else in America, are drowning in debt. Except for the obvious—that some of them have left his seminar with an extra $36 on their Visa card. For all of their good intentions, the financial gurus that Americans turn to offer just as many contradictions as solutions. A pastor I'd visited in South Central Los Angeles, for example, chastised his congregants for driving cars they couldn't afford—as we cruised South Central in his Range Rover. Suze Orman, the nation's bestselling financial adviser, has done ads for Cadillac (which have among the worst resale values of any automobile). Dave Ramsey has his sponsors (the pawnshop and discount luxury mattress place come to mind) because he's got to pay the rent too. And when Jerry Falwell holds himself up as an example for tithing 30 percent and being plenty prosperous, it's more than a little self-serving. When he tells his congregants that giving his ministry more money will erase their financial troubles—a strategy he calls "spiritual mathematics"—it's just plain slimy.

Yet, I've come to learn that, for all of their apparent contradictions, the financial gurus are a pretty accurate reflection of the times. We live in a country where the government tells us that the economy is getting better and better, but most polls show that we believe it's getting worse and worse. A country where foreclosures and bankruptcies have skyrocketed, while the numbers of million-aires and bank profits have increased year after year. A country whose citizens can afford the brand-new Hummer H2 and H3, but whose soldiers are expected to fight a war with the old ones (and with no body armor). Is it really possible that all of these catch-22s will be eliminated by holding biweekly garage sales and skipping the a.m. latte? Where is Susan Powter to jolt us out of our collective denial? *Stop the Insanity!*

Several months after I visited Tennessee, Hurricane Katrina rolled over New Orleans. A day later the city flooded. And then for seven long days, as the world watched, the people of New Orleans begged for help. Hundreds drowned in their own homes. Babies died in their mothers' arms for lack of water. And I watched in amazement as conservatives demanded answers to the questions many of us had been asking for some time. How could extreme poverty exist in a country of such enormous wealth? Why hadn't we taken better care of our infrastructure? Where was the money going to come from to fix it *and* pay for the war in Iraq *and* pay for Social Security *and* Medicare *and* all of the other entitlements? Was bankruptcy reform, which President Bush had just signed (really bad timing, Karl), too harsh? Katrina had changed everything, I told my-self. People were finally asking the tough questions. Americans were beginning to realize that credit was not the same as wealth—that a generation of debt surfing had left us extraordinarily vulnerable.

The president gave a dramatic and hopeful speech in the French Quarter, shouting out to the huddled masses who'd been ignored for too long. But then he seemed to lose interest. The telethons came and went. New natural disasters and new scandals took center stage. The death toll in Iraq passed 2,000. A bill to exempt hurricane victims from bankruptcy reform died in the House, as did a measure to offset the costs of rebuilding New Orleans with budget cuts. Insurance companies refused to rebuild homes because they claimed the damage resulted from hurricane-induced flooding and not from the hurricane itself.* Private companies, which owned most of the hospitals in New Orleans, expressed doubts that they would ever rebuild. The Small Business Administration offered loan guarantees, but only to those with near perfect credit—a cruel joke which has so far shut out 80 percent of those who have applied for help. The most hopeful sign was the return of white real estate speculators.

In other words, the status quo quietly eased back into place. The government would take on more debt to rebuild what it could. And the people would take on more debt to do the same. The only difference would be that that debt would be more expensive than before. In other words, we would surf the hurricane, even though the waters were getting far more treacherous. Why? We have no choice.

The federal government—and the majority of Americans—can no longer get by a single day without taking on additional debt. And as more borrowing goes to simply pay off old debt, or to make interest payments, the new debt does little more than increase banking profits. Eventually the higher levels of debt will lead to higher interest rates, which will lead to more debt, creating a cycle as vicious as it is inevitable. Over the past generation, banks and credit card companies have made trillions of dollars of high-interest, unsecured debt available, and Americans have scooped it up. Our incomes have risen an average of 1 percent in real terms, while our household debt has increased over 1,000 percent. As a result, we no longer save.† We have no choice but to keep spending until our credit is exhausted and

*Trent Lott, the former Senate majority leader, is among those suing the insurers.

†In the UK, a similar picture exists. Collectively, Britons owe 140 percent of their post-tax income—the average household is in debt to the tune of more than £8,000 excluding mortgages. Total debt in the UK is rising by £1m every four minutes.

we own nothing. As Marriner Eccles, the legendary Fed chairman during the Great Depression, noted, "The economy is like a poker game where only a few people control the chips and the other fellows must borrow to stay in the game. But the moment the borrowing stops, the game is over."

How did we allow this to happen? How could we be so short-sighted? How could banks keep lending to people who can't afford to pay them back? Doesn't that fly in the face of tradition, if not common sense? Don't bank executives realize that they are sowing the seeds of their own destruction? After all, when most Americans can no longer stay afloat, the banks will sink alongside them as they did back in Marriner Eccles's day.

The simple answer is that Americans are a lot like the cowboy with the guitar. While the banking industry has gone through its most profound change since the Venetians invented modern finance hundreds of years ago, Americans have clung to old assumptions. In particular, we've continued to believe that banks wouldn't extend us credit unless we could handle it, and that banks want us to save. Yet, the big banks realized more than a generation ago that they make far more money teaching us to *spend* than to save. They've also learned that making money upfront, mostly in the form of fees, is a lot more fun than waiting for a revenue stream to trickle in. The reason is simple: Fees can be booked as profits immediately; revenue streams take years. This is why most mortgages, car loans, and even credit card receivables are bundled together and sold off, sometimes instantly, to Wall Street.

Take Enron as an example. Enron executives didn't want to wait for their brilliant ideas to bear fruit. So they used an accounting gimmick called "mark-to-market,"* where they decided how much

---

*Ironically, mark-to-market was developed to prevent companies from hiding losses by compelling them to adjust their portfolios to market prices on a daily basis.

an idea was worth, booked it as immediate profit, and then collected a bonus on that profit—all in the same quarter. When these new businesses instead generated huge losses, executives turned to the world's largest banks to hide those losses—for a fee. Enron would "sell" the losses to a large bank before reporting its financial results, then buy them back afterward at a greater loss. The bank collected a fee without taking a risk, the bankers got a bonus based on generating that fee, and, most important, the Enron execs rewarded themselves with huge bonuses based on phony—but consistently growing—profits. Of course, mark-to-market guaranteed Enron's eventual failure. But consider that the top ten CEOs in America now earn more than $100 million per year, and you realize how quickly short-term gimmicks can create vast fortunes.

The same gimmicks are now being applied to consumer debt. Most mortgages, car loans, and credit card debt are packaged and sold off to investors at a profit within a short period of time, sometimes seconds. Banks create an estimate of how much the credit card debt is worth and sell it to investors, pocketing a profit. There is no banker carefully tending to your mortgage or your credit card down at the local branch, any more than there is a record executive strolling down Broadway Street searching for the cowboy.

But there is an even greater misconception at work. A misconception that debt is not what it used to be. That there is "good" debt, for example, and "bad" debt. Tune in to Suze Orman, for example, and she will tell you that a single number, your credit score (aka, FICO),* is the key to your financial future. But while a good credit score gets you better rates on your mortgage and credit cards, it also opens up the floodgates for more "good"—i.e., cheap—credit to pour into your life, and this credit does not usually remain good or cheap for too long. The idea that one should stay out of debt,

---

*Short for Fair Isaac Corporation.

period, is now considered unrealistic. After all, who lives without debt? The Unabomber, maybe?

Even more frightening is the notion that debt is our friend—a magical tool that allows us, in the words of Napster's new ads, to "own everything and have nothing." No less a fiscal conservative than President Bush has dismissed the federal debt as "numbers on paper." His vice president has flatly stated, "Deficits don't matter." But the apathy prize goes to two-term Florida senator Connie Mack, who was hired to give Bush ideas on reforming the tax code in 2005. Here's a recent exchange between the senator and the *New York Times*:

> Interviewer: Where do you suggest we get the money
> from?
> Sen. Mack: What money?
> Interviewer: The money to run this country.
> Sen. Mack: We'll borrow it.
> Interviewer: I never understand where this money comes
> from. When the president says we need another $200 billion
> for Katrina repairs, does he just go and borrow it from the
> Saudis?
> Sen. Mack: In a sense, we do. Maybe the Chinese.

Twenty years ago, when the federal debt passed the trillion-dollar mark, politicians, including Ronald Reagan, as well as economists, including Alan Greenspan, warned of dire consequences. Seven trillion dollars later, borrowing more has become the solution to every conceivable problem. Take Social Security as the largest, and perhaps most insidious, example: In order to reduce deficits, the past four presidents have borrowed $1.5 trillion from Social Security and the "trust fund" now holds nothing more than a very big IOU. In effect, we've been surfing, borrowing from Social Security to pay off the interest on the federal debt every year. In the 2000 and 2004 elections, George W. Bush promoted an idea called "private accounts." In theory, every American would own their Social Security account. The account would contain real money so it could buy real investments, i.e., not IOUs. In theory one could also borrow against it, of course. The trouble is that since the Social Security Trust Fund has no cash, no one can say where the money would come from to fund these accounts. The Chinese again? Probably. But Bush hasn't told us yet. He has, however, loudly warned working Americans not to count on Social Security. (Note to cowboy: Keep strummin'.)

The media never really took the president to task on the math of private accounts. It was the AARP* that killed the idea, and, ironically enough, they hated it because private accounts would have reduced the amount of guaranteed benefits to their members, not because it would have indebted their future members.

Pete Peterson, one of the smartest financiers among us, has correctly pointed out that "benefits" like personal accounts are simply deferred taxes if they're not paid for. Yet neither the anti-tax president nor his adversaries once questioned whether borrowing the trillions of dollars needed to fund private accounts was a good idea, much less possible. After all, Americans have accepted the surfing lifestyle in all of its absurdities. We have watched advertisements that say "Pay off your high credit card debts!" and we have called the 800 numbers and attached our homes to new loans in order to pay off our credit cards, then bragged to our friends that we are "debt free." We are encouraged to rent things we used to own—including music and, paradoxically, the down payments on our homes. We have accepted this new bargain that we will never be out of debt as inevitable, preordained by the God of our choosing. We have for-

*The American Association of Retired Persons, which offers a wide range of special products and services to the over-50s and is the largest lobbying group for seniors in Washington DC.

gotten the feeling of solid ground as we have taken on larger and more treacherous waves. We have ignored the greatest investor among us, Warren Buffett, who has derided our "sharecroppers society." He sounds old, cranky, and un-hip.

Until we wipe out. Until we lose our jobs, until we get divorced, until we discover that our health insurance doesn't cover thousands of dollars of "extras," or until our home doesn't appreciate at the anticipated rate. Until we can no longer surf. And then the "debt hell," as a consumer advocate I interviewed calls it, kicks in. The fees pile up. The interest rates increase. The bargain we accepted ceases to be a bargain. It becomes prohibitively expensive. We learn that we are not middle-class at all. We are poor. We own nothing.

And then, just maybe, we finally ask, "Well, how did we get here?"

One

"I think that there is a natural fascination that we all have in how rich and famous people live. People always want the larger than life. It's because those people still want to dream so they want to look upwards. They don't want to look behind them. They want to escape in a fantasy that says, 'Yes, I will be king for a day'; 'Yes, I will be queen for a day.' "
– Robin Leach

It is not yet fashionable to be in debt. I have no doubt it will be— soon. The must-see reality show will be *The Biggest Debt Loser* and Paris Hilton will be replaced by a maxed-out debutante who's learned how to take the bus and make homemade Christmas presents. But, for now, those brave souls who openly admit their financial troubles must shoulder a stigma just below that of a heroin addict and just above that of a registered sex offender. In other words, no one is bursting out of the closet just yet. So the stories I find in the public domain are the freak shows—the cases extreme or titillating enough to gather at least local news coverage. There is the Marine sergeant who used her military credit card to pay for a boob job; the college student with a weak spot for Mustangs and porn who shot and killed his family at point-blank range over a $5,000 MasterCard bill; the adolescent drag queen named Visa D'Kline; and, of course, there is Michael Jackson, who has managed to max out a $300 million personal credit line buying exotic pets and playing with his nose. In the process of filming my documentary, which I am calling *Maxed Out*, I will meet all of them, with the exception of Michael Jackson. But more on that later.

For now, the challenge is to find average Americans who are swimming in debt. I know they must be all around me, but where exactly? Who would be willing to talk to me? It's an all-too-familiar catch-22: you don't want the people who *want* to talk to you. There are too many publicity hounds, not to mention those with scores to settle, Web sites to sell, reality television careers to launch.

I ask Dave Ramsey for help. After all, he fields thousands of calls a week from normal people all around America. And for a long time I receive no response. But then, out of the blue, his publicist, a very nice woman named Beth, e-mails that she's found a family with a story to tell. As I read on, I fear that this story may be too dramatic, too severe, too tragic. Yet, this family's story—like all debt nightmares, I will learn—started small and compounded itself month after month until it had a momentum that was impossible to stop. Debt is a self-perpetuating prophecy. Once the snowball gains enough speed, you cannot reverse its direction.

Downtown Louisville, Kentucky, reminds me of a Chris Rock joke: "There are two malls in every city: the mall where the white people go and the mall where the white people *used* to go." I've booked a room in the part of town where the white people, like me, go. It's an old place, past its heyday but serviceable. Across the street is the city's attempt at bringing more folks like me in from the suburbs. It's called "Fourth Street *LIVE!*" There's a Hard Rock Cafe, a franchised steakhouse, a Borders Books, and a food court with—what else?—a Subway sandwich shop and one of those new old-fashioned ice cream parlors where the "small" starts at five bucks and the product is beaten to a pulp on a marble slab while you watch. The Louisville Slugger Museum is within walking distance, as are several gleaming high-rises occupied by large banks. But just around the corner from the hotel is another city: check-cashing stores, Popeyes Chicken & Biscuits with bulletproof glass, convenience stores with broken windows, and crack houses.

My destination is New Albany, Indiana, a suburb across the Ohio River. New Albany is strip malls and churches, and modest-size brick homes in cul-de-sacs, and white people. The largest employer is the UPS distribution center at Louisville Airport, where employees work at night sorting packages. The biggest news is still the Caesars Palace Casino, which opened a few years ago. When New Albany voted against gambling, the commissioners in the next county couldn't believe their luck. Hell yes, they wanted a casino! So Caesars built their casino megaplex a few yards from New Albany's county line and started wooing its citizens immediately. They had promised a boom in jobs and tax revenues, a quick fix to urban blight and the recession plaguing the burbs. But, according to the local paper, neither materialized. The neighborhood churches and service providers, however, *were* flooded with new charity cases who had somehow contracted all kinds of addictions, mostly related to gambling and alcohol, Caesars' top-selling products.

The house I'm visiting is a two-story colonial in the middle of a development of similar homes with large yards. An SUV and a minivan, both American-made and both gas guzzlers to be sure, linger in the driveway like red herrings. The home belongs to Yvonne Pavey and her husband, who drives a truck for FedEx. Six months ago Yvonne disappeared without so much as a note. That morning she dropped her grandson off at school in her blue Mercury Tracer, bought six dollars of gas at the Wal-Mart, and was never seen or heard from again. Yvonne's daughter Kathi immediately called the sheriff's department. A few days later, when she discovered the truth about her mother, she called the man that both women had turned to for guidance over the years in matters financial and otherwise: Dave Ramsey. Kathi's discovery was that her mother had secretly run up tens of thousands of dollars in credit card debt to feed a gambling addiction. Yvonne had disappeared the day before she and her husband's credit reports—ordered by her husband on Dave's advice—were due to arrive in the mail. The local police think that Yvonne panicked, drove thirty miles into the wilderness, led her car down a boat ramp into the Ohio River with the windows down, and drowned herself. They find a lot of cars in the river, apparently. When the water gets low enough, the police told Kathi, the antenna of her mother's car will show, or a barge will scrape the roof and then they'll send a truck to pull it out.

It's worth mentioning that "debt suicides" are occurring in the UK as well. Dereck Rawson, a 51-year-old forklift driver who owed over £100,000, took his life and left a note to his sister saying "I can't pay the bills and the credit card companies won't leave me alone." Father-of-two Stephen Lewis, 37, killed himself after running up £70,000 in debt on 19 credit cards. Most tragic, perhaps, is the indebted Wales student whose suicide has recently attracted a great deal of media attention.

Jon Ballew, Kathi's husband, greets me at the door. He's middle-aged but his buzz cut suggests younger. He wears a company polo shirt over a small potbelly and blue slacks. We sit down in the living room and Kathi joins us after leaving her two young sons to the jungle gym outside. She's dressed like a young mom: shorts and tennis shoes. Unpretentious. As it turns out, Jon and Kathi were college sweethearts. Now he works at a brokerage firm and she works part-time at the local movie theater. They go to their neighborhood church and take the kids to pizza buffets. They used to play dominos with Kathi's parents every Wednesday night. Kathi likes listening to Dave Ramsey. I like them both immediately.

Unfortunately, however, they do not have much to add to Yvonne's story except their grief. They are hoping that the documentary I'm filming may help lead to Yvonne, even though they seem resigned to the police theory. They just want to know. They show me the "missing" flyer they have posted at every church and restaurant within a ten-mile radius. Kathi and Jon talk about how Yvonne got the credit cards even though she was an unemployed housewife, only later finding a job as a parking valet at Caesars Palace, a job that paid the minimum wage. They describe a constant stream of harassing phone calls from banks and debt collectors and, now, the threat of lawsuits. I am amazed by their composure. They do not blame the banks, or else they swallow their anger very well. They don't want to make a spectacle of themselves; they just want to know where Yvonne has gone.

After college, Jon married Kathi and went to work for the local bank. At the time there were only two banks in his town, and they sat across the street from each other. The focus was on building long-term relationships, which meant taking care of the customer, which Jon did very well. He treated people as he would be treated. He was empathetic and honest. He worked his way up to manager and the potbelly grew from long hours sitting at his desk. Jon was the quintessential small-town banker, the one we like to think still exists.

But a glance at Jon's résumé tells me what's happened to the banking industry over the last twenty years. The independent bank where he began his career has become, over the course of no less than a dozen mergers, one of thousands of branches in the JPMorgan/Chase/Bank One/First USA empire. With each merger Jon gained a new title and lost a little authority until, just before he quit banking altogether, Jon was nothing more than a cheerleader for mortgages, car loans, credit insurance, credit cards, and all of the other financial products that banks package. True, Chase's long-time slogan was "The right relationship is everything," but twenty-first-century banking is as much about building relationships as Wal-

21

Mart is about building communities. The game is delivering credit (the enabler) as efficiently as possible to the maximum number of consumers and converting that credit into debt (the product). What's really important, then, is being the low-cost provider. And to do that, you must maximize your economies of scale: You must get bigger and bigger and you must become ruthlessly efficient at every level of the company. This is why Wal-Mart is trying so hard to build a bank, and why the big banks are so zealously lobbying against it.*

This also explains the wave of mergers and acquisitions over the past decade, the annoying ritual of having your cards replaced every other year so that you can advertise their new brand and logo. Ergo, the obsession with centralized decision-making and efficient customer "processing"—which, for the vast majority of us, translates into phone-tree purgatory and customer representatives with exotic Bangalorean accents. Ergo, the conversion of what we used to call "banks" into sales centers where we are hard-sold a credit card and second mortgage (otherwise known as a "refi") the moment we try to open a savings account. But apparently these initiatives haven't mustered up the desired response, for, at the end of the day, the banks always seem to raise fees—or create new ones—to make their numbers. There are fees for going over the limit (but only when the bank approves of you going over limit in the first place) and there are fees for paying early. Fees for paying by phone and for paying in person. There are fees for paying after a certain hour on a certain day. There are penalties for taking out too much debt and too little. By one estimate, the credit industry now collects $20 billion per year in fees that didn't even exist twenty years ago. Familiar fees, like returned-check and late-payment penalties, have gone up nearly two-hundred percent in the past ten years. These fees, incidentally,

*In the UK, all the major supermarket chains offer financial products such as insurance and pension plans. Most offer direct banking through exclusive partnerships with major banks, e.g. Sainsbury's/Bank of Scotland and Tesco/Royal Bank of Scotland.

cost the banks nothing. Similar scams have been gaining steam in the UK, where the banks are showing even less restraint. Consider a typical scenario: if you exceed your credit limit by £16, for example, most banks will charge you £39 for the privilege. They may also impose a £28 monthly "unauthorized overdraft fee" (though they have clearly authorized the overdraft by paying it) and, for good measure, would almost certainly levy interest at more than 30 percent per year—a total markup of more than 400 percent! No doubt shocked by the banks' audacity, the Office of Fair Trading has ruled that no charges should exceed £12 from now on. So, to Wal-Mart, I say, "Bring it on!" They've never charged me a processing fee for running my Cocoa Puffs over the scanner. And they let you use the bathroom.

In fact, the banks now seem to be pursuing the opposite strategy of Wal-Mart: Be the *high-cost* provider—just make sure to pass that cost on to the consumer. The key is to sell as much fee-generating product as possible and lock it in over the longest possible period of time. That's why, if you pick up the want ads, you'll find that the number-one qualification to work as a bank teller is not accounting or math or analytical skills: it's *suggestive selling experience.**

Jon and I are sitting in his mother-in-law's immaculate kitchen, talking shop over a cup of coffee. "I know for a fact," he tells me, "that they're not interested in anyone with a banking background or knowledge of how it works. They want people with retail experience, like people who have worked in stores at the mall. People who can sell, sell, sell."

"Sell debt?" I ask.

Jon raises his left index finger and ticks off an exhaustive list of financial products he had to sell: car loans, boat loans, vacation loans, refis, credit cards, overdraft protection, etc., etc. He pauses at

---

*Okay, most of these jobs also require a high school diploma or equivalent.

credit insurance, a profit workhorse that, unbeknownst to most customers, mainly protects the bank by guaranteeing payment of one's unsecured debts in the event of a job loss, illness, or death.* (A friend's grandmother was recently convinced to purchase credit insurance on a card she never uses, presumably because the word *insurance* automatically appeals to Depression babies.) Jon tells me how he was sometimes encouraged to increase the value of a refi by suggesting that the customer go on vacation or buy a new car. The cost of the vacation and/or the new vehicle would then be folded into the refi, making the loan amount much higher. "There's a lot more pressure to hit these numbers," he says. "And the standards have gotten so low, it's credit without good judgment."

So standards are down and pressure is up. If you fly Alaska Airlines, your cocktail napkin doubles as an advertisement for the Bank of America platinum Visa card and the flight attendants interrupt your nap to hand you an application in case you didn't get the hint. If you open any of those innocent-looking e-mails from people whose names, with their tinge of familiarity, just might be a long-lost college pal, you will be assaulted by rate sheets and urged to call now for a free quote or to claim the credit you deserve with no obligation. If you go to the doctor, you will find that Capital One would love to finance your next surgery. Fees have changed the way banks make money. But most people still believe in the good old days, when banks only lent you money if they thought you could afford to pay it back. We still see *approved* as a major validation. Getting a loan from a bank, even in the form of a high-interest credit card, means crossing the threshold into adulthood.

Why do we continue to believe this fairy tale? Because we want to and the bank tells us to. Any credit offer that holds back on the

*The banks get a commission from the insurer, or, in many cases, an affiliated company collects the premiums. Less than half of these premiums typically go to paying claims, versus one hundred percent for most forms of insurance.

love and adoration of a prospective client does so at its own risk. The envelope must look important, the copy must inform us of our preferred status, the vice president of marketing must personally congratulate us for being a valued customer and praise our responsible use of credit over the years, perhaps reveal that we are on a special list, that we are platinum or titanium or centurion or platinum select or preferred or whatever platitude we may not have heard—yet. The bank is not just *giving* us credit—oh, no. We have *earned* it and they are simply acknowledging our greatness. Our destiny. They are our humble servants. Their admiration is limitless and the credit will be ever flowing. Okay, so there will be a credit limit, but, then again, it can always be raised if we call them and beg, and it can be broken if we pay an overlimit fee.*

For those of us who receive our first credit offer in high school or college, it is as though we are leapfrogging the threshold into adulthood and realizing our ultimate destiny: to be a member of the American upper middle class. The late author Hubert Selby liked to say that Americans are taught that they are born assholes and the goal is to become an asshole with money. Yet, thanks to the new banking system, we are all assholes with credit by virtue of our eighteenth birthday.

I recently discovered, courtesy of a banking executive's deposition that was made available to me, what actually happens when a completed credit card application, er, invitation (priority processing!) arrives at its destination: a data entry clerk sitting amidst dozens of similar cubicles pulls it from a stack of identical envelopes, types in the name, address, and Social Security number, and presses a button that sends this information to a credit bureau, which returns a credit score in a matter of seconds. This score determines whether or not the application is accepted and how much

*See addenda to "Terms and Conditions."

credit is to be granted, within a matter of nanoseconds. If denied, a rejection letter is automatically generated, the applicant is referred to a "subprime" lender, and then the application is shredded (we can hope, anyway). If accepted, the clerk flips the full application (the personal stuff about your job and how long you've lived at your present address, yada yada yada) onto a scanner. Most of this information, however, will never be used or even seen by anyone at the credit card company. It is only saved, as the executive explained, to "get a jump on collections." Which reminds me of a beer cozy I got from a little gas station on the way back from Vegas: "If you think nobody cares, try missing a couple of payments."

By the end of our conversation, I am amazed that Jon has any positive memories of the banking business, but he does. Jon tells me of an older customer, probably Yvonne's age, who was living on Social Security. She had run up over $20,000 in credit card bills. How she got the credit cards in the first place is probably more troubling to us than to her: When you are of the age of hot flashes and senior moments and your home is about to be foreclosed, you don't dwell on details. What matters is that Jon convinced her to cut up the cards, refinance her modest house, and create a budget which she could afford by being vigilant and never wasting a nickel for the rest of her days. By doing this, he saved her from eviction and who knows what fate after that.

Jon had been her guardian angel and the woman had cried tears of gratitude. It was the kind of good deed that he had imagined doing when he became a banker. The fact that her problems had not been caused by drought or recession or widowhood but by Jon's own employer did not seem to bother him. What mattered was that he had cleaned up the mess and saved a life. Then, a few months later, the woman called the bank's credit card division and said there'd been a mistake, that she wanted her credit cards back. Maybe she'd grown tired of eating canned vegetables or maybe she was itching for a trip to Caesars. The bank didn't ask. They mailed her new cards out the next day.

Jon smiles and takes a sip of his coffee. Maybe it's not such a great memory after all.

I wanted to visit Las Vegas for three reasons. One, the present banking system seems a lot like legalized gambling; two, Paul Krugman was becoming famous for his observation that "Americans are making money selling each other houses with money borrowed from the Chinese" and there was no hotter real estate market than Las Vegas, where homes had shot up nearly 50 percent in the past twelve months; and three, it is the home of Robin Leach, of *Entertainment Tonight, Star Magazine,* and *Lifestyles of the Rich and Famous,* three pop culture phenomena that social critics and college professors love to blame for setting off the chain of events (*Cribs, Us Weekly,* Paris Hilton, etc.), which will eventually cause the meltdown—financial, moral, intellectual, and otherwise—of our civilization.

I meet Robin Leach in an upscale Italian restaurant at The Venetian, a glitzy megahotel/casino with its own canal system and singing gondoliers. Leach is heavier than he used to be and sports a salt-and-pepper goatee, but thankfully he has lost none of his ebullience. As anyone who's watched *Lifestyles* knows, Leach is not a pessimist. He believes in the greatness of capitalism and the reality of second comings. Wayne Newton and Debbie Reynolds, both of whom declared bankruptcy, only to reappear onstage in rhinestones, were two of his favorite guests. And then there's Donald Trump, one of the generation's most prolific debtors. A terrific marketer, according to Leach, and not a man to underestimate, by the way.

27

When I ask him if he thinks that *Lifestyles'* slow pans of The Donald's penthouse and helicopters caused people to become a little materialistic, he bristles. Leach believes the opposite: that his show promoted classic American values. As proof he offers up the story of an older black man he met by chance in a liquor store in L.A. The man thanked Leach for inspiring his two sons to change from Burger King–loitering homies to Brown University grads. When I look unconvinced, Leach cuts to the chase: "Nobody would watch *Lifestyles of the Poor and Unknown,*" he crows. Case closed.

So it's out to the suburbs for me, where the real action is. My producer has set up a meeting with Beth Naef, one of the city's most successful Realtors. Beth sells dirt parcels and multimillion-dollar spec homes in what are commonly known as master-planned communities—those themed kingdoms of miniature castles and golf courses barely hidden behind low fences and superficial "gates." A recent ad in *Vegas* magazine, squeezed between full-page glossy body shots of strippers, showcases nine of Beth's shiny new trophies under a vivacious photo of herself and the headline "Passion." Beth's company, Prime Realty, operates out of a newish strip mall seven miles or so from the Strip, at the base of a series of hills that developers are carving into lots and selling at a mind-numbing pace. The road itself is still under development but already nurtures a series of familiar franchises and big-box stores. A constant dust storm is fed by a hundred construction sites, and cars bake in the sun, barely moving. The heat is oppressive. I wonder if a view of the Strip and the chance to see Barry Manilow five nights a week could really make it worth living here.

Luckily, Beth is as dynamic and charming as my producer promised. She's middle-aged but seems far younger. The St. John's pantsuit and gold jewelry practically scream "upscale Realtor" but I'm a sucker for her tomboyish bent and easy grin. As it turns out, she's just moved into her new office, which she's designed to feel like one of the "custom" homes she sells. Or so she says. It feels more like an upscale Marriott Hotel than a place to raise children or fart on the couch. It's too clean. The surfaces are too hard and too polished, the fabrics too industrial, the colors too neutral. It's the kind of place you can imagine yourself leaving the moment you enter. You know that the perfectly placed throw pillows and pashminas aren't there for your comfort. You know better than to leave an impression anywhere.

Today is slow, meaning that Beth has time to talk. Her days are either feast or famine, she tells me. There is simply no knowing when buyers will suddenly outnumber sellers and vice versa. And this clues me into a simple truth. Her clients are not buying a home: They are *investing* in a home.* Timing is everything. If they don't call, this does not mean that they aren't there: It means they are waiting on the sidelines for the right moment to reenter the game. While they wait, the number of Realtors grows. Beth knows that a lot of her competitors are trying to build their own businesses by outpromising her but she seems more annoyed than threatened. She can afford to relax a little. What she can't do is get too comfortable.

Beth is, in her own words, "blessed." Six years ago, a newly single mother of two little girls, she stumbled onto the opportunity of a lifetime. A national real estate developer had just bought several hundred acres of desert overlooking the Strip and was looking for sales agents. Beth got a job as a receptionist at the sales center, but her potential as a Realtor must have been obvious to the developer. Within six months she'd gotten her broker's license and most of the listings in "Seven Hills," a brand-new development meant to evoke the serenity of the Italian countryside.

Beth sold most of the lots in Seven Hills. Then, as Vegas real estate started heating up, she sold many of them again—this time

*In March 2006, *USA Today* reported that 40 percent of home sales were for second homes, the vast majority of which were purchased as investments.

29

with houses. As interest rates fell and property values rose, Beth noticed something very interesting: Her clients weren't staying put, feeling smug they'd gotten in early and refinancing their mortgages at lower rates. They were selling and moving into bigger homes on bigger lots, sometimes in the same neighborhood. And they were making a killing. Prices in master plans like Seven Hills were skyrocketing. Developers couldn't build new homes fast enough to meet demand, giving the homeowners a seductive taste of easy money. Many became speculators. And there was Beth, smack in the middle of a nationwide real estate boom that made the tech craze of the late nineties look like pocket change. And unlikely as it had to be, Las Vegas, with its scorching weather and monotonous landscape, was becoming the hottest real estate market in the country.

"What's big in Las Vegas now," Beth explains on a tour of Seven Hills' larger units, "are home theaters, a wine room, elevators—because the homes are getting pretty darned big—two washers and two dryers, two dishwashers in the kitchen, huge kitchens." In other words, what's big in Vegas is *bigness*. When Beth started out, her clients were building 4,500-square-foot homes. Now a typical listing is 8,000 to 9,000 square feet. The largest home in Seven Hills is nearly twice that. "They're just making them as big as they can," Beth laughs. "And people want a gate. But more important, a gate with a guard. I had some wonderful lots for sale in Seven Hills that were clicker-gated. And people were, like, 'But there's no guard.' *What do you mean? The views are incredible!* But people want the guard. I don't know if it's for prestige value or security, but people want that guard." For the first time Beth sounds slightly exasperated.

Moving on, we exit the wrought-iron gates of Seven Hills. I am still wondering why it was named after, as Beth says, "someplace in Italy," because none of the homes seemed remotely Italianate, and then there is the glaring absence of Vespas and Fiats, but whatever.

We are headed to a newer development called MacDonald Highlands, an allusion to the lush rolling hills of my Scottish ancestors. Beth has scored her first listing at MacDonald: a $5.5 million spec home. Initially she wasn't interested, but suddenly prices in the Highlands have surpassed those in Seven Hills. This makes no sense to Beth or probably to anyone else, either, save the speculators. They have jumped in again, but onto a different field.

The gate at MacDonald Highlands has a guard, which I now know is a major plus. He even has an official-looking badge and pants, though the stain on his shirt and the Taco Bell bag behind him probably won't help Beth move real estate. There's something very airport-security about the guy, but I'm guessing that airport screeners make more money. His only purpose seems to be opening the gate very quickly, which pretty much debunks Beth's security theory—though, in his defense, we are white and in a big Mercedes. As Beth explains later, channeling Annette Bening's character in *American Beauty*, it helps to drive what your clients drive.

There are no kilts or bagpipes at MacDonald Highlands, though it does seem to offer all of the amenities one would expect of a master-planned community. There's the guard, of course, and a golf course, fresh pavement, themed street names, matching mailboxes, manicured lawns that look painted on the desert's ubiquitous shade of ecru, and no doubt a laundry list of homeowner association rules (no garage sales, no pickup trucks parked outside, no "estate" sales, *smarty-pants*, etc.) that guarantee that everything will stay this perfect forever, or at least until you're ready to trade up. As master plans go, it seems less cookie-cutter, more *authentic* even, though the Scottish name will gnaw at me a little, not least because the notion of two washers/dryers offends my ancestors' thrifty sensibilities.

For the past twenty minutes I've been very curious to know what a spec house approaching six million bucks on the outskirts of Las Vegas looks like. As it turns out, the answer is a massive shoe box with huge windows and very little yard. Beth barely gives the exterior a glance before leading me past a massive oak door whose weight is, I have to admit, pretty impressive.

The home's builder is a large man—Israeli, I think—who greets us in the spacious kitchen. He seems more than a little nervous. After all, nobody knows if the market has peaked. Homes are taking longer to sell. The big developers are offering incentives again—to buyers *and* agents. The word *bubble* is being tossed around at cocktail parties and has even appeared on the covers of respected business magazines. He needs to get this white elephant off of his hands, fast. . . . Who knows how much interest he's paying a bank every month it sits here, being big? Beth takes a yellow pad out of her bag and scans the Sub-Zero refrigerators and Viking stoves with a thoughtful eye.

Beth, I realize, has a great poker face. This drives the Israeli man nuts. He peppers her with questions, asking for some clues, but she won't commit to anything: whether the asking price is too high, whether the market is overbought or oversold, whether she likes the house, even. All she promises is to take some notes, design a glossy brochure (*Entertainer's Dream! Sunny Delight!* or some such Realtor euphemism), and wait for someone to bite. She turns the conversation to the home that she and her husband are building in Seven Hills. They had planned to do a concrete roof, she says, but the more she thinks about it, another $11,000 for the tile roof doesn't sound so bad. She asks the builder for his opinion. He takes us out onto the patio and points upward. Rubber. It's cheap, looks fine, and no one notices anyway.

Beth casts a thoughtful pose—she is a great listener—then leads me on a tour of the mansion, taking notes on the yellow pad as she points out the important features. There's the home theater (good) and the view (pretty good) and the sunken poolside bar with the built-in barbecue (very good, very *now*). The architect knew the formula. He penciled in two of everything that you would find in a home of half the size and he made the rooms twice as large. But then there is also the design (not so good) and a smaller-than-expected master bath (bad) and, finally, a bizarre wall treatment in the foyer that is supposed to resemble marble but looks more like the side of a frat house after a party (very, very bad but fixable).

After sharing some parting words and nervous laughter with the developer, Beth and I get back into the Mercedes and Beth's face softens a little. I can tell that she is underwhelmed. One of the negatives of a hot market is that expectations get out of control, she says quietly. Five and a half million dollars does seem pretty steep for a giant shoe box with an elevator, at least to my amateur mind, even if you can see a bunch of lights at night. Then again, if home prices rocket up another 50 percent in the next twelve months, it's probably a steal.

But then I realize that what we have just walked through is not a home at all: It is an investment—or, to steal an analogy from the tobacco industry, it is a *debt-delivery mechanism*. Houses—homes, if you want to get quaint—used to be the savings vehicle of the middle class. The mortgage was a sort of layaway program guaranteed and closely regulated by the federal government. The obvious advantage to home ownership as opposed to putting money in the bank or under a mattress was that it protected you from the ravages of inflation—and, by default, destitution. But no longer. Now an entire, increasingly unregulated industry exists to ensure that the house is not a vehicle for saving but for spending and even for speculating. Armed with euphemisms like "Release the hidden value of your home" and fueled by Americans' gratitude for credit and our short memories, this industry has become hugely profitable and almost unfathomable in size. The total amount of mortgage debt in the United States is now greater than the value of all the stock markets combined. It's a similar story in the UK, where consumer debt recently passed the £1 trillion mark for the first time. Along the way, familiar phrases like *home ownership* and *American Dream*—simple terms whose goodness once seemed self-evident—have become hopelessly obscured. The goal is no longer to be free of debt, to own something of lasting value. The goal is simply to be free of "bad debt." Debt that buys you a bigger house is "good," because the home will always appreciate and you are simply leveraging your earning power to generate the maximum profit. "Bad" debt is the credit card junk and the other high-interest, unsecured balances you've accumulated,* but those can now be magically transformed into "good debt" by refinancing your home and using the proceeds to "pay off" those "bad" debts. Presto!

In reality, of course, there is no difference between good and bad debt. Debt, by definition, is nothing but a liability, a promise to pay. And, to put it simply, if you can't afford an expensive house now, you still won't be able to afford it when that same house becomes even more expensive.

Our last stop of the day is the office, where Beth has scheduled a meeting with a lending consultant. He is an older gentleman, maybe early seventies. He was probably born during the Depression. He has definitely lived through boom and bust and boom again. After admiring Beth's new digs, he sits down with her and explains why mortgage debt is "good" debt: The interest is tax deductible![†] He knows that most people don't fully understand the math of the tax deduction, but he also knows that most people hate paying taxes, which is his ace in the hole. He can whip out a calculator and quickly show them how buying a bigger house actually *saves* them money, because the more interest you pay, the more you can deduct! Sha-*zam*! It doesn't hurt that one local bamk's new mortgage calculator encourages folks to spend up to

---

*Perhaps by furnishing the house, or maintaining the house, or, God forbid, paying the mortgage with cash advances.

[†]This is not the case in the UK.

55 percent of their income on the mortgage, more than double what Realtors used to recommend. Bad credit or no credit? No problem! This consultant can fix his clients' credit ratings in a matter of weeks, sometimes days, by paying the credit bureaus special fees to expedite the erasing of negative items.

Beth interjects with an interesting question. She's heard that you should never cancel a credit card because it hurts your credit rating. True, says her guest. You want to show as much available credit as possible, though you should maintain at least a little balance, presumably to show the credit card companies that you enjoy paying interest.* Beth nods her head to show that she either understands this rather counterintuitive fact or else she needs him to speed things up.

When the consultant starts talking about building a relationship together, Beth finally cuts to the chase: What can he offer her clients? He responds that the only question on most people's minds is "how big of a house can I get for the lowest payment?" So his job is to get them the biggest bang for their buck by hooking the biggest loan possible. How can he help Beth? By up-selling her customers into bigger mortgages and, by default, more expensive properties.

Beth wonders out loud how most folks can afford to buy a house these days. After all, the average listing in Vegas is now over $250,000. So later on I decide to call a mortgage broker I'm friends with in Los Angeles, where homes are *really* expensive. His chief assets are that he is attractive, enthusiastic, and very friendly. Like Beth, he also happens to live in one of the hottest real estate markets in the country. Locals are now saying that property in Southern California never goes down, even though that's precisely what happened a decade ago. But for the moment they're right. Home prices have been increasing by at least 20 percent a year for as long as anyone cares to remember.

*This is later confirmed on an episode of *The Suze Orman Show.* Suze says that lowering your credit card limits automatically lowers your credit score.

Last year my friend pocketed $70,000, mostly in commissions. This year he'll do even better. That's more than double the median wage in America and far more than he made selling expensive jeans at the mall, his previous job. But, unlike Beth, his clients aren't rich. Sometimes they aren't even what we would traditionally call middle-class. His newest client is a cashier at Home Depot. She wants to be a homeowner—or, more precisely, a condo owner. The tiny slice of the American Dream she craves is priced just north of $400,000—a bargain by L.A. standards but unrealistic, given that her take-home pay is around $1,300 per month. In other words, she earns half the mortgage payment she would have to assume in order to buy the condo. It doesn't take a calculator to figure out she can't afford it.

Yet, the mortgage industry has created a product for her and the millions of other earnings-challenged Americans like her. It's officially called the "stated income" loan, though mortgage brokers like my friend refer to it as the "liar's loan." And it works like this: The Home Depot cashier writes down whatever income my friend tells her the bank needs to see on her application (wink, wink) and both the broker and the bank promise not to verify it by asking for tax returns or paycheck stubs (nudge, nudge). If needed, she will find a "tenant" to mitigate her rent "shock," i.e., the fact that her mortgage will be four times her previous rent payment, a fiction that he or she will put in writing for the bank (wink, wink). If she has no friends, or if she has friends who are unwilling to commit fraud on her behalf, friends may be appointed for her, probably by the mortgage company (triple wink). All the cashier needs to do is provide a decent credit score and her signature. The bankers will provide the money, and their sense of imagination/denial will reach new heights. "Who knew that cashiers at the Home Depot netted $6,000 a month?" they will ask each other incredulously at the water cooler. Must be one hell of a union!

But the application is just a bump on the road to the dozens of new products that make that monthly payment seem within reach. By far the most popular is the interest-only loan, in which the "buyer" pays only interest for the first two or three years at a very low short-term rate, then is "converted" into a traditional payment plan with a much higher long-term rate. In London, where prices are exorbitant even by US standards, things are even easier. You can get an interest-only loan for as long as you desire, as long as you repay the full amount by retirement. And, if your income isn't sufficient to qualify, you can apply for "fast-tracking"— meaning that the bank won't bother to verify how much you earn. There is also the "negative amortization" loan, in which the mortgage becomes larger every month because the payments aren't high enough to cover the interest and principal. And then there's the 125 percent loan, in which the bank lends the borrower 25 percent more than the value of the property. That extra money, I assume, can be used to make the mortgage payments the borrower could otherwise not afford. As Beth later explains with deadpan understatement, "These lenders are having to be very creative." So are their ad agencies. NIG's latest ad, for eample, asks 'What if a mortgage could make you richer?"

Every one of these loans rests on a simple principle: property values will only go up. My friend's client, for example, is betting that her condo will appreciate fast enough so that the equity she accumulates can be cashed out to make her future mortgage payments. Of course, cashing out the equity means that her total mortgage payment will have to get larger. She'll be surfing decades from now, and that's if everything goes according to plan. If the condo doesn't appreciate in the double digits, or if interest rates rise, or if she can't find a real roommate with real money, or if she decides to eat or put gas in her car, she'll drown very, very quickly.

Officially, more than half of the new mortgages in California are some variety of interest-only loan and the average down payment has fallen from 20 percent to around 3. This means that the notion of home equity—the percentage of your property that actually belongs to you, as opposed to the bank—no longer exists for most new homebuyers. My friend tells me that nearly all of his clients are getting interest-only loans and estimates that 85 percent of them "have to" misrepresent their income. Similarly, in the UK, around 30 percent of mortgages taken out today are interest-only mortgages, compared with only 12 percent in June 2003. He assures me that the banks know this is happening. After all, with home prices increasing so rapidly in California, lying is the only way that most people can afford to buy a home. Does he understand that this will help no one, least of all the desperate souls being approved to assume thirty-year liabilities? Does he understand that these amateurs are surfing a tsunami?

According to the Federal Reserve, 12 percent of young families—those whose head of household is 35 to 44 years of age—were more than two months behind on their debts in 2004, twice the percentage from 2001. It's worth noting that, in 2004, home prices were booming. By 2007, will that number have doubled once more?*

The next afternoon, Beth offers to take me to the site where she and her husband are building their dream home. As we get in the Mercedes, talk again turns to how blessed she is. She has three girls whom she worries about spoiling. She owns her own business. She

---

*Again, the UK is no different, although the problem appears to be growing at a slower rate. There, around 280,000 mortgages are one month or more in arrears. That represents an increase of 4 percent from the same period one year ago.

has a personal trainer. She is happily married to a man who also works in the real estate business—for a master plan called Alliante, which sounds suspiciously like the car that was supposed to make Cadillac hip. Her daughters are in Catholic school even though she says that the public schools in Vegas are terrific. (I think she has to say that.)

She and her husband recently sold their 4,500-square-foot house for close to a million dollars, doubling their money in a few years. They will move into the new 11,000-square-foot dream home in April, which reminds her of the roofing dilemma. She interrupts our conversation to call her husband from the car, meaning that I finally get to observe Beth sell something. She goes in quietly, as though she herself has not made up her mind yet, as though she is also weighing the pros and cons. But then she starts leaning toward the tile, thinking out loud. After all, tile looks nicer than concrete. And the large homes in Seven Hills are mostly doing tile. They can fold it into their construction loan (and tile will automatically increase the resale value of the house; that's the real beauty of it: it's kind of free in a sense, really) and the difference in monthly payment won't be noticeable—well, everything is relative. When she hangs up, I ask her if she's already thinking about flipping. "If I can make a profit," she replies, "why not?"

When I finally meet Beth's husband, a soft-spoken man who drives a matching Mercedes, he asks me if Beth has told me about the new house. When I reply in the affirmative, he mumbles, "Crazy."

The home is little more than foundation and framing, but one can just begin to imagine angles, textures, places for windows and doors. In front of us, the sun is setting. The desert glows in rapturous oranges, yellows, and auburns through the beams. At night the air in Vegas turns cool and the desert can seem like paradise. Beth and her husband walk amid the sawdust and discarded soda cans and fast-food wrappers. They point at different areas, imagining rooms. I overhear Beth say something about how excited the girls are, but I know that it's their mother who is most excited. She is living the American Dream. More important, she has apparently sold her husband on the tile roof.

Later, Beth will try to explain her own mortgage product to me. The bank calls it "loan to value" because it bases the loan amount not on the value of the land or even the land and the cost of the house, but on the value of the house *after* it is built. Beth calls it "a very ingenious way to get people to keep building expensive homes." The result is that Beth was able to borrow far more than she could have with a traditional loan. Of course, the future value of a mansion that hasn't been built yet in the middle of the desert, and in the midst of a speculative real estate bubble, is more than a little subjective. "I'm very lucky they had that loan," Beth gushes, as though this were all an utter coincidence, the stars aligning to make her dreams come true, "though if that interest rate goes up by the time we move in, I might not be able to afford the house anymore."

She giggles at the absurdity for a moment, but I catch a glint of hope in her eye—the glint of a speculator—before she adds, "I guess if you look like you make money, eventually you will, you know."

Two

"In the land of the blind, the one-eyed man is king."

– Anonymous

Dee Hock didn't invent the credit card. He did something far more important: He *believed* in it. Really believed. Believed that it had the potential to free human beings from rules and regulations (Hock's definition of *hell*). Believed that it would thwart the ability of large financial institutions to impose uniform standards because every bank, no matter how small or how large, would have access to the most powerful brand ever created. Believed that a tiny plastic card with a magnetic stripe could become *the* store of value, linking every human being with his or her wealth instantly. Believed that, in doing so with nothing but electronic signals racing through his computers from one bank to another, the credit card would create its own currency so universal that the dollar, the yen, and the British pound would all be made obsolete. Finally, he believed that the organization he created, Visa International, would save the world. How? By, in a typically new-agey rhetorical flourish, "allowing spontaneous interconnection into an equitable, enduring, twenty-first-century society in harmony with the human spirit and the biosphere."

Of course, none of these beliefs came true. The credit card has shackled individuals, imposed uniformity, destroyed value (i.e., savings) at an unprecedented rate, and, so far at least, has replaced neither the pound, the yen, or the dollar. And credit cards (with Visa at the forefront) have arguably been the most powerful force behind a massive redistribution of wealth that has left this country less equal than at any time since the Great Depression. If anyone besides Hock believes that credit cards have contributed to the harmony of their spirit and the biosphere, I have yet to meet them.

So what does Hock think of the credit industry he helped to create? That's a difficult question to answer, because Hock does not wish to discuss the past with me. When I requested an interview, he declined with a succinct note: something about no longer doing those kinds of things. Today Hock lives on a small farm in Northern California where he spends his time tilling the soil, discussing philosophy with his tractor (which he has named "Thee Ancient One") and his subconscious (which he has named "Old Monkey Mind.") He is a grand philosopher, the kind of guy who can write something like "Until our consciousness of the relational aspect of the world and all life therein shall change, the problems that crush the young and make grown people cry will get progressively worse," as though it were self-evident. Like Ross Perot, he likes to state his beliefs as facts. And, also like Perot, Hock never thinks small. His latest hobby is leading a movement he calls "chaordism,"* which will remake corporate America in the image of Visa International, and, by doing so, save the planet from rigid, hierarchical, oppressive, and bureaucratic organizations. This is not a joke.

For all of his eccentricities, one cannot deny that Hock was a great visionary, and, like all great visionaries, Hock found himself

*The conflation of chaos and order. Visit www.chaordic.org to become part of the movement.

42

surrounded by doubters at a time when he himself felt absolute conviction. The year was 1968 and Hock, who had been fired from several jobs and was facing an increasingly desperate financial situation, talked his way into a job at Seafirst Bank in Seattle, Washington. For some time the bank's president shuffled him from department to department, because there was simply no work to be done and no job for which Hock was particularly qualified. He recalls one task—digging through the garbage of a branch, looking for a lost deposit—with particular bitterness. So when the bank decided to become a licensee of the "BankAmericard," the country's first bank-issued credit card, Hock was tapped as one half of a two-man team overseeing its rollout. It was a job that no one, including Hock, wanted. Banking was then about servicing large corporations. Consumer credit was left to the loan sharks and pawnbrokers. Yet, as Hock rolled up his sleeves, there was something about credit cards that instantly seduced him. Perhaps it was the magnitude of the task (which roughly matched the size of his ego), or maybe it was the new technology, which fascinated Old Monkey Mind, or perhaps it was the fact that Bank of America, the card's creator, was the embodiment of everything he hated and the antithesis of everything he stood for. In Hock's eyes, Bank of America was not just bigness but management charts, uniform standards, titles, stupidity. In his new role working with this organization, Hock would get to be an agitator. He would have a platform to try out some of the philosophy he and Old Monkey Mind had been discussing on their long walks in the lush, soggy hills of Seattle. In other words, he would be able to cut the largest bank in the world down to size. David versus Goliath.

As Hock tells it, the Bank of America turned out to be even more incompetent than he could have dreamed. Thanks to the mess they'd created, Seafirst, like the other BankAmericard licensees, was losing vast sums of money on the credit card business. Why? The banks were being defrauded by customers, merchants, and criminals alike. The technology was primitive and the accounting was, by all accounts, a nightmare. This was back in the days when every transaction was recorded by hand on extremely thin strips of carbon paper, which were then sent to a warehouse to be sorted and reconciled. Inevitably the warehouse became a paper jungle, many of the receipts were lost or illegible to begin with, and reconciliation was wishful thinking. Bank of America had promised its licensees access to the future of banking, but most of them—like Hock's boss at Seafirst—had signed up mainly to preempt their competitors. Now they had simply saved their competitors a huge amount of money and time. Credit cards had become their albatross.

Within a year of rolling out the credit card for Seafirst, Hock was dispatched to a BankAmericard convention in Ohio, where two Bank of America executives were supposed to give a pep talk to their disillusioned—and angry—licensees. Or so thought the licensees. Not only did the Bank of America execs on the stage offer no insights as to how they might fix the crisis, they wouldn't even acknowledge a problem existed. The situation came as close to a riot as bankers get—that is, until one of their own, Hock, took to the stage and, with the now terrified B of A executives' blessing, promised to clean up shop.

Hock created an advisory committee composed of his fellow licensees on the spot. Within a few years he had formed a cooperative owned by all of the banks that issued BankAmericards, which became the organization that would blossom into Visa International, which would become the most ubiquitous organization in the history of capitalism. It was a brilliant idea, a company devoted to issuing credit as quickly and as efficiently as possible: instantly was the ultimate goal. This company would be composed of its members, the banks, so that there would be no infighting or other conflicts to slow Hock's grand plan. Finally, Visa would exist not for profit but ultimately to fulfill Hock's vision of a world where tangible currency (Hock was one of the first to see paper money going the way of stones and beads) was replaced by trillions of electronic signals moving through his mainframe computers. In theory, Visa would become the ultimate store of value. In practice, it was nothing more than a massive marketing campaign and an electronic switch that routed money from the bank of the payer to the bank of the payee. For practical purposes, Hock had two main priorities: one, that Visa would truly be ubiquitous ("everywhere you want to be"; "life takes Visa"); and two, that transactions would occur with lightning speed ("faster than cash").

Looking back in his memoir, Hock professed feelings of reluctance and even fear that day in Ohio, but he was clearly the man for the job. Hock wasn't a bureaucrat, like the banking guys. He wasn't scared of challenges. He was obsessed with the technology that would be needed to process small transactions on a grand scale. But, most of all, he truly believed that the credit card would empower the masses, that it would give them a freedom they had never known. They could reserve hotel rooms and rental cars without sending a check in advance! They could buy things instantly without waiting for funds to clear! They could hand over a card and get something in return *and* get their card back to use again! Best of all, they would no longer be forced to interact with nosy, judgmental bankers! Credit cards could indeed create a new currency—an abstract currency of numbers that only existed on statements, a currency that flowed through computers without ever being touched or felt, a currency that no government or central bank could control. Dee Hock saw the big picture.

In other words, Hock was the industry's Moses—and he knew it. He would lead the trembling bankers, so comfortable in their suits and corner offices, to the Promised Land, a place of infinite possibilities and untold progress. He would not waver or compromise, but he was bad at compromise anyway. His vision was absolute, his conviction was absolutely convincing—if misplaced. Visa International, would, as his mission statement put it, become "the premier store of value in the world," even though Visa never stored anything: It simply routed transactions from one bank to another. Had the bankers known that Hock's vision was about creating a twenty-first-century society in harmony with the human spirit and the biosphere rather than about making them boatloads of cash, they might have balked. Luckily for Hock, and for them, he kept that grandest of notions between himself and Old Monkey Mind. If the bankers ever wondered if the guy was a little different from them, they kept their mouths shut.

Indeed, the suits whom Hock longed to replace with mainframes worried far less about technology and grand visions of the future (which they probably didn't understand anyway) than they worried about the past. What they knew (and what Hock's theory failed to appreciate) is that banking is about selling a single product: debt. That product can be packaged a million different ways—car loans, mortgages, lines of credit, overdraft protection, credit cards, cell phones, etc., etc.—but, in the end, the product is an obligation to be repaid, with interest. And the price of that product is however much interest and fees can be charged on the original amount. The more interest and fees a bank can charge, the more profitable the product. This is a fairly academic concept.

When Hock had taken the job at Seafirst, banks were in the business of borrowing money from individuals (this is back when people actually saved) and lending that money to corporations at a slightly higher rate. Consumer lending was not profitable for two major reasons: one, processing small loans was too time-consuming, mainly because bankers actually reviewed the applicant's financial situation and thereby determined their ability to repay the loan; and two, the government, acting in its traditional role as consumer protector—a role that had grown out of the massive bank failures in the 1920s and 1930s—regulated how much banks could both pay and charge in interest. So not only was there only one product, but by law every bank had to sell exactly the same product.*

Furthermore, banks were forbidden from crossing state lines and, in some instances, city lines. A bank in New York City, for example, could not open branches outside of the city. A bank in Texas could only operate one branch in the entire state. Accumulating millions of customers was next to impossible, even if they could be managed profitably. All of the conditions that make the modern credit card industry so profitable—high rates, a national market, efficient processing—did not exist.

But the greatest obstacle facing Hock was not regulation or technology: It was tradition. Handing a customer the "noose with which to hang himself financially," as one of his peers at Seafirst put it, was generally acknowledged to be immoral. More than anyone else, bankers understood a simple truth of human nature that Hock, in his zeal to create a brave new world, never seemed to appreciate: If you give someone credit, they will probably use it. The banks had learned this lesson in the Roaring Twenties, when Americans had overextended themselves buying all of the shiny new trophies of the Industrial Revolution on credit. So had begun the first race to create an American middle class—or at least the appearance of one—and its violent crash in 1929 nearly took down the American banking system. Since then, the role of the government regulators and the banks themselves was primarily to ensure that the Great Depression was not repeated. Indeed, the banker's most sacred duty was to rein in his customer's appetite—in other words, to say no.

---

*Though it is true that banks could, and did, offer "free" gifts under a certain dollar amount (e.g., toasters) as a signing bonus. Citibank was the first institution to fully exploit this loophole, tempting New Yorkers with particularly desirable appliances whose value exceeded the government-imposed limits.

There are two things that make consumer credit in general and credit cards in particular different from any other product. One, demand is a function of supply. In other words, the more credit you supply, the more demand you create. The more people become dependent on credit, the more they need to keep going. Once Americans began using one credit card, for example, they tended to need another. And then another. And then higher credit limits. And then they needed to refinance their homes to pay off the credit card bills. And so on. No other product creates that cycle (well, crack and heroin come to mind, but . . .).

The other difference is that a credit card is the only product whose price changes after the purchase has already occurred. Is there any other product for which, after you've purchased it, you are suddenly told that you have to pay more? Or that the terms and conditions of the product have changed? Imagine that someone calls you one evening, just as you are sitting down to watch your favorite television show, and tells you they need another twenty bucks for the suit you bought last month or five bucks extra to cover the meal you ate at Red Lobster three years ago. Presumably you'd tell them to go to hell, or maybe you'd be more diplomatic. What you wouldn't do is pay them. Yet, the cost of credit and its terms are changed constantly. And not very many people protest, by the way. Why? Presumably because they know that agreeing to this bargain is a condition for getting more credit. This became Hock's greatest weapon.

Visa was what economists like to call a "natural" monopoly. Its growth was limited only by the reluctance of consumers to spend. In fact, one of Hock's most daunting challenges in the early days was convincing retailers to pay Visa its 5 percent transaction fee, but that reluctance was overcome by studies showing that customers spent far more—usually 30 percent more—when they used plastic rather than cash. This is the same argument that finally convinced fast-food companies to accept credit cards—a frightening thought in a country already confronting record levels of obesity. (Suze Orman's favorite guest is a young woman who claims to have accumulated nearly $30,000 in credit card debt by eating at Kentucky Fried Chicken.)

Citigroup Center consumes an entire block of midtown Manhattan between Third and Lexington. Its trophy is a fifty-nine-foot brushed-steel-and-glass tower designed by the late Cambridge architect Hugh Stubbins Jr. The tower's distinctive angled roof, which has been featured in countless Citibank ads, is supposed to resemble a gigantic number one; however, the building can just as accurately be described as the world's tallest—and shiniest—erection. When it was built in 1975, a seventy-year-old church had to be destroyed and neighbors tried to block its construction. But Citicorp prevailed, with one director assuring the community that the complex was designed "as a life force . . . as a source of energy and commitment back to the city and the people." The day I visited, Citigroup Center was a fortress guarded by dozens of New York police and National Guardsmen toting M16s and Starbucks Caramel Macchiatos. The public spaces had been closed indefinitely due to one of those catch-22s of the war on terror that many Americans find so disconcerting. Although the bank's largest shareholder, Prince Alwaleed bin Talal bin Abdul Aziz Alsaud, is a Saudi citizen, Middle Eastern terrorists were apparently bent on car-bombing the place as well as several other Citigroup facilities around New York City.

Citigroup Center was the brainchild of Walter Wriston, who retired as Citicorp's chairman in 1984. Wriston was a gigantic man physically, a man who literally stood out, who had to have his suits specially tailored to his odd and outsized dimensions. He was hyper and always uncomfortable in his skin. But he was also an

49

intellectual, the son of a history professor who became president of both Lawrence College and Brown University. Though Wriston grew up in considerably plusher surroundings than Hock, his parents had raised him with the same frugal sensibility and he'd developed a similar, almost obsessive, hatred of bureaucracy. In other words Wriston, like Hock, saw himself as an outsider and would ultimately become a revolutionary. Unlike Hock, however, Wriston realized that it was very much to his advantage if the rest of the banking world stuck to tradition: It would give him a head start. Wriston was probably the first modern American banker to realize that his job was not to teach his customers how to save but how to spend as much as possible.

In his early years Wriston tried to work within the industry's framework. He earned his chops at Citibank loaning money to airlines and shipbuilders, forging close friendships with Ari Onassis and several American presidents, nurturing those relationships on private yachts and exclusive golf courses. It got him the CEO job in 1970 but, once installed in the corner office, Wriston's appetite for growth proved insatiable. He promised his shareholders 15 percent annual increases in profits—unheard-of in the banking business*— just before a perfect economic storm of inflation, war, and technology bust ravaged the economy in the midseventies. Wriston weathered the storm by reaching out to smaller and riskier customers.

While, because of banking laws, Wriston could not expand beyond the boroughs of New York City, he could expand everywhere else in the world with few to no restrictions. Indeed, other countries were delighted to receive his credit. They were used to being treated with condescension and caution by the ivory towers of American banking. Which made a lot of sense: After all, the countries

*John Reed, who succeeded Wriston as CEO, called the promise irresponsible.

that needed the most tended to be the poorest. Who wanted to lend to a bunch of peasants? Wriston stepped up to the plate and smaller banks followed him. If he felt any of the traditional banker's intuitive sense of caution, he purged it by endlessly repeating his new mantra: *Countries can't go broke.* The mantra seemed to satisfy Wriston's conscience, attracted a devoted circle of shareholders and dictators, and, most important, allowed Citi and the rest to lend more and more money to countries that could afford it less and less. Pretty soon, the "less-developed countries," as Wriston was fond of calling them,* were using new money to pay off old debt. The trouble was that a large chunk of the money was coming from the same source: Citibank and its partner banks. The familiar term for what Wriston's strategy became in practice is a "reverse pyramid scheme", so named because larger and larger liabilities must be piled on top of the original debt in order to avoid default. Eventually the amount of new cash needed to service the old debts and the new debts becomes too burdensome and the whole thing collapses beneath its own weight. The only exception is where the player prints the currency with which the game is played, which makes the United States government unique among debtors.

When the inevitable happened, there were only two solutions: one, squeeze the working classes of these countries harder (the wealthy made sure that their own assets were not available when the bills came due, which seems to happen a lot in "developing" countries); and, two, swallow your pride and allow a larger entity— say, the United States Treasury—to bail you out. Ultimately, both happened. There were the expected outcries from competitors, consumer advocates, and even some members of Congress, but most

---

*Wriston was one of the first bankers to get the power of verbiage. Thus were "third-world" countries simply "less-developed" nations. He was also the first to understand the importance of flattery, discovering that a *President's Office* or *Special Processing* stamp on a credit card offer increased the response dramatically.

Americans accepted the wisdom that Citibank was too large to fail. Wriston kept his job and his company treaded a little more carefully—at least for a couple of decades.*

Wriston had been humbled, but he never abandoned his audacious growth ambitions. Indeed, failure seems to have sharpened his sense of focus. Now there was only one market that could approach the scale he needed to produce that double-digit growth he'd promised, but that market, the American middle class, was unavailable by virtue of regulation. The solution was obvious: Get rid of the laws. For that to happen, both the banking industry and its customers would have to be radically reprogrammed.

Wriston hired Robert Kennedy's Harvard roommate to head up a new lobbying effort designed to obliterate any law which restricted his bank's activities. He couched his new crusade in terms of personal frustration and a fervent patriotism. Sears, JCPenney, and a host of other large retailers, he pointed out, were charging 18 percent a month on their store credit cards, while Citibank was restricted to charging roughly half that amount. Why should retailers be allowed to act like banks *and* charge pawnshop rates, while banks were prevented from acting like banks? It didn't make any sense. Armed with considerable moral influence as the world's leading banker (these were the days before *financial executive* equaled *scandal*) as well as an unflagging and convenient belief that banks should be allowed to do whatever they wanted (this was America, by God, let freedom ring!) and, most important, a remarkably limited deference to history, Wriston set out to conquer the American middle class.

Over the previous ten years Hock had stayed busy popularizing the means to Wriston's end: a tiny plastic card that was already

---

*In 2005, Citigroup paid more than a billion dollars in fines and settlements with investors—and wrote off a multiple of that amount—for promoting a similar scheme. The only difference was that this time Citi had engaged corporations—Enron and Dynergy, among them—not nations.

being used by millions and that would soon be ubiquitous. For all of the problems Hock had encountered, getting people to use the card had never been one of them. There was something seductive—addictive, even—about instant credit. The challenges were techno-logical in nature: making transactions faster, processing more effi-cient, and the brand more recognizable. But Hock had made impressive progress on all of these fronts. Computers were becom-ing more and more powerful. Telecommunications had reduced the time needed for an authorization from minutes to seconds. Hock had convinced the stodgy old guys to rename their BankAmericard "Visa" because it was one of the only words whose definition and pronunciation were the same everywhere in the civilized world. The Promised Land was in sight.

Wriston, meanwhile, laid out his own vision of the Promised Land—a land in which millions of customers charged all of their purchases to a Citibank credit card and paid high, unregulated inter-est rates and fees for the privilege. A land where the same govern-ment that had indirectly bailed out his company was told that any oversight was equivalent to socialism. A land where he could oper-ate anywhere he damned well pleased. Wriston attacked a half cen-tury of tradition from his phallic bully pulpit in midtown Manhattan, agitating and cajoling his way out of the straitjacket of regulation that constrained his grand ambitions.

Wriston's and Hock's separate visions were on a collision course, yet they turned out to be a brilliant tag team. At no time was this more evident than when Hock decided to re-brand the BankAmericard as Visa in the mid-1970s—a giant step toward uni-versality. Millions of BankAmericard customers were sent letters explaining that their "new" Visa card would soon arrive in the mail and instructing them to destroy their "old" BankAmericard, even though the two cards were identical in every aspect except the art-work. Back then, an outsized Visa logo occupied the front of the card while the name of the customer's bank—the institution that issued the card—was printed in very small letters on the back. Not very many people bothered to look at the fine print on the back, and it didn't take a genius to realize that customers would rush to use the first shiny new Visa card that arrived.

Up until that point Citibank had mainly issued cards under the MasterCharge brand,* but Wriston sensed an opportunity of epic proportions. By signing up as a Visa bank and by ignoring the spirit of Hock's rebranding scheme, Wriston could send out millions of Citibank Visa cards to his competitors' customers *before* the replacement cards from their own banks arrived. Thanks to Hock's letter, most of those customers would immediately destroy their BankAmericard and start using the Citibank Visa card. When the Visa card arrived from their own bank a week or two later, those same customers would probably assume it was redundant or, ironically, from a competing institution and destroy it.

And that's exactly what happened. Wriston preempted his competitors by a couple of weeks and they never recovered. The gimmick not only exceeded Wriston's expectations, poaching millions of accounts and instantly making Citibank the largest credit card issuer in the country, it taught Wriston an important lesson: When it came to easy credit, the average consumer was lazy or lovestruck or both. They used the card and they didn't ask questions. Creating a sense of confusion was therefore an extraordinarily effective weapon.

Wriston had effectively hijacked Hock's Promised Land and made it his own. Now he turned his attention to reaping the har-

*MasterCharge had been formed in the late 1960s by a competing group of banks in response to the BankAmericard system. For a brief time, MasterCharge counted more banks as members than BankAmericard, but Dee Hock consistently outmaneuvered MasterCharge in the all-important areas of branding and processing technology. Today, despite Citigroup re-allying with MasterCard, Visa International, has retained a wide lead over its competitor.

vest. Wriston knew that his customers wanted credit, especially since they knew that the bank tended to be stingy with it. The more credit you gave them, the more they would want and, eventually, the more they would need. It was the same with the American middle class as it was with the less-developed peoples who had ultimately stiffed him. Wriston used his customers' collective appetite to his advantage, painting the issue in patriotic stripes. Doling out instant credit was an issue of *freedom*. How could a democratically elected government deny Citibank the freedom to give its customers what they wanted? The simple answer was that they could not. It was repressive, anticapitalist, and un-American. One by one, Wriston succeeded in demolishing the laws restricting credit, laws that had been designed to protect the banking industry every bit as much as the individual. The financial industry's record of legislative and judicial victories since Wriston began his crusade is simply too impressive to list in full. Here's a brief summary:

1972:	In *Worthen Bank & Trust v. National BankAmericard, Inc.*, the United States Supreme Court gives banks the right to use both the MasterCharge and Visa systems to issue credit cards, cementing the natural monopoly.*
1978:	In *Marquette v. First National Bank of Omaha*, the United States Supreme Court gives banks the right to "export" interest rates across state lines, i.e., to charge whatever interest rates they so desired anywhere.
1981:	The Federal Reserve and the comptroller of the currency approve Citibank's credit card office in South Dakota, effectively killing the McFadden

*Hock himself was vehemently opposed to what was called "duality," fearing that it would reduce competition. As it turns out, he was right.

Act, which prohibited banks from making loans across state lines.

1996:   In *Smiley v. Citibank,* the United States Supreme Court allows banks to charge whatever fees they see fit.

1997:   Congress approves the merger of Citibank and Travelers Group, effectively killing the Glass-Steagall Act, which prohibited banks from cross-selling insurance and other investment products.

Needless to say, Wriston emerged victorious, maybe even more so than he could have imagined. But in retrospect it's a little hard to see how he could not have. Consumers had been taught to see credit both as a free gift and as a validation of themselves. Legislators quickly understood how credit could fuel an economy that, by the early eighties, had become overwhelmingly consumer-driven. Equally important, both Congress and the American people shared Wriston's disregard for history. Only the stodgy old bankers whose fathers and grandfathers had warned them about the need for regulation—the ones who were quite comfortable operating the small banks in the small towns and granting credit to individuals only with great caution—only *they* resisted. And by the time they caught on, *their* customers were using Citibank cards and Wriston was opening branches across the street.

Wriston and Hock revolutionized the world of banking, though their motives could hardly have been more opposed. And in the end they both received startlingly little in return. Hock's starting pay as chairman of Visa was $40,000 a year; what Wriston earned in his best year at Citi today wouldn't get a mid-level analyst to pick up the phone. But both Hock and Wriston were ultimately recognized by the young Turks they led to the Promised Land, the modern-day bankers, financiers, and politicians who have since plundered its waters with the efficiency of piranhas. In 1996, as Americans charged a record $1 trillion on their Visa cards, Hock briefly abandoned Thee Ancient One to be admitted into the Business Hall of Fame. And in 2004, with foreclosures, bankruptcies, and defaults all at higher levels than during the Great Depression, President George W. Bush awarded Wriston the Presidential Medal of Freedom.

Three

"We see names like 'Bank of America' and we think, 'Those guys aren't going to take advantage of me.' But the truth is, those are exactly the companies that will take advantage of you."

– Bud Hibbs

Rochester, NY is one of those places I never intended to visit—ever. Three hundred miles west of New York sounds cold and not particularly glamorous. Whenever I hear someone mention a city like Rochester, it sounds like a relic from the industrial revolution, when cities were actually producing things rather than just selling them. Like most Americans, I find the consumer hubs—New York, L.A., Miami—far more appealing. Rochester does sound vaguely familiar—was it Kodak that was founded there? Or Xerox, maybe? Both?—but it also sounds dead, stale.

Yet, I have made the trip, via Philadelphia, because of a unique opportunity. Bob Manning, a professor at the Rochester Institute of Technology and probably the world's foremost expert on the credit card business, has offered to explain how the modern financial industry really works. I have already visited his Web site, which is chock-full of salacious industry secrets: how credit card companies refer to people like me as "freeloaders" and "deadbeats" for paying our bills on time; how they pay lip service to responsible borrowers but fight over the "revolvers"—those who pay all of the interest and fees—because those are the customers who generate the real profits; how they've severed the logical link between income—i.e., how much you can afford to borrow—and credit—i.e., how much you are allowed to borrow; how their lobbyists have taken over Congress to abolish a decades-long tradition of consumer protection.

The RIT campus is a collection of angular brick-and-glass buildings anchored by one of those impossibly ugly modern steel sculptures that is de rigueur at most universities. Bob's office is a cubbyhole in a one-story building near the main parking lot, packed full of souvenirs: a MasterCard Teenie Beanie Baby, an advertisement for the Smithsonian Discover Card (which he finds particularly distasteful), a board game that teaches girls ages 3 and up how to use a charge card, and so on. Bob, wearing a beret and a necktie silk-screened with $100 bills, urges me to shut the door as he turns on his computer and reminds me how privileged I am to receive this information. So begins my indoctrination into the underground world of financial industry dissidents—which, for the beret, the cramped office (blinds drawn), and the slightly paranoid undertone, I thus christen la Résistance.

We begin with a PowerPoint presentation of images that Bob has collected over the years. Each has been used in the class he teaches or in testimony to the United States Congress, where he is frequently summoned as an expert witness. When we come to a slide of Manning's book, *Credit Card Nation*, he claims that the financial industry attempted to buy it from his publisher so they could bury it. When that proved unsuccessful, he claims, their PR machine launched a massive campaign to discredit both Bob and his book. They needn't have worried: the book never sold very well. It is, like Bob, extremely thorough but sometimes very hard to follow.

But Bob is more than a financial guru. He is a cultural anthropologist and, like Dave Ramsey, blames a shift in behavior as the source of our addiction to credit. In particular, Bob cites the death of what he calls the "puritan ethic," i.e., thrift, for consumers' willingness to take on debt. Then there's the "cognitive connect"—his term for the traditional relationship between people and their money—which has been decimated by plastic. According to Bob, consumers don't make the connection that when they whip out a piece of plastic, they are spending real, hard-earned money. Whether the loss of these two key values represents a failure of the individual or a massive hoodwink by the advertising-financial complex seems to be an open question, but there is much to suggest that Bob blames the financial industry.

Bob finally hits his stride when discussing what has become his cause célèbre: credit card marketing to students. He tells me how the industry has raided universities and high schools for new victims, eliminating the requirement of a parent's signature in the early nineties when they realized it would cost them customers. But when students inevitably defaulted, the companies still sued the parents, knowing they didn't have a case but guessing they'd win anyway because no good parent would allow his or her child's future to be compromised by a youthful indiscretion that would squat on their kid's credit report just as junior was interviewing for that all-important first job. The credit card business has become so predatory and the competition for young borrowers so cutthroat, Bob says, he's begun receiving e-mails from financial executives encouraging his crusade. Apparently, credit card execs have teenagers, too, and they don't like them being preyed on, even if their own hands are tied by competitive pressures.

Similar tactics are deployed in the UK. But here, at least, the industry has occasionally broken ranks. In 2003, Mark Barrett, then CEO of Barclay's, owner of Barclaycard, one of the UK's biggest credit card firms, shocked the assembled media at a press conference by admitting, "I do not borrow on credit cards. I have four young children. I give them advice not to pile up debts on their credit cards."

Without some popular backlash, without some checks and balances handed down by Congress, Bob thinks the industry will consume its customers and then itself. Until then, things will only get worse. Bob's most shocking claim is that in 2001, some credit card companies lobbied against the $600 income tax rebate checks, fearing that the revolvers would use the money to pay down their credit card bills.*

When I sit in on Bob's graduate-level credit class, I discover one reason he's so pessimistic about the future. Most of his students possess the attention spans of squirrels. For today's lecture Bob has projected an episode of *The Simpsons* in which Bart gets a credit card in the mail. Bob's either trying to relate or maybe he's just trying to get them into the subject (cartoons!), but they're not reciprocating. When he switches gears, projecting a table comparing the lifetime costs of mortgages at varying interest rates, the eyes in the room start to glaze over. Bob tries for audience participation but none of his kids can calculate 40 percent of $500,000 (yes, these are graduate students). Worse, when he makes a point about credit card issuers' systemic use of purposely confusing language and small type to pull one over on their customers, a smart-ass in the front row finally engages, dubiously asserting that he reads and fully understands his credit card agreement, so if other people don't, well, that's their problem. Case closed. They're tough, these kids. And entitled. For some reason I picture them, these lambs, slouching coolly toward the financial slaughterhouse, iPods in ears. No wonder credit card executives love them so much.

I leave Rochester with an autographed copy of Bob's book and the feeling that college is a far more distant memory than I'd like to

---

*Though, on its face, this may seem counterproductive, it makes perfect sense when you consider that such an eventuality would convert many interest-paying "preferred customers" into "responsible deadbeats."

think. The professor has been kind enough to contact a few people for me, including the mothers of two college students who committed suicide after running up credit card debts. Bob took their case to *60 Minutes* but nothing more has come of it. The mothers still want to talk, are still hopeful that something positive might come of their children's deaths. So, with a heavy heart, I head west.

Janne O'Donnell remembers when she took her son Sean to college. A National Merit Scholar from a small town in Oklahoma, Sean, she remembers, "was so excited to be in the big city. *Dallas.*" As they carried Sean's belongings across the relatively small campus of the University of Texas at Dallas, she noticed a number of tables advertising credit cards. "But I didn't worry," she recalls. "Sean was 18, he didn't have a job. Who would give him a credit card?"

The beginnings of a smile appear on Janne's face. What she has learned since that day makes the question seem impossibly naïve. Not only would they give him a credit card, they would practically shove it down his throat. And as soon as he maxed that one out, they'd reward him with another one, and another. In the industry's parlance, he was "building his credit history." "Sean was a smart kid," Janne says, "but he didn't know how he got in, or how to get out." Barely out of college, Sean would find himself working two minimum-wage jobs, paying down $12,000 in debt on ten credit cards (including Neiman Marcus) and saving money—to declare bankruptcy. "I just didn't understand," Janne says. "It was something that was never in my world." Back in Janne's day, you and your husband could both work full-time jobs and still not qualify for a single credit card.

The Visa and MasterCard offers Sean received as he was digging himself deeper and deeper into desperation describe an extraordinarily responsible young man, one who had "graduated into adulthood," whose "responsible use of credit" was to be rewarded by a coveted spot on a number of VIP lists—in short, a platinum young man who deserved a limitless supply of credit. What exactly he did to deserve that credit remains a mystery to his mother.

"If you're working, or if you're in a trade school," Janne tells me, "they don't want you. Maybe they realize that you know the value of a dollar. It's the *college* students who get the credit card offers. So we're setting up a two-tiered system and I believe that they're manipulating the students. An easy market."

Several years ago Janne met another mother, Trisha, from the Oklahoma City area whose daughter had hanged herself in her dorm room after racking up a modest $2,500 in credit card debt (the young woman, Mitzi, didn't leave a note but did spread her credit card bills on her bed by way of explanation). Trisha and Janne had separately written their children's schools demanding that credit card companies be kicked off campus, and they had both been ignored. Then they took their stories to the newspapers, to *60 Minutes*, and finally, with the help of a local congressman, to the Oklahoma state legislature. A bill was introduced prohibiting credit card companies from marketing on college campuses, an idea which has since been made law in several other states. When it came time to testify, Trisha and Janne found themselves opposing the financial industry and its lobbyists. "We were sitting across a table from them," Janne recalls, "and they were discussing how much money they contributed to each congressman's campaign. That bill didn't have a chance. They didn't want to listen to these two mothers. They wanted to listen to the money." As it turns out, Janne was right: congressmen have their own preferred customer lists.

In one of her last appearances before Congress, Julie Williams, the comptroller of the currency and thus the nation's top banking regulator, assured the Senate Banking Committee that credit card companies have not only developed complex models that determine exactly how much credit to extend to a particular student at a particular school, but that these models have appropriate risk metrics built in. I would be curious to see her explain this to Janne and Trisha. I would be even more curious to know the magic number these banks and credit card companies had assigned to Sean and Mitzi—in other words, their price. What that company expected to make over a lifetime from Janne's and Trisha's kids by selling them more credit—not just credit cards but home mortgages (and then equity lines of credit), auto loans, student loans, credit insurance, late fees, and so on. No one has ever asked the credit card companies for that particular number, but one thing is certain: it is much larger than most people realize, and the competition for young customers is getting more and more intense.

Ten years ago, First USA paid the University of Tennessee $19 million for access to its students—their telephone numbers, Social Security numbers, and addresses—setting off a bidding war for access to college students. In 2000, the company raised the stakes again by purchasing two high school students from New Jersey who'd offered to sell themselves as human billboards to any company willing to pay their college tuitions.* If positioning the two friends—"Chris" and "Luke"—as a couple of hip surfer dudes who just happened to love First USA seemed a tad corny, the two students, who were working at a public relations firm, had already developed the perfect angle. Chris (who was photographed driving a brand-new BMW convertible) and Luke (the edgier one, with the mutton chops and board shorts to prove it) would position themselves as spokesmen for financial responsibility (wink, nod)! Even for a credit card company, this was an

---

*This in itself raises an interesting question: With all of the credit card money now flooding into universities, why is tuition still skyrocketing? The answer seems to be that that money is going mainly toward expanded sports programs, real-estate purchases and better food service.

act of extraordinary chutzpah, meaning that the media ate it up. Chris and Luke appeared on FOX News, the *Today* show, and *Good Morning America*, to name a few of the more prominent outlets. Their Web site, www.chrisandluke.com, was featured on Yahoo! and received millions of hits. The financially responsible "celebrity surfers" from New Jersey who were ferried to photo ops in limos were a hit, at least for a few months. My experience with them suggests that a few months of celebrity was probably a stretch for First USA's young champions of financial responsibility. Here's one brief exchange, taken from my filmed interview with Chris:

> James Scurlock: What does surfing have to do with being financially responsible?
> Chris: I think it's a cool image.

In the end, the marriage of credit card behemoth and surfer-dude students turned sour. Chris dropped out of Pepperdine to start a career in the independent film business, and Luke tired of being manipulated by bossy PR people from First USA, though he does admit that being flown in a private jet for lunch at the company's headquarters in Chicago was pretty cool, *dude*. Plus, First USA was more about boring business mags like *Forbes* and *BusinessWeek* than about MTV and *Rolling Stone*. "We wanted to delve deeper into the aspect of financial responsibility but we got the feeling that First USA was just a little more interested in getting credit card sign-ups," Chris relates in one of the less shocking confessions I've heard in my lifetime. He estimates that, in exchange for the $50,000 First USA spent on the duo's freshman-year college tuition, the company has received roughly $20 million in free publicity and hundreds of thousands of new, college-age cardholders. Despite this appearing to be a fairly awesome deal for First USA, Luke says the company paid their tuition weeks late, nearly causing an early end to both his and Chris's college careers. "It was just weird," Luke says with a straight face.

Ultimately, there is one customer far more valuable to the corporations than the 18-to-24 demographic, and that customer is Wall Street, which supplies the funds that lenders like First USA resell in small chunks to people like Chris and Luke and Sean and Mitzi. At the time Chris and Luke were being hyped on the pages of *The Wall Street Journal* and *Fortune*, First USA had just been acquired by a larger bank, Bank One, for close to $8 billion. One of First USA's major selling points had been its access to the student market. Perhaps Bank One recognized the perfect opportunity to justify its big purchase, to show analysts that its new brand was hip with the kids, that it would continue to aggressively pick the low-hanging fruit— the easy market, as Janne put it.

Like Chris, Janne's son eventually dropped out of college. Sean moved back home and tried to figure out a way to declare bankruptcy, finish school, and somehow get a law degree, his dream. Living at home and working more low-wage jobs must have been humiliating for a National Merit Scholar who'd left for the big city with so much potential, but it was harder on Janne and her husband, who were forced to choose between bailing out Sean or helping their younger son through college. In the end Janne couldn't see denying her other son the same opportunity they'd given Sean. Sean accepted the decision, told his mother he felt like a failure, and two days later hung himself. Thereafter Sean's memory was commemorated by a constant stream of phone calls from bill collectors, threatening letters, and more offers for credit, one of which read, "We want you back!" One day a collector called up and suggested that Janne should pay up to honor Sean's memory.

"I gave you my son," she replied. "What more do you want?"

* * *

Several months after I interviewed Janne, Bob Manning called to let me know that the Senate Banking Committee had agreed to hold the first hearings on the credit card industry in more than ten years.* Since I hadn't had any luck getting anyone from the industry to talk on the record, this seemed like great news: The senators would do the interviews for me. Bob was scheduled as a witness, as were a few other consumer advocates, several senators, and executives from the major credit card issuers. So, when the day came, I called up a friend with cable and TiVo and prepared to learn the other side of the story Bob had told me.

On television I could barely make out Bob, squirming in his uncomfortable wooden chair behind the first panel of witnesses, side by side with the credit card executives he battles in the press and the other leaders of la Résistance who, like him, have made careers of trying to stem a tidal wave with their charts and graphs and sob stories. I wanted to see the look on Bob's face when one of the first witnesses, Senator Dianne Feinstein, a liberal Democrat from California who was appearing before the committee to share her personal frustrations with the industry, sparked a lighthearted exchange about how confusing this whole credit card business could get.

> Sen. Feinstein (D-CA): I tried the other day to figure out, if
> I only made the minimum monthly payment, how long it
> would take me to pay it off. I couldn't figure it out. There is
> so much fine print. [Laughter]
> Sen. Dole (R-NC): You shouldn't need a magnifying glass
> to figure out your credit card statement.
> Sen. Bennett (R-UT): Senator Sarbanes can't figure out his
> credit card statement. I don't say that in the pejorative. I
> can't figure out mine, either.

*The hearing was a quid pro quo for passage of the Bankruptcy Reform Act, but more on that later.

> Sen. Sarbanes (D-MD): I've decided that the only answer is
> to pay my bill off every month, as soon as it comes in, to
> avoid getting caught in any of these traps.*

These traps are familiar to most of us. They include changing
the date that payment is due, in order to trip us up and incur a late
fee; holding our checks until after the due date, again to incur a late
fee; and a uniquely convoluted accounting method called "double-
cycle" billing, which has confounded no less an authority than an
MIT math professor and whose only practical purpose seems to be
that it allows the bank to lop on finance charges even if you paid
your bill in full the previous month.† But I digress . . .

The second panel consisted of Comptroller of the Currency
Julie Williams and Ed Gramlich, a Federal Reserve Board governor. It's worth repeating that Julie Williams is the nation's top
banking regulator, meaning that her job is to make sure that
Americans don't get screwed by their bank. Gramlich's role is a
little less clear. In theory, the Fed, which is actually a private corporation,§ protects the solvency of the banking system and over-
sees the economy's steady expansion by regulating the money
supply, but it is also the de facto lobbying arm of the big banks.
Whenever the interests of the big banks and the American people
collide, it is difficult to say whose interests the Fed will protect,
but it has largely solved that problem by deciding that what
is good for big banks is good for Americans, and therefore the

*Unlike the vast majority of United States senators, approximately 70 percent of Amer-
icans cannot pay their credit card bills off at the end of the month.

†In the UK, the FSA legislates against firms doing this.

§This may come as news to most people, but the Fed is actually owned by a fairly small
number of very large banks. Its most important function is the creation of currency,
which it accomplishes by printing money but also by purchasing and then reselling
Treasury notes, i.e., the national debt. The Bank of England, on the other hand, is
wholly owned by (and accountable to) the government.

interests of the big banks is the same as the national interest, and therefore there is never any conflict.

The senators quizzed Ms. Williams and Mr. Gramlich for less than an hour. The two witnesses agreed that, despite record defaults, bankruptcies, and foreclosures, everything was just fine. Ms. Williams told the senators how handing out credit cards to unemployed teenagers is actually a very responsible thing to do (because the banks have computer models that allow them to figure out which students have the wealthiest parents, or something like that) and Mr. Gramlich assured everyone that the Fed would "look into" the rising flood of consumer complaints (the financial industry is now the largest source of complaints to the Better Business Bureau, beating out cell phone providers and car dealers—no small feat).

Strangely enough, no senator asked about the rising bankruptcy rates or how it was that the banking industry could be reporting record profits while record numbers of Americans were going broke. It just never came up. In fact, there were only two moments of any drama (banking regulators are not, in general, a dramatic bunch): when Julie Williams was asked how much interest a customer who made minimum monthly payments would ultimately pay and she lapsed into an impression of a human phone tree, sifting through documents, keeping the senators and the rest of the room "on hold," before revealing the awful truth;* and when Gramlich was forced to admit that the Fed had purchased a vast amount of information on Americans' credit card habits from a private corporation, a practice that required no Congressional oversight or authorization. As soon as it spilled out of his mouth, Gramlich seemed to fear that he'd screwed up big-time and quickly declared that he would have to speak with his attorneys before divulging any more information and he really shouldn't have

---

*Approximately twice the original loan amount over the twenty-two years that it would take to pay off the balance.

divulged the private corporation thing to begin with—even though the Fed, as I mentioned, is itself a private corporation—and then he turned around to an aide, who looked very concerned that the Fed had revealed too much to the American people already.

Bob, like the class genius in the room of dumb kids, must have found himself in a special kind of misery. Every time a senator asked a question of a witness, I'm sure that Bob knew the answer. If only he were allowed to raise his hand and be called on, he would tell them everything. No doubt he'd wanted to nail Julie Williams on the minimum payment question. Yet, Bob kept his cool. For the first time in ten years, he was about to have a seat at their table. He would stack his notes and charts in front of him—not that he needed them, but he'd done enough media appearances to know they didn't hurt—and he would explain how the system really worked. He would have a microphone and at least some of the senators, like Sarbanes, would ask him the right questions. If the professor just kept his composure for a little while longer, played the senators' game, he would finally get his turn.

Inexplicably, the consumer advocates and the credit card executives—la Résistance and the Gestapo—were consolidated into the third panel and seated "boy-girl-boy-girl" style, as though they were all on the same team. Bob was squeezed between the vice president of customer relations for Capital One, Marge Connelly, and the vice president of marketing for JPMorgan Chase, Carter Franke, who, I should disclose, sends me what she euphemistically calls "convenience" checks every month. To Ms. Franke's left was Ed Mierzwinski, consumer program director for the US Public Interest Research Group (PIRG), and on Mr. Mierzwinski's left, Louis Freeh. Mr. Freeh, you may recall, was formerly the head of the FBI under President Clinton. His new position is chief counsel to MBNA. This revolving door works both ways. In 2002, President Bush tapped Larry Thompson, a former director and compliance committee chairman of Providian Financial Corp., to become his corporate crime czar, even though Providian had earlier paid $400 million to settle charges that it had defrauded its valued customers.*

Each witness was allowed four minutes for an opening statement, which was bliss for the polished credit card execs and absolute torture for the scrappy consumer advocates. It was especially taxing on Bob, who was constantly interrupted by the committee's long-time chairman, Senator Richard Shelby, the senior senator from Alabama and a reliable Southern Republican, taunting him about how little time the verbose professor had been given to speak. Meanwhile, precious seconds ticked by on the digital clock. Bob smiled his awkward smile and tried to get something on the scoreboard before it was too late, but he seemed overwhelmed by the brevity required and also a little intimidated by Shelby's malevolent smiles. Bob had to relinquish the mic before he'd finished his statement and cede the floor to the slick VP from Capital One, who magnanimously allowed that people were complaining—a lot more—but assured the committee that the credit card companies were now listening. "I just want to say that at Capital One," she crowed, "we're committed to re-earning our customers' trust every day."

Then it happened: Shelby's coup de grâce. Before the committee could ask a single question of Bob or the others—before the professor even had a chance to straighten his print tie or make one self-deprecating remark about his penchant for long, exhaustive answers—the hearing was over. Shelby apologized profusely, singling Bob out for his sympathies. The senators had an important vote in the chamber. Shelby understood that the panel members had traveled some distance and was terribly sorry if he'd wasted their time. He flashed his best Southern smile—what my dad calls a shit-eating grin—and slammed down the gavel. Hearing adjourned. It would not

*The company did not admit to wrongdoing, but acknowledged vague internal "issues."

reconvene. If the senators had any questions for the credit card companies, they would mail them. In a coup de grâce de coup de grâce, Tom Carper, the Democratic senator from Delaware (where MBNA is based), apologized to the credit card companies for not having time to question them and further explained that he wished he could find a way to "put a spotlight on all of those good practices" without explaining what those practices could possibly be.

The credit card executives must have been ecstatic—Shelby had rung the school bell before the teacher could administer the test—but I didn't notice any of them gloat. Bob must have been beside himself, but I think he hid it well. Maybe he saw it coming from years of playing flea to the industry's dog. Or maybe he never really expected anything else from the masters of bait and switch. So he bundled up his reports and graphs and his unused speaking points, and maybe he put on his beret and his scarf and his coat, and then he walked out of the heavily fortified building, which from the outside now resembles nothing so much as a bunker, into the heat of summer in Washington. If he'd taken the flight back to Rochester, he could have looked down at the Justice Department, the White House, the Federal Reserve, and both houses of Congress—all run, in varying degrees, by the financial industry, which was now officially immune to the most basic oversight, the most elementary scrutiny: a single question. In Bob's pocket, incidentally, was an MBNA MasterCard with a credit limit of over $50,000, a card he told me he'd used to buy a new condo.

Shelby and his honorable colleagues returned to the Senate chamber and promptly approved a $300 billion (give or take) transportation bill, which included the so-called bridge to nowhere, a $250 million contraption that will connect a sparsely populated island to a sparsely populated town in an especially remote part of Alaska. The project was the brainchild of the state's senior senator, Ted Stevens, who is known for taking care of his constituents to the detriment of the United States Treasury. This was the important business that prevented the government from examining the largest industry in the nation for the first time in a decade.

Four

"The trick is charging a lot, repeatedly, for small doses
of incremental credit."
– Andrew Kahr, founder, Providian

The Four Seasons Hotel Beverly Hills is not actually in Beverly Hills but tucked away in a residential neighborhood very close to Beverly Hills. Though unimpressive from the outside—it looks like one of those newish mid-rises in Miami Beach advertised in airline magazines—the hotel boasts one of the most exclusive clienteles in the world—celebrities, movie moguls, and billionaires among them—and does a steady business in women recuperating from plastic surgery. The hotel has kept its clientele by offering both legendary service and legendary discretion. The newest owners of the Four Seasons empire are Bill Gates and Citigroup's largest shareholder, Prince Alwaleed bin Talal bin Abdul Aziz Alsaud. The prince possesses an almost maniacal devotion to detail and a connoisseur's appreciation of luxury. Four Seasons has a new deal with holders of the American Express Centurion Card—also known as the "black card"—which gives them special discounts and upgrades. Not that they need them. Centurion cardholders like Steven Spielberg and Britney Spears are chosen on the basis of their wealth and their proclivity to spending it. They pay $1,000 per year for the card, twenty-five times the average annual credit card fee, but the prestige value is priceless.

I arrive at the Four Seasons Beverly Hills dressed in a black suit and new shoes. I have worn both exactly once—for a wedding at the Beverly Hills Hotel (which is owned by Prince Alwaleed's neighbor, the Sultan of Brunei)—a few weeks previous. The groom was an agent, the bride a publicist. It was very L.A., as my mother likes to say.

I park on the street rather than disappoint the valets with my ten-year-old car. Then, being compulsively early for meetings like this, I take a brief tour of the hotel's gardens and lounge. The staff is discreet and attractive, yet I am subtly impressed with the uncomfortable feeling that I'm being watched and that I should not linger anywhere for too long.

At the appointed hour, an attractive young man appears to collect me and I am escorted to a suite on one of the higher floors. The assistant's name is Johnny. He, like myself, is dressed impeccably (though more Savile Row than Nordstrom) and he sports slick hair tied back into a barely noticeable ponytail. He speaks with a slightly Irish British accent and tries, ever so gently, to prepare me for meeting royalty.

The suite is smaller than I would have expected, but it is impeccable, and freshly cut flowers lend the elegant touch that Beth's office in Vegas lacked. On the polished dining table is a basket of pastries as well as a spread of thinly sliced fruit. Johnny offers me a cup of tea and encourages me to fix myself breakfast, but as perfect as the slices of pineapple appear and as clear as it is that some sous-chef has gone to great lengths to choose strawberries of just the right color, the idea of eating in front of a royal audience is just too daunting.

Fergie, as she is known to most Americans, now goes by the title Sarah, Duchess of York. (She does not like the name Fergie, Johnny warns. Commoners like me should call her Duchess or Your Royal Highness.) The duchess, of course, became famous around the world when she married one of Prince Charles's younger brothers, became Princess Diana's best friend, had a couple of beautiful young daughters, gained a lot of weight, fell out of favor with her mother-in-law, and got divorced. There is a country song in there somewhere, and while the British cringed at her behavior and even vilified her as unfit to be a royal, much less a royal mother, when she was photographed having her toes sucked by a Texan in the south of France, Americans remained fans. Unlike her snooty, starched in-laws, Fergie kept it real.

The duchess greets me with a brilliant smile and, to my dismay, encourages me to eat something. She is a very pretty woman, wild-eyed and bursting with energy of the Tony Robbins/Dave Ramsey variety. She now makes her living promoting shopping centers, Wedgwood china, and, as most people know, Weight Watchers. She has also written a couple of children's books—the most famous about a talking helicopter—and published a memoir and, most recently, an inspirational book. Two years ago she filmed a pilot for a network talk show that she still wants to do despite having been passed over, according to my friends in the biz, for Sharon Osbourne, whose show has since been canceled. She has agreed to meet me because she is still trying to break into reality television and I have several ideas for her, including a television show in which various commoners vie to become her next assistant (Johnny's calling it quits) and a film in which she and a dozen other recovering spendthrifts relate their tribulations, which will somehow, hopefully, lead to their redemption. Fergie has her own ideas, including a television show called the *Fergie Factor*, in which the duchess intervenes in the lives of people who are severely traumatized or who suffer from low self-esteem. How? By being Fergie (I am reminded numerous times in our meeting that she "connects" with people) and, sometimes, by taking them shopping.

Shopping is something that Fergie knows very, very well because it nearly led her to bankruptcy ("I was minutes from bankruptcy, James," she tells me, still shocked) and is currently steering her toward reality television, which some people might consider scarier. The problem was that the duchess's husband, Prince Andrew, the Duke of York, made $50,000 per year at the height of his career in the Royal Navy, an impossibly modest sum for someone with as many social commitments as his wife. Matters were made worse when her mother-in-law, aka the Queen, built the newlyweds a 20,000-square-foot mansion but declined to furnish it. By the end of her marriage, Sarah was $7 million in the hole. She received $250,000 in her divorce settlement. Ergo, the endorsement deals and the meetings with people like me, who may or may not find a way to repackage the Fergie brand or transform her limitless ideas, her passion, her travails, her *story*, into something profitable.

Breakfast lasts for forty-five minutes, in which time she consumes half a croissant from the pastry basket—an illustration of the self-control she has learned from Weight Watchers, I am told—and I manage to down a slice of pineapple and a few strawberries without initiating any of the bodily functions associated with digestion. She shakes my hand, tells me that we have made a special connection in our brief time together, and memorializes the occasion by having Johnny fetch one of her "Little Red" dolls, pulling down its underwear, and inscribing a personal dedication with a Sharpie. According to Little Red's ass, the duchess and I are destined to do great things together. Johnny leads me out of the room as two more guests are led in. He tells me I did well, mainly because I dressed better than anyone else so far. I leave the Four Seasons holding Little Red and contemplating an Egg McMuffin.

Later, as I relate my royal encounter to friends and family in exhaustive detail—my grandmother is particularly convinced that I have now made it in the world—I am asked, again and again, how could someone so famous, someone with the appearance of so much wealth—*a duchess, for God's sake*—be maxed out? The answer is quite simple. Fergie is a perfect example of what the credit industry refers to as a "preferred customer": young, unemployed, highly impressionable, confronting expenses grossly out of line with her salary. She also has rich relatives with an assumed interest in bailing her out,* a definite plus. Indeed, what distinguishes Fergie's experience from that of most Americans is not that she was showered with easy credit but that she had to seek it out herself. I'm fairly certain that no zero-interest "introductory" offers or courtesy checks arrived at the palace. Instead, the duchess had to pick up the phone on her own initiative and call an officer at Coutts, the royal bank, to inquire about a loan. That being said, she was rarely, if ever, declined. For America's preferred customers, the process is very different, though the end result is the same.

Macon, Mississippi, is worlds away from the Four Seasons Beverly Hills. A ghost town in the midst of southern Mississippi's backwoods that even the fast-food chains have deserted, Macon is home to the grandchildren of sharecroppers, many of whom work at the giant catfish farms and processing plants nearby and many more who are unemployed. A generation ago the Amish set up a small community here. They run a popular bakery and country store off the interstate, the only business of any consequence for miles. Macon's most

*This assumption has proven incorrect.

famous resident and national hero, Thomas Hamill, has just written a book describing his ordeal in Iraq. Hamill, a dairy farmer who'd fallen on hard times twice—once because of low milk prices and a second time because of his wife's medical bills—had taken a job with a division of Halliburton, driving a fuel truck, which was promptly attacked by RPG-toting insurgents. He'd had the good or bad fortune of being kidnapped on camera and his ruddy, mustachioed face is now familiar to millions of Americans. When he escaped a few weeks after the attack, busting out of his prison when his captors left him unattended and flagging down a military helicopter, the soldier-like Hamill captured the imagination of a media still jaded by the Jessica Lynch and Pat Tillman scandals—or so his publisher hopes. There are flyers advertising his book signing taped to the windows of the few open businesses in downtown Macon.

I have been brought to Mississippi by Mike Hudson, an investigative reporter for the *Roanoke Times*. Mike used to cover a police beat, but now he reports on crimes that are much more complex and insidious: crimes committed by lenders against their customers. Mike's latest piece, titled "Banking on Misery," has just won a prestigious journalism award. Basically, it explores how the largest banking institutions in the world are making huge profits off of a new niche: the very poor. And there are plenty of those in Macon, Mississippi.

Our host is a talkative attorney named Eason Mitchell. Mitchell is a huge man, shaped like Humpty Dumpty, with a cherubic face. He drives us around Macon in a massive SUV with leather seats that he calls his "old farm truck." In another life, Mitchell had one of the best workers' comp practices going between Montgomery and Birmingham. Then, in 1992, Mitchell tried cocaine for the first time. He was instantly addicted. The first year, he recalls, was wonderful, but the year after was a hell he describes as impossible to understand unless you've been there—worse than death. Mitchell ended up in treatment, thanks to the intervention of his fellow attorneys and a few judges, and he didn't practice law for nine months, but was brought back to the land of the living with the support of the bar association. Once he got out of rehab, Mitchell realized that he had been given a unique opportunity to start a practice from scratch with no ties to the past.

Finance had always interested him, so one day, while sorting through the files of his mentor, Mitchell picked out an intriguing insurance case: a bank accused of cheating a mobile home owner out of $132. Still on disability and not technically practicing, Mitchell took the file to Farmers Insurance, which had a policy on the trailer. Mitchell had a simple question, but the first person he talked to at Farmers couldn't answer it, nor could the second. Mitchell, with all the time in the world to work on a file that no practicing attorney would have wasted more than one billable hour on, eventually reached a secretary who looked him straight in the eye and said, "I've been waiting two years for somebody to ask me that question."

The case involved a bank that had forced a mobile home owner who already had insurance to purchase additional credit insurance as a condition of getting the loan—a violation of the Fair Lending Act. When the owner defaulted, the bank had gone to Farmers and collected the credit insurance, while the customer lost his home. The secretary's son had coincidentally fallen victim to the same ploy by the same bank but, fearing retribution, didn't file suit. His mother had retained all of the records of her son's case and even done a little investigating of her own, waiting for someone like Mitchell—someone who had nothing to lose, someone who wasn't afraid of the bank—to come around asking questions. What Mitchell eventually discovered was a massive scheme to sell mobile home owners credit insurance they never needed or asked for. The additional premiums often forced the customers into default, and, when that happened, the bank collected the insurance money—and the trailer.

In theory, credit insurance is supposed to protect consumers by paying off their debts in case of a job loss, disability, or death. In reality, credit insurance is almost pure profit and has thus become the banker's version of crack—a product they've grown so addicted to that they routinely stretch the limits of morality and credulity. Mitchell discovered policies insuring goldfish and WeedEaters, among other things. Customers, oftentimes illiterate, were told that the "insurance" was required to get a mortgage or loan—a blatant lie. The premiums went straight to the banks' bottom lines. In the UK, credit insurance is sold under the euphemism "Payment Protection Insurance" or PPI. A report by the Office of Fair Trading recently found that the claims ratio—i.e., the amount paid out as a percentage of the premiums earned—is only 19 percent for PPIs, versus 55 percent for household insurance and 74 percent for motor insurance, making it an even greater cash cow (read "rip-off") than in the United States. The Office of Fair Trade is investigating...

Mitchell discovered how quickly small numbers, like the $132, added up. He also realized that he had two major things going against him: one, the financial industry itself, which had inserted clauses into customers' credit agreements denying them their constitutional rights;* and two, the desperation of his clients. Uneducated and dirt-poor, they were easily seduced by salesmen promising quick cash. If a bank told them to sign, they signed, no questions asked. There was the sharecropper's daughter who had been convinced to take out a $500 loan to buy a hog, later converted to a $5,000 loan for home improvements, which later became a $40,000 loan she could never hope to repay. There was the schizophrenic woman—the chief of police's mother—who had been checked out of the psychiatric hospital for two hours so she could sign refi documents for CitiFinancial, which was now threatening to

---

*If you're looking at your credit card statement or mortgage, this can generally be found under the paragraph titled "Arbitration Clause," but more on this later.

post a foreclosure notice on her home in the newspaper. There was the retired bathroom attendant who had received a $20,000 loan through a contractor who never did any work but had apparently convinced the bank to pay him anyway, because a collection agency was now calling her and threatening foreclosure if she didn't pay.

There were too many victims for Mitchell to handle, and they were almost always black. His beloved South was reverting back to a sharecropper economy, albeit one where the people worked for the banks and not the landowners, and there was nothing he could do about it but fight small battles here and there, wondering aloud how much human suffering the American people were willing to tolerate. "Don't they understand," he asks me rhetorically, "that a society is measured by its lowest common denominator? We're not defined by how high we set the bar, but how low. You know, third world countries have a lot of rich people too."

Mitchell maneuvers the SUV past the empty shells that form downtown Macon, past the white cemetery, down a long dirt road and into a small cul-de-sac of one-story brick homes. Along the way he and Mike discuss a story that ran in *Southern Exposure* magazine in 2003. On its face, the story seems too absurd to be true. CitiFinancial, the "sub-prime"* unit of the world's largest banking institution, is suing a mentally retarded woman and her severely retarded son for default, hoping to force them out of the modest house they've shared for years. And Citi is winning.

John and Katherine Brown live in a two-bedroom, immaculate brick house on the outskirts of Macon. Katherine, like many black women in the Deep South, is obese and suffers from diabetes. She also happens to be mentally retarded and nearly deaf. Her first son, a private in the U.S. Army, died while stationed in Germany. Her second son, John, was born almost totally deaf and severely

---

*I.e. *high-interest.*

retarded. Though John is now 44 years old, he has yet to finish second grade. Mitchell likes to call him a "special child of God," meaning that when the short bus rolls down the dirt road, John jumps on board. But it also means that John is blissfully innocent, a lamb. Pure. As Mitchell points out, John is probably the only middle-aged man he's met who has never told a lie and never committed a sin. John is all that Katherine has in the world, and vice versa. Mitchell pities whoever dies last.

A couple of years ago Katherine began receiving credit card solicitations. Although she has no income besides a government subsidy and lives in one of the poorest zip codes in the nation, Katherine had somehow made it onto someone's preferred customer list. It is unclear whether Katherine knew that by returning the application she was assuming a liability or not: there is not much in the literature to suggest the money will ever have to be repaid, just a lot of superlatives and numbers like 0 percent. In any case, Katherine managed to rack up a few thousand dollars' worth of expenses on the card, mainly buying things for John.

Within a short period of time, Katherine found herself on the receiving end of some very nasty phone calls. All she knew now was that she couldn't afford to pay her credit card bills. Since credit cards are unsecured debt, she could easily have ignored the phone calls and kept her home and her government income. But this was not in Katherine Brown's nature. Instead, she did what any good Southern woman would do: She asked God for help.

According to Mitchell, a church friend of Katherine's just happened to work for a unit of Citigroup and just happened to know the solution: a refi. It was apparently of no consequence to the friend that there was nothing the credit card companies could do to Katherine—besides call her incessantly—nor did it matter that she already had a low-interest mortgage subsidized by the federal government. All that mattered, as Suze Orman might have told her, was that

Katherine protect her credit rating—even though her credit rating was the very thing that had attracted the credit card companies in the first place. No matter that having no credit would be the best thing for someone like Katherine. The friend presented her with a false and absurd choice that preyed on her sense of pride: Declare bankruptcy and ruin your reputation, or refinance with Citi, pay off all of your bills, lower your mortgage, and save your credit.

Citi replaced her low-interest, government-subsidized mortgage with a more expensive and much longer mortgage—with credit insurance, naturally—and Katherine happily signed because her friend told her it was the right thing to do. At closing—which is the proper time to reveal the real terms of the deal, or so I have learned—Citi demanded that John also sign his name on the mortgage. Though absurd on its face, Katherine never questioned this. She wrote out J-O-H-N B-R-O-W-N in large block letters and John copied them onto the contract slowly, one by one, looking up at his mother for approval when each letter was finished, just as he did in school. Thus "executed," Citi faxed the documents back to New York. Katherine breathed a sigh of relief and thanked the Lord that she'd just averted bankruptcy. Instead she had made it inevitable. Within a few months the phone calls weren't coming from a collection agency but directly from Citi's attorneys—and they weren't cajoling her for a small monthly payment; they were demanding the roof over her head. When Katherine finally realized that she needed help, she says, Citi tried to bully her out of seeking legal advice: Which is more important to you, they asked, having a lawyer or keeping your house?

Katherine and John are standing in front of their home when we arrive. John is as tiny as Katherine is large. He seems to have waited for us for a very long time and can't restrain his excitement when Mitchell's red truck pulls into the driveway. Sitting down in the tidy living room—*visiting*, as my Southern grandmother would call it—

84

Mitchell implores Katherine to stop paying the credit insurance on her refi, which is now several months in default. But Katherine clearly doesn't understand. Citi told her the policy was worth $10,000. If she dies, she thinks John's going to collect $10,000, which sounds like a lot. Mitchell counters that even if John did collect that $10,000—and he wouldn't beacuse Citi would get there first—it would simply make him ineligible for his government benefits. But Katherine still doesn't get it. Citi promised her $10,000! Mitchell nearly goes ballistic when she admits that she has used the money earmarked for her homeowner's policy—which would come in handy in the event of a fire or tornado—to pay for the useless credit insurance. But, short of becoming her legal guardian, there is nothing Mitchell can do.

As obvious an injustice as this appears to anyone who's met Katherine or John, Mitchell is losing the case. Like most lenders, Citi has inserted an arbitration clause into its documents. In theory, this is supposed to spare lender and consumer the tedious, expensive, and time-consuming process of going to court by agreeing, in advance, to subject any grievances to an impartial mediator—a single decision-maker who reviews the arguments of each side in a matter of days or weeks and hands back a binding decision. In theory, it is supposed to be fair. In practice, because arbitrators are nearly always paid by the financial industry, it is often nothing but an end run around consumers' constitutional rights. Mitchell was not terribly surprised when the arbitrator in the Browns' case ruled in Citi's favor. The arbitrator's reasoning? Because John is clearly incompetent, he could not have been manipulated. In other words, if you are unable to understand what you are signing, if you are a special child of God, you cannot claim to have been duped. Ignorance is bliss. So sayeth the arbitration industry.

Mitchell has taken the case to federal court, though he is not particularly optimistic. Most of the judges on the bench were appointed during the Reagan-Bush era. Almost all come from corporate backgrounds. They are good people, according to Mitchell, who simply never gained an appreciation for what it's like to be poor and uneducated. They do not understand why people like John and Katherine can't pull themselves up by their bootstraps. Why they don't stand up for themselves. Why they sign documents they don't understand.

Mitchell has one ace in the hole. Over the years, land titles have become so manipulated in Mississippi that it is often hard to determine exactly who owns what. If the title to the Browns' land has been obscured enough times, perhaps he will be able to delay foreclosure indefinitely. It is a precarious way to live, but Katherine seems resigned—happy, even. She is used to living at the mercy of others. She does not question the will of God or the wisdom of the law. She simply accepts it and sends the bank everything she can each month.

As we leave the Browns' house, the mail arrives—including a letter from CitiFinancial. It reads, in part:

> DEAR KATHERINE BROWN,
>   BECAUSE YOU'VE BEEN SUCH A VALUABLE CUSTOMER IN THE PAST, YOU'VE REMAINED ON OUR PREFERRED CUSTOMER LIST. JUST SIGN THE ENCLOSED CHECK FOR $5,000 AND PAY ONLY $129.68 A MONTH!

We, the educated white men, are appalled. "They keep sending you these even after all the trouble you've been through," Mike, the reporter, says incredulously, holding the letter as though it's not quite real.

Katherine laughs it off. "That ain't the first one I got," she says. Citigroup has declined to comment on the case.

* * *

For the next couple of weeks, Mike takes me on a tour of the America he has spent his recent past getting to know. I meet consumer advocates and attorneys in the Deep South, in Pittsburgh, in Queens and Brooklyn. And I meet their clients, generally lower-middle-class Americans whose biggest enemy turns out to be access to easy credit. The scams are eerily similar. The client, usually a minority or immigrant, is approached by a mortgage broker or a contractor or anyone else with a product to sell, and they are offered a loan—a mortgage or a refi, typically—on terms they can barely afford. They are promised that the loan will pay for itself, either by lowering rates on credit card bills (consolidation) or increasing the equity in their house (in the case of home improvements). At closing, as with Katherine and John, they find themselves pressured to sign documents they do not understand on terms far less favorable than promised. The excuses for the bait and switch are varied—rates have gone up, the "special" deal is no longer available, they are suddenly required by law to buy credit insurance, etc.—but the result is always the same. The monthly payments are much higher and the "cash out" has disappeared. Still they sign, either because they are now counting on the money or because they are promised that the terms will be renegotiated in a few months' time. Some are told that if they do not sign now, they will no longer be able to get credit at all. So sign they do. And within a fairly short period of time, they find themselves facing foreclosure. By the time this happens— sometimes in a matter of months—the loan has been sold off to a large institution that has no idea, nor much interest in, what kind of promises or threats the broker made to get the documents signed, a process one attorney calls "mortgage laundering."

I hear this scam described so many times I become convinced that somewhere there must be a script, though I never find it. What I do find are communities, particularly minority communities, where blacks and immigrants have lived frugally and saved, have built solidly middle-class neighborhoods on the back of thrift and decades of hard work, communities and neighborhoods that have been decimated in a few years' time by a flood of "easy" credit they never asked for in the first place.

And I realize that the modern "financial services industry," as it likes to be called, is changing the landscape of this country dramatically. In Manhattan and other wealthy areas, it is evident in the number of bank branches that have opened over the last several years, replacing mom-and-pop businesses and chain stores alike with stunning efficiency. In less wealthy areas, check-cashing joints, pawnshops, title loan establishments, and personal-loan stores are replacing banks. But, in reality, the banks and their sub-prime cousins are simply two sides of the same coin. Consider that the largest pawnshop chain and the largest check-cashing outfit in the United States are both largely financed by some of the largest banks in America. Whether the bankers are educating their loan shark partners or vice versa is a question that should be of great interest to every one of their customers, and there is more than a little evidence to suggest that the bankers are behaving more like their less esteemed counterparts, not the other way around.

The country's largest sub-prime lender, CitiFinancial, is owned by Citigroup, the largest financial services company in the world. CitiFinancial is the brainchild of Sanford "Sandy" Weill. Mr. Weill, whom his biographer succinctly describes as "the chubby kid who became the chubby billionaire," built the financial institution called Citigroup, an institution so large he correctly bragged that it was too big to be regulated by Congress. Indeed, Citigroup has commanded the blessings of politicians from Alan Greenspan to Bill Clinton to George W. Bush with an ease that must surely have awed even Walter Wriston.

Like Wriston and Hock, Weill saw himself as an agitator, an outsider, an iconoclast, from the beginning of his career. Perhaps because he was a middle-class Jew in a world run by blue bloods or perhaps because his ambitions were so outsized for a man of his relative youth, he pursued his goals with an aggressiveness and focus that tended to offend his Waspy rivals on Wall Street. Weill learned the banking business from the back office, and he used that knowledge to make every organization he controlled leaner and more profitable than its competitors. The pinnacle of his career might have been being named president of American Express, a company then run by a genteel Southern Methodist named James Robinson, but Weill wanted more than prestige. He wanted to build an empire.

Weill resigned from American Express and, in the throes of middle age and at the height of his powers, found himself unemployed. It could have been worse. According to Weill's biographer, he spent an entire year sitting in a plush Manhattan office paid for by American Express, taking long, three-martini lunches at the Four Seasons Restaurant, being pitched deals that were inevitably smaller versions of past achievements. The hardest thing about reaching the top early is that there is very little left to excite you.

When two executives from a fledgling finance company in Baltimore called Commercial Credit rang asking Weill to save their company, it was surprising that Weill even took the call. But enough time had passed for Weill to see past the veneer of prestige and respectability those insecure elitists on Wall Street clung on to so tenaciously. What Weill saw in Commercial Credit was hugely exciting: a large company that made small loans to millions of customers at high interest rates. Like Hock, Weill knew that efficiency was the key to reducing costs. Like Wriston, he understood the profitability of lending to the masses. After all, Sears had charged them 18 percent for decades and they had never complained. Weill's Commercial Credit was a portal to the best customers in the world; he would transform it in the image of both Hock's and Wriston's grandest visions.

When Weill told his longtime assistant what he was up to, she protested. Like the bankers in Hock's day, she probably knew the game he was about to play. Screw the little guy. Weill brushed her off and bought the company anyway, made it hugely profitable by slashing the payrolls and selling more "products," i.e., high-interest debt, to his customer base. But Commercial Credit was much more than a windfall to Weill. It was a platform to build the world's greatest financial empire. In less than a dozen years, Weill acquired the nation's largest sub-prime lender, The Associates, one of the largest brokers, Smith Barney, the largest bond trader, Salomon Brothers, as well as the largest consumer insurance company, Travelers, and finally, in 1998, merged them all with the country's largest bank, Citibank. A decades old antitrust law had to be destroyed, but that was easy since Wriston had put Congress in its place. Thus was Citigroup, the first trillion-dollar financial giant, created, and it would be remade in the image of Commercial Credit, not the other way around. As one of Weill's deputies explained, Citigroup's strength was its ability to appeal to everyone, not just a certain segment of society—i.e., not just the sophisticated and wealthy and the literate. When the CEO of Weill's old company, American Express, countered that AmEx only wanted the most profitable customers, he must have had a good laugh. Weill's preferred customers—he called them the "people who eat at McDonald's"—*were* the most profitable customers. His old enemies on Wall Street still didn't get it.

I have developed a new understanding of the term *preferred customer*. The best definition I have heard yet—and this is from a vice president of MasterCard—is an individual who has a "taste for credit," i.e., someone "willing to make minimum monthly pay-ments—forever." Now I know why, if I fail to pay off my balance in full, my credit limit is increased. I know why the world's largest bank is trolling the poorest backroads of Mississippi, looking for new business. I know why the same bank will simultaneously sue to put you out on the street and then, unsolicited, send you a check for five thousand bucks.

Credit, as Janne observed, is a two-tiered system: There are those who pay interest and those who collect it. But it has always been thus. What has changed is the *marketing* of credit, the notion that credit is not a tool but a lifestyle. The financial industry spends vast sums of money spreading the myth that debt is good, that what matters is a good credit score, *approval,* as though that ap-proval still means what it did a generation ago when denial was the norm. That it is more important to take your mother on a tour of the old country than to take care of your financial future. That doing without is immoral. That debt is freedom. That wealth is spending, not saving, and that there will always be more credit as long as one remains on the preferred-customer list.

It is disturbing enough to many of us that the largest institu-tions in our culture spread this propaganda every second of every day—that the taste for credit is being systematically cultivated into a voracious appetite among those who can least afford it. But it is more disturbing that an institution far larger than Weill's or even Hock's has echoed all of these lies until the most reluctant have agreed to believe them—an institution that has traditionally pro-vided checks and balances over exactly such abuses of power. That institution is the United States government.

Five

"The scope of the problem is very large."
– Alan Greenspan

The stretch of Interstate 5 between Los Angeles and San Diego starts in an industrial ghetto, cuts southwest through miles of vast shopping complexes and newish housing developments and nearly touches the Pacific Ocean at the southern tip of Orange County. From then on it hugs the coastline, dissecting dozens of small towns with Spanish names whose smallest shacks are now worth millions, as well as the barren landscape of Camp Pendleton and its sister town, Oceanside, whose quaint stores seem frozen in the 1950s. Finally, you enter San Diego from the far northwest, grazing the Mc-Mansions of La Jolla and just missing the dramatic cliffs of Del Mar. On a sunny day, which is most days, the two-hour drive is a revelation, a journey that takes you out from under the shadow of a big city and into the eternal warmth of a shimmering ocean. At night, the interstate becomes a speedway for the *coyotes* and their desperate clientele who are packed into vans or stuffed into the trunks of cars, rushing north back into the shadow—always with the lights off, often on the wrong side of the road. The most fortunate will begin new lives as day laborers or maids or hotel employees. The bodies of the unluckiest are collected from the brush off the shoulder after the inevitable head-on collision. There is probably no other highway in the country where the American Dream is chased so frequently in opposing directions, or where it collides with itself at such high speeds. There are still those who cannot afford the *coyotes* or who have learned to distrust them; these risk the journey north in the light of day, and dozens of diamond-shaped roadsigns warn you to watch out for them: a husband and wife running, the wife's hand attached to a child struggling to keep up. They are painted in profile against yellow backgrounds, like wild deer.

I hardly need an excuse to make this drive, especially on a Sunday morning, when the traffic is light and the sun is gently blessing everything around me with warm, golden rays. Yet, there is something discomfiting about it, something unexpected about my journey—something, as Dave Ramsey might say, that "just isn't right."

For several months my producer and I have been searching for the notorious overspenders, those Americans who we all know are living beyond their means, who are abusing credit, who live the high life on our dime and then walk away from it all without so much as a wave good-bye. We can be fairly certain they are laughing at us— *suckers!*—as they steal a fresh start, courtesy of some bleeding-heart bankruptcy judge, while we, the responsible, pay for their free ride in the form of ever higher interest rates and ever more numerous fees. Thanks to the moral vigilance of our congressmen and the relentless public relations execs working for the financial industry, these ingrates have become as infamous as the "welfare queens" of the eighties: You may remember them as the "lucky duckies"* who make $80,000 a year by having twenty children. And, as I have

---

*A.K.A. the working poor, at least according to the *Wall Street Journal*'s editorial pages.

discovered over the past several months, the spendthrifts are also just as hard to locate.

But I have finally found a live one. How? Not by entering *credit card whore* into a Google search or loitering with the other losers around that stretch of Robertson Boulevard where Lindsay and Paris and Britney are always photographed stepping out of tiny boutiques with absurdly huge shopping bags or trolling the O.C.'s many Starbucks cafés for semiretired reality-television celebrities.* No, I have discovered a veritable treasure trove of overspenders in the personnel files of the country's largest employer: the United States military. Despite having their health insurance, meals, and educations paid for, the bankruptcy rate for military personnel is currently twice the national average, and the General Accounting Office estimates that one out of every four military credit card transactions is fraudulent—spent on staples of war like Vegas vacations, DVD players, fur coats, and, my favorite, lap dances. It could be that the men and women of our armed forces are particularly irresponsible, bad human beings. Or it could be that, since the midnineties, the Defense Department has made high-limit credit cards standard issue to hundreds of thousands of our troops. Why? Credit cards increase efficiency.

The Navy Consolidated (NAVCON) brig Miramar is located in Building 7684 on the Marine Corps Air Station (MCAS) base in Miramar, a small town northeast of San Diego which has developed around the needs of the modern military-industrial complex, meaning there are plenty of fast-food outlets, discount stores, and check-

*A relative term in this instance.

cashing joints. The NAVCON Web site boasts of "setting the standards of excellence in military corrections" and features links to the Federal Department of Corrections as well as something called "Brig Industries, Products and Services." Visiting hours are from 1 to 3 p.m., Saturday and Sunday. You may not schedule visits in advance. You are warned that you will need a driver's license, current vehicle registration, and proof of insurance to enter the base.

I present my credentials at the north gate and receive a pass and directions. Driving along a manicured golf course and past a Burger King, it is difficult to imagine that this is, at its core, a launching pad for war. Even the brig, it turns out, has a distinctly suburban flavor. It does not resemble a prison at all. It is a single-story brick building that could just as easily be a Marriott Residence Inn or a medical office.

Once inside, I receive a pass and a locker for my keys. The receptionist places a call to a guard who will retrieve my prized interviewee from her cell. Then I am buzzed past a thick steel door into a holding room with a metal detector, frisked, and finally escorted out the final door, into a small gymnasium where dozens of plastic chairs have been arranged into little circles. Already several uniformed prisoners are visiting with their loved ones, mainly young women with children. On the perimeter, armed soldiers monitor the activity, but the mood is relaxed.

I have never met Staff Major Sheila Bryan. I was allowed to send her a letter, though I don't know whether she received it or not. And even if she did receive it, I don't know that this will make her want to talk to me. I have no idea what she looks like, if she is white or black, thin or fat, diminutive or larger-than-life. All I know is that she is roughly my age, 34, a sixteen-year veteran of the Marine Corps who gained notoriety by charging $130,000 of personal expenses, including a Cadillac Escalade, a boob job, a wedding, and two years' worth of tanning sessions, to her military credit card.

Sheila appears fifteen minutes later in green camos. She is a tiny woman, not white but not black, either, with a thick Cajun drawl and the wary eyes of a frightened animal. She has received my letter and decided to receive me. As it turns out, I am the only visitor she has had in her eleven months here. Her husband and her three children cannot afford to visit. The rest of her family thinks she is in Iraq, fighting what her commander in chief calls the global war on terror.

Where to begin? Sheila grew up on the streets of New Orleans fending for herself. Her parents had no money and, for the most part, she was raised by her grandmother, but they didn't get along. It was a tough life for a 14-year-old trying to survive in one of the country's bleakest cities. But survive she did. When you are a homeless teenage girl, you develop instincts. At 18, Sheila joined the Marines because it offered her a way out. She applied her street smarts and learned to love discipline. She married, had two children, got divorced. Along the way she received promotions. She was a good Marine, always loyal. The military had given her a life and in return she devoted her life to the military. Several years ago she married another soldier named Carlton who had ambitions of becoming a rap mogul. They had a young daughter together and Carlton left the service to pursue his dream. But Sheila stayed in, only a few years shy of retirement and the generous pension that would allow her to pursue her own dreams.

That had been the plan until a year and a half previous, when her commanding officer and two MPs had walked into her office and told her they had something to discuss. A chill ran up and down Sheila's spine but also a cool wave of relief. She knew what was coming and she was ready to deal with it. In truth, she was tired of looking over her shoulder, tired of not being able to sleep at night, tired of being afraid. She sensed that she would be found out from the beginning.

Yet, if it hadn't been for a bit of bad luck, Sheila would have gotten away with her crime. The military's budget is in excess of $700 billion, and her theft did not even come close to a rounding error. Sheila had another advantage: Having risen to become the officer of her division overseeing procurement, there was no one above her checking statements or signing off on her purchases. As astonishing as this may be to anyone who has ever had even a modest expense account, there is apparently no automatic internal auditing process in the Marine Corps. Had it not been for a less careful soldier in her unit attracting attention and ultimately a team of accountants from Washington, Sheila could have remained the unit's most beloved poster child, the tough girl from the streets who the military had made good, just like in the ads.

In a voice that is both humble and matter-of-fact, Sheila tells me she can still remember the day the credit cards arrived. Previously, all purchase orders had been routed through a central procurement office, where they were reviewed and approved. Whether you needed a tank or a roll of toilet paper, this was the procedure. Getting supplies often took weeks, sometimes months. It was tedious, time-consuming, and annoying. It wasted paper. It felt draconian in a world where one is accustomed to getting what one wants instantaneously—where, as the mortgage lender ditech.com advertises, refinancing your home is easier than ordering a pizza.

So the Pentagon had decided that government should imitate business and that soldiers should have expense accounts. What they had neglected to install were the checks and balances. Indeed, what is commonly referred to as "fraud protection" was entirely outsourced to the credit card issuer, Bank of America, which according to published reports had been very liberal with its credit limits and very tight with questions. After all, countries, particularly the U.S.A., don't go bankrupt.

The potential for abuse should have been obvious from the start—if not to the Pentagon, then at least to the Bank of America. Here was a population of low-paid, highly charged young men and women who liked to travel, a population that had chosen the military, to some degree, to teach them self-discipline, to be a surrogate parent. But if anyone of authority at the bank considered these rather scary facts, they kept it to themselves. Soldiers were full-fledged adults and would thus be treated like any other valued client, i.e., the more they spent, the more credit they would be given. Moreover, Bank of America hadn't installed any special red flags on the purchases themselves, so a $500 bar tab at Hooters was approved as expeditiously as a $50 toner cartridge from Staples. When Senator Charles Grassley of Iowa finally got wind of the mess and started asking questions, the media had a field day doing his work for him. There were plenty of salacious details to unearth: huge tips to Hooters girls, expensive clothes for girlfriends, rounds and rounds of drinks for Vegas strippers and prostitutes. The resulting imbroglio dominated the "Fleecing of America" series on NBC News. Local newspapers rode the coattails and uncovered similar scandals in local government. Governors, mayors, and city councilmen magically turned into hedonists when they received their government-issued MasterCards. (Similar outrage was stirred in the UK when Colleen McCabe, a headteacher from Bromley in Kent, went on a five-year spending spree with her school's credit cards and chequebooks. The former nun was sentenced to five years in prison and the press dubbed her "The Imelda Marcos of Bromley.") But the media's hype and Grassley's measured outrage (love the troops, hate the fraud) hit a stone wall. The Pentagon insisted that credit cards were necessary because they increased efficiency, i.e., they allowed soldiers to buy stuff faster, and, therefore, they saved money. End of story. Even a

United States senator knows not to press the military-industrial-financial complex. You are either with them or against them.

Sheila had a revelation the day the Marine Band needed a bus to tour in. She realized that, rather than schlep around for a cheap rental that the bean counters in procurement probably would bitch and moan about anyway, she could charge a top-of-the-line bus with a flick of the wrist and no one would notice or care. So that's exactly what she did. And when the band realized it would be a nice bit of brand-building to have their photograph airbrushed on the sides of the bus, she charged that too. The credit card was magic. For someone like Sheila, who had scraped by her entire life, charging was not only fun but therapeutic, addicting.

And it was all completely legal, as long as the purchases were military-related. But what did that mean, exactly, military-*related*? Her friends at the base had become very interested in the answer to that question. Was a laptop or a DVD player that they could take home after work military-related? What if they neglected to return it for a while, or what if it somehow ended up in the local pawnshop? Was a buddy trip to Las Vegas a vacation or a team-building exercise? Fact-finding mission, anyone? The line between military expense and personal indulgence began to blur, and Sheila was the decider, a duty for which she was uniquely unfit. Because, although she had lived a life of abject poverty and self-denial, Sheila still possessed a remarkably potent guilty conscience—an inner voice that constantly reminded her it was more blessed to give than to receive.

Guilt nudged Sheila from blurring the line to crossing it, and guilt overwhelmed both conscience and common sense. Guilt caused her to move over an hour's drive from the base in New Orleans where she had been stationed so that her husband could be close to his mentor. She could not bear the thought of limiting her husband's ambitions, even though her car was too old to make the trip reliably and she would have to quit the cocktail waitress job at Harrah's that was making ends meet. It was guilt again that caused her to charge recording equipment and a digital video camera for him so he could record his music and shoot videos. It was after a blistering fight with Carlton, when she thought her marriage was over and her second family destroyed and her guilt plunged to new depths, that she called up the Cadillac dealership and recited the familiar sixteen digits of her credit card to the salesman over the phone because her husband was always talking about how nice the neighbor's truck was, and if she could provide this for him, then maybe she could save their family. It was the residual guilt of junior high school—emerging from her grandma's beater in worn, generic clothes—that further justified the Escalade with its pearlescent paint job and the designer clothes she could suddenly buy her kids at the mall. It was guilt when her husband noticed the extra flab after her pregnancy and she realized that the credit card could get rid of that and perk up her breasts to boot.

Looking back, Sheila can trace every illegal charge she made to a fight with her husband. Each crime was an attempt to make things right and save their relationship. Yet, she does not blame Carlton, nor does she blame the military or Bank of America. She blames only herself, and the time she is spending in the brig is deserved, necessary. She tells me that she's determined to right herself. She has found God, and He has told her not to shirk her responsibilities, as she didn't shirk them when her commanding officer came into her office that day and she readily admitted to everything. She is scared of seeing her family again, scared by the prospect of bankruptcy, which she somehow hopes to avoid. Sheila wants to repay her financial debt every bit as much as her debt to her fellow Marines for betraying them. Yet, every day she sits in the brig, Sheila is accumulating interest on a sum of money that already seemed overwhelming eleven months ago. By the time she gets out, this will have compounded with itself and with fees she probably can't imagine. Being fairly good with numbers, it's hard for me to figure Sheila redeeming herself with her creditors, even if she is somehow able to transcend the guilt that threatens to consume her once she returns to her husband and children.

Sheila is aware that she has always been her own worst enemy. She tells me that the day she was discovered, when the Marines removed every piece of furniture and every appliance from her home, her biggest worry had not been arrest or jail time or even public humiliation. Her overriding fear had been telling her kids why there was no more stuff. So when they returned from school that day, she told them that she had cleaned their home to make way for even better stuff. *Brand-new stuff!* The next morning, Sheila dialed Rent-A-Center, and within a few hours the Bryan house was transformed to resemble a collection of those dioramas you see people win on *Wheel of Fortune* and *The Price Is Right*, complete with a big-screen television and mass-produced objets d'art. All for no money down and triple-digit interest. A week later Sheila was led off to prison.

A large soldier interrupts our conversation. The hour is up. One of his peers will escort Sheila back to her cell, where she will spend more hours pondering her mistakes and talking to God. We shake hands and agree to meet again the following Sunday, and then she disappears. I drive off the base, passing several golf carts driven by men in bermuda shorts and polo shirts, marveling at how comfortable the MCAS is, how safe it makes you feel, like one of Beth's master-planned communities. The drive north is just as beautiful and just as unsettling as the one that preceded it. Sheila, after all, is a criminal, and one must therefore be cautious of the veracity of any tale she has to tell. Yet, there is something indisputably honest about her, as though physical confinement has finally relieved her of the need to live a life confined by lies. I wonder what our founding fathers—the idealists who wrestled with the morality and practicality of debtor's prisons so inconclusively—would think of

Sheila. I wonder what my corporate friends, who write off their vacations to Southern California as business trips and who classify their attempts to catch a glimpse of Britney or Lindsay or Paris while dining on $11 onion rings at The Ivy as a business expense, would make of her.

The next Sunday I present my credentials but the mood at NAVCON has clearly changed. Two burly and not particularly fit naval officers confront me. Where am I from? What is my agenda? Documentary film, eh? I don't look like Michael Moore. Their bad cop/bad cop routine is clearly meant to intimidate, but all I can think about is shutting down that Burger King on the base before everybody looks like these jokers. After a few minutes of browbeating they tell me to leave. Sheila doesn't want to talk to me. She doesn't know who I am, anyway. My clever attempt to pull one over on the United States military has thus been thwarted.

In the 1950s, the big tobacco companies sent free cigarettes to soldiers as a way of expressing their gratitude to the men in uniform. Much to the soldiers' dismay, the industry's altruism was ultimately rejected by the Pentagon and the free cigarettes stopped coming. Even in a day when advertisers managed to fit *clean fresh air* in the same sentence as *unfiltered* without causing the American Medical Association fits of apoplexy, the powers that be felt pretty sure that sending young men and women free samples of an addictive product might be a bad idea. Later in the decade, the United States Congress reinforced this principle by forbidding banks from sending Americans credit cards they never asked for—a practice begun, as I mentioned in a previous chapter, with the BankAmericard. The principle is fairly simple: If people want to purchase an addictive product, they are capable of asking for it all by themselves. And for a long time this principle has not been seriously questioned. If anything, it has been taken to extremes. At the convenience store, cigarettes are now tucked behind the counter and sometimes behind locked glass; ditto for porn and even a sinus decongestant; finally, crack houses are located in neighborhoods that most of us find more than a little inconvenient and somewhat intimidating.

The point is that even if the government allows us to have these things, they want to make sure that we need them *enough* to wait an extra minute and to use that minute pondering why we would waste our hard-earned dollars on something that is not particularly good for us, something that will only make us want more of it. The good folks who manufacture hard liquor and tobacco are not even allowed to advertise their wares on television and they rarely, if ever, complain. When Congress told big tobacco to print warning labels on their products, labels which would scream *cancer* and *death* every time an already stressed customer reached for a little respite, cigarette manufacturers magnanimously agreed. In return, the attorneys general of all fifty states and the federal government have sued them relentlessly, demanding hundreds of billions of dollars in restitution for hoodwinking the masses.

The credit industry has enjoyed a very different reception in Washington. For the past forty years, the federal government has helped private corporations sell debt to its citizens and guaranteed them a profit. Starting more than fifty years ago with the Small Business Administration (SBA) and continuing two decades later with the Federal National Home Mortgage Association, aka Fannie Mae, Freddie Mac (FRE), and Sallie Mae (SLM Corporation), politicians have created enterprises to give lenders special status as partners rather than private industrialists. In return, each entity has been allowed to sell trillions of dollars of debt with little to no risk. Fannie Mae alone has either guaranteed or sold nearly $5.7 trillion in home loans in its relatively short history and currently, with its sister company, Freddie Mac, counts nearly $4 trillion in home loans either outstanding or guaranteed (the companies receive a fee for the guarantees, which are implicitly backed by the full faith and credit of you and me); Sallie Mae boasts a $123 billion portfolio of loans to students—which is very different, by the way, than loans for education because students are allowed to fold their credit card debts into these loans; and the Congress has blessed the SBA with a $28 billion war chest to be dispensed in modest sums to small businesses, which most of us like to think of as entrepreneurial ventures but which more often than not are nationally franchised behemoths. The top two beneficiaries of the SBA's largesse are Burger King and Super 8 Motels.

On its face, guaranteeing bank profits seems an absurd public policy in a free-market, capitalist economy like ours. Why would the federal government assume trillions of dollars of risk on behalf of a hugely profitable industry whose purpose is to shoulder exactly that kind of risk? Or, put another way, why would the federal government give banks an incentive to make risky loans?

The answer becomes abundantly clear when one reviews any State of the Union speech of the past twenty-five years. Guaranteeing private debt, rather than paying for goods like education (as do many other industrialized nations), saves politicians from making risky choices while allowing them to toss around what sound like very impressive achievements: increases in home "ownership," particularly among minority groups; leaps in college enrollment, particularly among the disadvantaged; a wave of entrepreneurship, i.e., lots of new fast-food restaurants and cheap motels; and so on. Politicians, like consumers, hate making difficult choices. Debt offers the illusion of having it all—now. Take the UK, for example. The government has set targets for the end of the decade of 50 percent of all school leavers attending university. But the average student leaves higher education owing £12,000 on credit cards, bank overdrafts and student loans. By 2010, it is estimated the average level of student debt will be £33,000, a figure that will be enlarged mainly by the pending introduction of "tuition fees"—effectively a government-imposed tax for attending university. So-called "graduate loans," marketed as a crutch to debt-laden university graduates confronting the divide between salaries and expenses, will no doubt increase that figure substantially.

Over the past several decades, at the same time that the financial industry has argued that market forces should be allowed to rule exclusively and that regulation has become irrelevant, the same industry has jealously guarded their special relationship with Washington by donating generously to the reelection campaigns of powerful congressmen, governors, and other would-be regulators. In 2005, Fannie Mae alone spent more than $7 million on lobbyists, and in 2006, Freddie Mac was fined $3.8 million by the Federal Election Committee for making illegal campaign contributions—the largest fine ever levied by the FEC. In the interest of fairness, I should mention that Freddie Mac did not actually admit to any wrongdoing, and an attorney for one of the company's executives, Robert Mitchell Delk—who was cited for holding over seventy lavish campaign fund-raisers that benefited the all-powerful chairman of the House Financial Services Committee—denied that there was anything improper about his client's activities, describing these fund-raisers as "personal events."

So successful have executives like Mr. Delk been at convincing politicians that what is good for their profits is good for America that I can only once recall hearing the conventional wisdom of "good debt" challenged, this during the vice presidential debate between Lloyd Bentsen and Dan Quayle in 1988. Quayle, the dashing young heir to a publishing fortune, regurgitated the industry's talking points when Bentsen, the silver fox, stopped him in his tracks. "If you let me write $200 billion worth of hot checks every year," he admonished, "I could give you an illusion of prosperity too."

It was a stunning remark. I remember silently cheering at the time, even though I was volunteering for Bush/Quayle (I actually watched the debate at Bush/Quayle headquarters in Seattle). But the media didn't pick up on it. Later in the debate, Bentsen outdid himself with the remark about Quayle being no John F. Kennedy, and that became the cover of *Time* magazine.

But the free ride is only one reason politicians have been so reluctant to put down their pom-poms and get real. The other is denial: They have their own debt problem, after all, one that is variously calculated at $8 trillion (the national debt) and north of $40 trillion (the national debt plus the future cost of all of the promises Congress has made over the last sixty years, e.g., Medicare, Social Security, and government pensions). One does not hear much about America's addiction to debt in the State of the Union, though one is treated to tantalizing visions of glory—trips to Mars and democratic crusades, etc. Inconsistencies, i.e., the application of mathematics to said speeches, tend to be explained away by underlings and with an arrogance that makes Sheila look like a realist. Here's one particularly telling exchange from the same *New York Times* interview with Senator Connie Mack that I quoted a while ago:

> Interviewer: If we keep borrowing at this level, won't the
> Arabs or the Chinese eventually own this country?
> Sen. Mack: I am not worried about that. We are a huge
> country producing enormous assets day in and day out. We
> have great strength and we have always adjusted to difficul-
> ties that faced us, and we will continue to do so.

This sounds quite a bit different from President Bush's explanation, a short time earlier, on why debt actually *is* a bad thing—for Iraq:

Interviewer: I know you don't want the Iraqis to be bur-
dened with a large amount of debt, but why should Americans?
President Bush: Let's not burden the Iraqi people with debt.
All they've got to pay the debt with is the oil.

One might expect the president of the United States, a former
wildcatter himself, to know that oil-producing nations tend to be
pretty wealthy. One might also expect a higher level of concern—
and awareness—from the nation's economic guru, the man whose
job it is to look glum and fret about the future and otherwise
restrain our inherently American "irrational exuberance": Alan
Greenspan. But then one would be sorely disappointed. Watching
one of his final appearances before the House Banking Committee
in 2005, I was struck by how well Greenspan manages to expose the
crisis without ever compelling anyone else to notice it with him. He
will agree with a Democrat who mocks Bush's modest budget cuts
as irrelevant, reminding him that the crisis is of such magnitude
that "I regret to say the word *billion* does not encompass the nature
of the problem." Then, poker-faced, he will agree with a Republican
who suggests that tax cuts are a wonderful way to stimulate the
economy and the government doesn't really deserve the money
anyway. Greenspan's schtick reminds me of a story my father used
to tell of a wise man who is confronted by two men in a heated argument. When the first man tells his side of the story, the wise man
looks at him and says, "You're right." The second man goes nuts
and demands that his side of the story be told. When he is finished,
the wise man replies, "*You're* right." When the men protest that
they cannot both be right, the wise man smiles and says, "You're
right."

So if the government was suddenly to announce that debt was a
liability after all and not a wonderful, magical thing, as we had all

assumed it to be, it would not only smack of hypocrisy but, after so much water under the bridge, it would probably not be taken seriously anyway. The culture of debt is therefore left unchallenged. What is open to debate are the ancillary issues, the tactics. But even these debates have proven remarkably one-sided. When thirty states sued mortgage lenders for fraud and racial discrimination because they were charging minority customers higher rates than they qualified for, the comptroller of the currency intervened and said the states had no legal authority to protect their citizens. When the California senate tried to slap a box on credit card statements that would explain how long it would take to pay off the balance if only the minimum payment were remitted, the banks, after publicly agreeing to do so voluntarily, changed their minds and killed it. Must have smelled too much like those health warning labels on cigarettes.

Of course, the founding fathers bestowed us with three branches of government in this country for a reason. If the Congress and the president somehow get it wrong, there remains one last hope: the judiciary. Judges, more so than politicians, tend to respect both the Constitution and the notion of tradition—or, as they call it, precedent. It was therefore with great interest that I started digging around the United States Supreme Court, reasoning that the highest court in the land must surely have weighed in on these matters. And, as it turns out, they have.

I meet Pamela Hood in a modest apartment complex on the outskirts of Memphis, Tennessee, where she shares a single bedroom and tiny living area with her grandmother. In her early twenties, she is already pushing up against obesity. She is also sweet and terribly nervous—the last human being you would expect to win a major case before the United States Supreme Court.

Pam apologizes for her jitters, then disappears and returns with several photo albums. There are pictures of Pam in Australia and the Philippines, trips paid for by the United States Navy, and there are photos of her with her late grandfather, who was a career sailor as well as her best friend. She has always been restless, she tells me, partly because she is young and Memphis is not exactly bursting with opportunity, but also because she suffers from depression and spent most of her early years trying to escape from it.

Before the Navy, Pam attended the University of Texas at Dallas, the same school Sean attended. Unlike Sean, she was lucky to get in and did not qualify for grants, so she did what most young people in this country do: She went to the bank and got a student loan, guaranteed in full by the United States government. It was, she remembers, probably the easiest transaction of her life. They were even willing to give her more than she asked for, and if she ended up needing more in the future, well, she could always just pick up the phone. No one at the bank told her the reason for their generosity: that Pam was a risk-free client.

Pam learned all of this several years later when, working at a nursing home for close to the minimum wage and supporting her widowed grandmother (the Navy has been slow to transfer her grandfather's pension), she chose to pay the rent and utilities rather than the interest on her student loans.* Pretty soon Sallie Mae started calling. She explained that she couldn't afford to pay, but they wouldn't take no for an answer.† Pam declared bankruptcy to

*As for London, don't get me started … It is probably worth noting that 2005 was the first year in which anyone working a full-time job at minimum wage would not be able to afford an apartment in any city in the United States.

†Incidentally, Sallie Mae now owns one of the largest—and fastest-growing—collection agencies in the United States.

make the calls stop. It was then she learned the one debt she could not put in the "discharge" column was the roughly $5,000 in student loans—the only substantial debt she had. Of all the horrific crimes you can commit in this country, only two have a statute of limitations of more than ten years: one is murder, the other is not paying your student loans.*

Pam decided to ask for a discharge of her student loans anyway. The judge told her it couldn't be done. But Pam decided to fight. An eccentric attorney in New York City named Lenny took on the case as a matter of constitutional law. He was supported by consumer advocates and at least one historian. The Supreme Court agreed to hear the case in 2004, and Lenny, to the great surprise of most of his colleagues, emerged victorious. The ruling was a watershed, not only because it gave Pam the chance to discharge her student loans—she would still have to prove to the judge that paying them constituted an undue hardship—but because, more generally, it struck at the core of the government-banking duopoly. If the government could not claim a special right to squeeze its citizens when they fell on hard times, how could it continue to guarantee the repayment of those loans? And how could its leaders continue to gloat about the always expanding economy and the vibrancy of the American Dream if the easy credit stopped flowing? How could they claim, as Senator Mack put it, that "we have great strength and we have always adjusted to difficulties that faced us, and we will continue to do so" knowing full well that both the primary engine of that strength and the mechanism that always bridged the difficult gaps were both based on a false assumption?

---

*By contrast, student loans are "dischargeable" from bankruptcy proceedings in the UK. So far, over one thousand students and graduates have cleared their student loans by declaring themselves bankrupt, but they may be the lucky duckies. In 2004, the governments of England and Wales responded by proposing laws to close this loophole. Similar proposals have since been introduced in Scotland and Northern Ireland.

The answers arrived in 2005 in the form of two serendipitous events for the duopoly: One, the United States Congress passed the Bankruptcy Reform Act, which makes discharging debts far more difficult, if not impossible;* and two, the Supreme Court issued a controversial ruling that Social Security payments can be garnished in order to repay student loans. So the government's special status, and its special relationship with lenders, will remain intact. And the 20 percent of Americans who, like Pamela, are in default on their student loans will never live in peace. The phones will ring until they die.

Sheila stands behind a bar in a dark club on the outskirts of New Orleans, chatting up a couple of old men from the neighborhood who have stopped by for Long Island iced teas. When she came home, the first thing Carlton did was take her to the mall to get her hair cut and highlighted. Then she went to the tanning salon, and now she's working behind the bar. After fourteen months in the brig, she is a free woman again, yet she looks more imprisoned than before.

Carlton sits in the corner of the bar, feeding dollar bills into a video poker machine. He developed a gambling addiction in the military, which operates casinos on many of its bases around the world, and now he can gamble in his own establishment. It's not much—a dozen tables and a worn bar with just enough bottles of liquor on the shelves to justify its existence—but Carlton is an optimist. He's held on to the Escalade, which suits the oversized jerseys that hang over his jean shorts and the gold caps that make him mumble. The old men eventually leave and then Sheila remembers to call back

*A bankruptcy judge in Austin, Texas, recently called the act "inane," "absurd," and incomprehensible to "any rational human being."

her kids, who've been left at home watching television. They call incessantly, driving her nuts. At eleven she and Carlton will shut the place down and go to the local IHOP to eat something, calm their nerves. Then she'll get up at eight to attend pedicure class at beauty school, where she is training to be a beautician. The school has applied for a government-sponsored student loan in her name.

The past two weeks have been tough. There have been moments of joy, like when she arrived at the airport and got to hug her children for the first time in more than a year, and when her fellow ghetto-girl-made-good Fantasia Barrino became the third American Idol, but there have been many more moments of despair. Carlton kept a box for the bills and collection letters that had piled up, but Sheila couldn't bear to open them. She guesses they total around $100,000, but she can't conceive of ever paying them, so why bother? She doubts she will own anything again, despite Carlton's constant pep talks that things will be better than before. Sheila is, at last, facing reality. It's a new day: There are bills to pay and mouths to feed before tending to Carlton's dreams, but she doesn't even know where to begin. One night over a pot of homemade jambalaya, she mentions shoplifting, then looks over, ever so subtly, to gauge my reaction. Is it immoral to steal food when your kids are hungry?

A year from now, every talking head in America will be asking this question. A massive hurricane will have flooded the city of New Orleans and the suburb where Sheila and her family live, will have wiped out both their home and their fledgling business—washed away the beauty school, even. And for a brief moment the media, as a cartoon in the *New York Times* jokes, will rediscover the poor. But then the bloodied water will be pumped out of the city, and the media will move on to other matters, and the American people will hope and pray that something is being done for those poor people who lost it all.

I have tried calling Sheila and Carlton since the hurricane, but their numbers no longer work and going back seems pointless, since there is nothing left to return to. I thought of them the other day, when the president was delivering his latest State of the Union speech. The Pentagon, he promised, would receive a 7 percent raise, upping its annual budget to nearly $800 billion—not counting another $120 billion or so for the Iraq war, which is considered an off-budget item for some reason. The president did not actually mention Hurricane Katrina, the greatest natural disaster in our history, by name, and barely alluded to it at all toward the end of the speech. The most ambitious government plan to help the residents of New Orleans remains a home loan program that the vast majority of the city's residents do not qualify for—partly because of their address.

It is possible that the president feels we simply cannot afford to help these people. Or maybe, as Eason Mitchell says, he's just a good guy from a privileged background who doesn't understand why they can't pull themselves up by their bootstraps. There is another reason not to mention them, however, and that is because they no longer exist. They have already maxed out. They have nothing left to contribute because their credit has run out, their chips long since passed into the hands of others.

Six

"We're just bringing people together, almost like a dating service . . .
but for debt."
– George and Frank, www.DebtOutlet.com

When I was 16 years old I inherited a quarter of a million dollars from my grandfather. There was only one condition: No part of it was to be spent on a Ferrari. But as much as I liked Ferraris, I was already exploring a more expensive habit: investing. I had read the *Wall Street Journal* since my early teens. I was obsessed with the lives of self-made men and devoured their biographies at the local library. Looking back, I was a very ambitious and rather scary young man.

My senior year of high school I applied to the Wharton School of the University of Pennsylvania, the country's oldest business school, not because of its founder, Ben Franklin ("A penny saved is a penny earned") but because of its most famous graduate, Donald Trump, whose autobiography, *The Art of the Deal*, I had read twice and whose net worth was then negative $900 million, give or take a million. My choice of school, and the reasons behind it, would turn out to be more than a little propitious.

I was one of the real lucky duckies: the kids whose families can pay for college. The small fraction who don't have to start their adult lives with the equivalent of a mortgage hanging over their heads. In fact, my parents had been so determined that I graduate with no financial encumbrances whatsoever that they had covered absolutely everything, including living expenses, in my college fund. All I had to do was fax the bank an estimate of my expenses for the following year and a week later I received a check, usually in the neighborhood of $25,000. And because my grandfather had shrewdly invested my inheritance in high-yield municipal bonds, I was receiving another $25,000 every year, tax-free, to cover any additional expenses that might pop up.

Wharton taught me that economics is not business, that finance is not hustling. Everything I had learned in my favorite books became irrelevant. Most of my classes either dealt in the arcane, like accounting and insurance, or in the theoretical. My teachers' ideas, which they taught as self-evident, often contradicted what I'd learned from my idols—a phenomenon that drove my adolescent mind to a state of constant distraction. After all, how could a professor claim that all stocks were perfectly priced, as is taught by the "efficient markets theory," when George Soros said you make a killing because stocks are anything *but* perfectly priced? How could my teachers say, with straight faces, that we must always assume that people act rationally in their own self-interest when The Donald had told me how he'd become a gazillionaire by exploiting people's irrationality—their greed, their fears, and their egos? I was miserable.

But the wonderful and terrible thing about having a lot of money is that, when you are miserable, you can do something about it. So it was that after enduring my freshman year, a year in which I was accepted into the school's elite as a Benjamin Franklin Scholar, I decided to get on with things and prove my professors wrong. My motives were pure. The trouble is that I, the Benjamin Franklin Scholar, decided to make my fortune in the worst business imaginable: fast-food restaurants.

115

I'm still not sure what qualified me to be a restaurateur, except that, like most people, I enjoy eating. At the time, *Entrepreneur* magazine (which is basically an advertisement for a handful of franchises) had named Subway Sandwiches & Salads the number-one business opportunity in America for five years. I signed on, ponied up the $80,000 necessary to open a sub shop (without telling my family), found a location a short drive south of campus in Wilmington, Delaware, and spent two weeks of my first college summer learning to make something called the "Bigger, Meatier, Tastier" at Subway's headquarters in Milford, Connecticut. I have no doubt it was at this moment that my grandfather began turning in his grave.

My Subway store turned out to be a success, which only stoked my appetite for more. I dropped out of my fraternity and quit the rowing team, scheduled all of my classes on Tuesdays and Thursdays, and moved to Delaware. My landlord would soon introduce me to the next big thing: a bustling quick-service franchise called Boston Chicken that had just opened its first "unit" in a suburb of Philadelphia. Boston Chicken was then a chain of thirty small food stores based in Newton, Massachusetts. The entire concept could be summarized as Thanksgiving Dinner every day: homemade mashed potatoes with gravy, butternut squash, stuffing, cornbread, rotisserie fowl, etc. In retrospect, the wisdom of replicating a day that leaves most Americans in a food coma for twenty-four hours seems inherently unsustainable. But back then all I noticed were long lines of customers forking over twenties.

I summoned all of my creative accounting genius, conjured up a bunch of spreadsheets that showed how Boston Chicken was the path to millions of dollars in EBITDA,* and even managed to hook an investor, a short bald man who'd made his fortune in a leveraged

*Earnings before interest, taxes, depreciation, and amortization.

buyout. I then convinced the company to sell us the exclusive rights to build Boston Chickens in Delaware. I neglected to account for two eventualities: One, Boston Chicken was then being sold to an investor group that would promptly decide to increase the cost of building a store by approximately 400 percent; and two, my investor would decide that paying the IRS was more important than meeting his commitments to my fledgling company.

Not surprisingly, my adventure in the chicken business turned out to be a disaster, though at least it turned out to be a disaster relatively quickly. Within two years I had built two stores, which were profitable, and was about to start construction on a third. However, start-up costs had more than consumed all of my cash. I was broke. My investor panicked and wanted his money back—fast. Boston Chicken's new management could not have been more delighted. As it turned out, they wanted Delaware for themselves and they'd never liked the arrogant teenager from the Ivy League school anyway. I had no option but to sell out and they knew it. So, after enduring a hardball negotiation in which I held no cards, I ended up with a deal that gave my investor his money back plus 10 percent and left just enough to pay all of the company's outstanding liabilities. Then I waved good-bye to my inheritance and moved to Texas. My grandfather was now spinning in his grave, no doubt, but my dad was more philosophical, telling me he'd been pretty sure I'd lose anything I'd been given at such a young age. Anyway, I don't remember being upset, just relieved that my employees' final checks had cleared, my investor had been made whole, and the bank had been repaid.

Was I a fool? Probably. Boston Chicken's IPO in November 1993—the month I sold out—was the second most successful public offering in the history of Wall Street.* The shares more than

---

*The most successful was the biotech firm Genentech, which had more than tripled its first day of trading, setting a precedent for technology companies for years to come.

doubled in one day. But a few years later, the company declared bankruptcy. Their gleaming new stores were simply too expensive to make any money. And the franchisees who had stayed on, much older men than me with much more to lose, lost everything. One of them, a man who'd sold the Burger King franchises he'd spent most of his life nurturing into a successful business in order to make his fortune on the next big thing, had a heart attack and died shortly thereafter. The spectacular crash of Boston Market—the name was changed in 1992 in order to appeal to a broader demographic, or so went the theory—also wiped out over a billion dollars of stockholders' equity and banks were left holding hundreds of millions of dollars in bad debt. Boston Market's CEO, the guy who'd promised to make shareholders and franchisees rich and whose dream in life was to own a professional sports franchise, became a born-again Christian. Boston Market is now a division of McDonald's.

It was, my mother told me at the time, a terrific learning experience.* And, of course, she proved to be right. I managed to sell my Subway store at a profit and, over the next several years, I published a successful newsletter called *Restaurant Investing* and made a lot of money trading restaurant stocks. I've also found comfort in a truism from the media mogul Sumner Redstone: Success is not built on small successes but on very large failures.

Yet, there is something that my mother does not know, that I have, in fact, never told anyone and never intended to tell anyone. Even now I hesitate to reveal it. Maybe it's because of what Dave Ramsey calls the intense shame that everyone feels about debt—the false certainty that everyone *else* has got it together. Or maybe it's what Bob, the Debtors Anonymous member I interviewed, told me: debt is simply not a socially acceptable topic; one can talk about

*As opposed to college, which I dropped out of in my senior year.

118

one's sex life or even one's drug addiction as though it were fashionable, but owning up to one's financial troubles means being ostracized from the world of polite conversation. Maybe it has taken my journey around the country to know that what Dave and Bob told me is as true of myself as of the dozens of people I've interviewed. After all, I live in the same culture of debt as everyone else—which, at it's base, let's face it together now, is a culture of fear. If I've let myself believe that a deeply held hatred of secrets has exempted me from the culture's golden rule, then I've been very naïve indeed.

For five years after handing over the keys to my chicken empire's ruins, the aftershocks rippled through my life every month. I always felt them at the beginning of the month, but they could also occur in the middle and on very rare occasions, at month's end. They always started with the ringing of my phone and, if I chose to answer, they continued with a stern salutation from "Mr. Johnson," a man I came to know very well, though Mr. Johnson was not his real name. Mr. Johnson knew a lot about me—his knowledge of certain aspects of my life was actually quite amazing—and he was immediately comfortable calling me by my first name. In each of our many conversations, he did his best to set a tone that was both urgent and intimidating, taking care not to alienate me or let me off the hook. An appeal to my sense of honor was his weapon of choice, though Mr. Johnson could whip out the occasional threat of character assassination, e.g., the obliteration of my financial and professional future, especially if our conversation occurred toward the end of the month. He was more patronizing than my father has ever been. Mr. Johnson worked for a company I had never heard of, a company called Wyndam Associates. It was his job to collect the final debt from my days as a fast-food mini-tycoon.

I have never told anyone about Mr. Johnson, I now realize, because his tactics worked. He made me feel terribly guilty; he wounded my sense of pride. And ultimately he got what he wanted: the $25,000 I had promised to pay the University of Pennsylvania for my senior year of college but which I had instead spent making sure the payroll checks didn't bounce. As a reward for his persistence, I was generous enough to throw in the fees and interest to which he felt so entitled without questioning, either.

I think of Mr. Johnson frequently as my research turns to the collections business, the underbelly of the financial industry that no one likes to think about. For weeks I have been trolling industry Web sites* and I have even struck up a fledgling e-mail relationship with a collector who could very well be Mr. Johnson for all I know. But he calls himself Dave and we quickly develop a nice rapport.

Dave is in his early forties, old for a collector. He began working for a midsize agency in college because the money was good and because collectors work mostly at night, when their clients are home. He never intended to make collecting a career, but twenty years later that's what it's become. He left the business once, but they pulled him back in. The collection business employs nearly three million Daves, a 100 percent increase over the past decade. Business is up only about 70 percent since then, meaning more collectors chasing fewer dollars.[†]

Over the course of our brief relationship, Dave changes companies. Turnover in the industry is remarkably high, mainly due to

---

*My favorite is www.CollectionIndustry.com. They send me e-mail blasts with headlines like "Collection Agency Takes Advantage of Consumers' Foolishness." Tell me about it.

[†]In the UK, the amount of debt passed to debt collection agencies exceeds £5 billion every year. The search for that money is shared by around 500 debt collection companies, although no exact figure exists.

the monthly purges. If you don't meet your quota on the thirty-first, another warm body will be deposited in your cubicle the following day. If the collection agencies themselves don't meet their clients' quotas, they are out of business in a matter of months, sometimes weeks. It is not uncommon for credit card companies to change agencies several times a year. I suspect that Dave's old firm, a smaller, family-run operation, got cycled out of a big account. His new employer is one of the larger collection agencies in the country and I can tell that Dave's mood has taken a decidedly negative turn. His e-mails begin to sound less like a defense of the business and more like confessionals. Yes, he tells me, the industry thrives on pressure and it tends to bring out the worst in people. Yes, the few laws designed to protect consumers from harassment are routinely broken. Yes, consumers are unaware of their rights and tend to believe the threats, which is why they are so successful, which creates a self-perpetuating cycle that will probably never end. Why they tend to believe them is something I know all too well. Across the pond, numerous attempts have been made in recent years to strengthen regulation of the debt collection industry, mainly by the government's Office of Fair Trading. They recently introduced new "guidance" on their expectations of firms' activities, but flouting of these undoubtedly continues for the simple reason that the financial industry tends to believe that it is immune to regulation by virtue of its size and political might.

Dave thinks it's hilarious when I ask him if I can film him at work. No collector and no collection agency would ever allow the cameras in, he chortles in text. Dave stops writing a few days later. He's given me a taste of the business but ultimately I am left feeling more hopeless than before. After all, why would a collector talk to the media? They have nothing to gain and everything to lose. They would have to be so incompetent or so egotistical as to be ridiculous. And neither one is my cup of tea. I want to film a modern, successful operation. Dejected, I press forward on other fronts, leaving one more posting on www.CollectionIndustry.com, no longer hopeful that anyone will bite.

Bob Johnson loves Minneapolis. He loves the music scene here. He loves driving around in his black BMW 540i and hanging at the hip clubs. He loves his hot fiancée, who looks like Thandie Newton. He loves the Green Bay Packers and he loves sushi. But most of all, Bob Johnson loves being a debt collector.

Bob and his partner Chris are the cofounders and managing partners of Big Ten Capital Management, the parent company of People First Recoveries, which at the moment consists of five college students calling people who owe their clients money. Several weeks ago, when I received the following e-mail from Chris (attached to an eight-page full-color corporate summary), I could hardly believe my luck:

HELLO JAMES.
WE WOULD NOT MIND FINDING OUT MORE ABOUT WHAT YOU ARE DOING AND SEEING IF WE CAN BE OF ANY HELP.
MY PARTNER AND I ARE BOTH COLLEGE GRADS (1993 MADISON, WI MYSELF AND I BELIEVE 1996 U OF M TWIN CITIES FOR MY PARTNER ROBERT) WHO STARTED OFF IN THE INDUSTRY AS FIRST JOBS OUT OF COLLEGE AND NOW LESS THAN 10 YEARS LATER WE OWN OUR OWN DEBT PURCHASING AND COLLECTION BUSINESS LOCATED IN MPLS.
I WILL FORWARD YOU OUR MARKETING INFO THAT WE USE FOR OUR COLLECTION AGENCY AS IT GIVES A

BACKGROUND OF WHAT WE DO. WE THINK WE HAVE A UNIQUE BUSINESS THAT REALLY WORKS TO TREAT PEOPLE FAIRLY AND WE HOPE THAT IDEA WILL HELP DRIVE OUR BUSINESS AND MAKE US SUCCESSFUL. IT ALSO HAS SOME BACKGROUND INFO ON BOTH OF US ON WHAT WE DID BEFORE STARTING OUR OWN BUSINESS.

OUR DEBT BUYING COMPANY IS CALLED BIG TEN CAPITAL MANAGEMENT BECAUSE WE BOTH ATTENDED BIG TEN SCHOOLS AND WE FOCUS MOST OF OUR DEBT BUYING ON PURCHASES FROM BIG TEN STATES.

IF ANY OF THIS INFO IS USEFUL OR IF YOU WOULD LIKE US TO HELP YOU IN YOUR DOCUMENTARY—LET US KNOW. I AM SURE IT WOULD BE A GREAT MARKETING OPPORTUNITY FOR US IF YOU WERE TO INCLUDE US (AS LONG AS THE DOCUMENTARY IS NOT A NEGATIVE ONE ON OUR INDUSTRY) IN YOUR PROJECT. WE CAN BE A HELPFUL RESOURCE FOR YOU I BELIEVE AS WE ARE WELL CONNECTED IN THE INDUSTRY AND WE HAVE SOME EXTENSIVE EXPERIENCE TO DRAW FROM.

GOOD LUCK AND WE LOOK FORWARD TO HEARING FROM YOU.

CHRIS WINKLER
PRESIDENT
PEOPLE FIRST RECOVERIES

We meet at their office, which is no more than 3,000 square feet in an industrial building that overlooks downtown Minneapolis. Their neighbor is a sports bar. The office is centered around a large room—the "collection floor"—with five cubicles beneath a dot-matrix printout blaring *Post Some Money!* On the other wall is a white board that keeps score of who's posting and who's not. Chris, a dimpled young buck who could pass for under 20 and bears an uncanny resemblance to Howdy Doody when he smiles, loves keeping score. He was a wrestler in college—only because he's too small to play football—and a framed photograph of Vince Lombardi watches over his modest office. As far as I can tell, the happiest day of his life was running into a professional baseball player on the Chicago subway.

Bob was also an athlete in college, a runner, but he doesn't talk sports much. He does, however, talk about the collection business relentlessly and passionately—mostly about how and why Big Ten is a new kind of agency. He reminds me of the guy I was when I entered Wharton on Donald Trump's coattails: idealistic, but in a very nonidealistic kind of way. I can't dislike him because I know that he believes everything he's telling me. When you are on the cusp of untold riches, it's hard to see the contradictions, even the glaring ones.

Not that Bob and Chris are unaware of their industry's image problem: They know what most of us think. But they blame such hostility on the old collectors—the "billygoat gruffs," as Chris calls them—who would beat you up over the phone and steal your money. People First Recoveries is different. They work with people, get to know them, try and figure out why they got behind and how they can help. They don't use pseudonyms (a practice started by the Internal Revenue Service, by the way), though they do set arbitrary deadlines. Plus, they are young and attractive and they wear pressed white shirts and ties. They are emulating the new industry standard set by none other than Capital One, which, Bob tells me, will give you a new credit card the moment you pay off your old one, no matter how delinquent. How generous, I guess I'm supposed to think. How twenty-first-century of them.

Debt collectors, it turns out, spend most of their time tracking clients down, not talking to them. And what has changed a great deal is not the tactics—I witnessed one of their collectors get testy with a client—but the technology. Now the moment a debtor* answers the phone, his or her credit report is automatically generated onto the collector's screen. This serves two very important functions: One, it allows the collector to appear very familiar with the debtor's life, which is intimidating; and two, it shows the collector any credit cards with open balances that could be used to pay off the debt in question. The first thing a collector looks for is credit cards that haven't yet maxed out. If the debtor has credit left somewhere else, they can pay. This is a little scary, considering that many Americans use their open credit card balances as their emergency funds to cover unforeseen illnesses, job loss, etc. But while savings can be hidden away from view, credit card balances remain in plain sight of anyone willing to pay a few bucks for a credit report. For a collector, an open balance is almost begging to be snatched away.

The goal is getting the person on the other end of the line to pay—anything. Even ten or twenty dollars a month is a score. Chris explains that these payments add up over time, they get people with the program, they start the debt snowball rolling. But there is another reason: The statute of limitations for most debts is only seven years, *unless* you make a payment—any payment—in which case the clock resets itself. So Chris and Bob are not only in the debt *collection* business, they are also in the debt *extension* business, which may turn out to be more valuable for their clients.

But what if the debtor cannot be reached? Well, then there is a brilliant program called "skip trace," which Bob and Chris have purchased.[†] Skip trace pulls up every bit of information that has ever been known, or could be known, about the debtor, including their relatives and neighbors, who are fair game for a collection call. "How embarrassing is that, to get a call from your neighbor?"

---

*I use this term rather loosely. Perhaps *alleged debtor* would be more accurate?

[†]This tactic doesn't fly in the UK due to the strict Data Protection Act, which effectively prevents the sharing of information on individuals.

Chris asks with his Howdy Doody grin. Of course, the law doesn't allow them to say what the call is regarding, so they must make do with euphemisms like "This is Mr. Johnson from People First Recoveries and I have a very important message for so and so . . . " Often they will call the neighbors or the relatives first because it just seems to be more embarrassing, er, effective.

And what if the caller cannot be reached *and* they cannot be shamed into calling back? Generally, the account is sold down the line to another collection agency, and if they are unsuccessful, then to another and then another. What it never does is die. I suspect that there are plenty of billygoat gruffs out there waiting for such scraps to be thrown their way. What they do with them is anyone's guess.

Watching Chris and Bob's college kids skip trace and coerce for beer money makes me wonder about Mr. Johnson, who was probably younger than me, the threatening persona he'd created probably no more real than the laughable name.* It's amazing how non-threatening these kids really are. If the people on the other line knew what they were up against, they wouldn't send in a dime. The most valuable asset of a collection agency, I realize, is deceit. It's making someone think that they owe *you* the money. It's amazing how many people believe that some disappointed or angry loan officer at Citibank is calling to remind them of their moral obligation to repay their debts, as opposed to some frat boy who doesn't like waiting tables. Why? Because debt collectors are *conditioned* to take it personally. They are *conditioned* to believe that they are the creditor. Yet, this is almost never the case.

Some banks and credit card companies do have in-house collection departments, but these almost never handle serious delinquencies. By law, after a bill has gone 180 days without payment, the

---

*It now occurs to me that, in college, *johnson* was a euphemism for a certain part of the male anatomy, which makes my collector's choice of pseudonym particularly illuminating.

bank must write it off. This does not mean that they forgive or forget, it simply means that that amount can no longer remain on their books as a performing asset. So what the banks do is jack up the balance with interest and fees during those six months, take a generous tax write-off, and hire guys like Chris and Bob to start scratching the bottom of the barrel. Collectors get to keep anywhere from 20 to 50 percent of what they bring in, but the business is intensely competitive. Collecting is a black-and-white kind of deal—you either score or you don't—and banks have their own scoreboards. The size of most collection agencies vacillates wildly according to the accounts they're able to get and keep. Collecting can be a fast track to small fortunes, but it is a very difficult way to build a business. Which is why the future of People First isn't debt collection; it's something that Chris alluded to in his e-mail: debt *purchasing*.

Off the collection floor is a smaller room with a conference table and a giant map of the United States covered in colored pins. Every pin represents a state where Chris and Bob can buy debt—which is most states—and, taken as a whole, they represent the young guns' strategy to strike it rich. If they can buy, say, a million bucks' worth of bad auto loans in Texas for three cents on the dollar and collect just 10 percent, they've made seventy thousand bucks. And then they can resell the rest for pennies on the dollar again. Debt, like no other product,* has an infinite capacity for reincarnation. And debt buying is the new frontier, the Wild West of the financial world. Last year, banks and loan companies sold over $75 billion worth of bad debt to collection agencies, investors, and individuals, making it the fastest-growing business on Wall Street. Dan Quayle, whose net worth is estimated north of half a billion, recently joined the board of a large agency that specializes

*Cher and Madonna may be other notable exceptions.

in collecting unpaid medical bills. There's a lot of gold to be mined from the bad fortune of your fellow traveler to the grave. All you need to get started is a little cash, a telephone, and an easily conjured sense of moral indignation.

When the work day is done, I meet Chris and Bob for sushi at one of their favorite restaurants. Over Amstel Lights and California rolls, I ask them how People First intends to strike it rich in this brave new world of debt-buying. As it turns out, not by putting people first.

Chris, not surprisingly, is quick to cough up a few sports analogies. Getting someone to pay is like winning a wrestling match or scoring a touchdown. It's great! How many other jobs, he asks me, let you do something competitive and, at the end of the month, reward you for scoring and give you cash that you can use to buy stuff for your family and for yourself? How many jobs allow you to imagine you're a sports hero? "That's what makes this a fun industry for collectors," he crows, the semicrazed smile of a true believer spreading across his dimpled cheeks.

Bob seems to approve of Chris's analogy, though he imagines himself in somewhat different terms: as a pirate. Collecting is all about walking people on the plank, he says, gesticulating wildly with his hands as his bloodshot eyes become scarily animated. The trick is knowing how far you can push them. You've got to push them just far enough to the edge where they get really freaked, and then pull them back to get what you want. What you want, of course, is their emergency fund. How you make them imagine that they are facing death is a little harder for me to figure, so he continues. There's a lot of things you can attack, he says, a person's honor, their fear, *pride*. There are also special situations, like if someone hasn't told their spouse. That's where putting people first finally comes in handy. "You talk to people," Chris explains, "you get to know everything you can about them. I become your best friend.

And you know what? It gives me power. Information is power. And just when I've gotten to know everything about you then I turn it on you, use it against you."

If I had to choose, I'd rather be on the receiving end of Chris's full nelson than the tip of Bob's sword,* but I leave dinner with a new understanding of what makes the collections biz so fun for some people: It appeals to the inner sadist.

I visit People First again the following evening. There is a mini-crisis in the office. Chris and Bob have purchased a large chunk of debt in southern Florida, yet they have neglected to realize how few Miamians—especially those who can't pay their bills, apparently—do not speak English. Watching Bob and Chris's college kids try like hell to get on the scoreboard using Cancun-level Spanish is pathetic and appeals to my inner sense of poetic justice. *¡Chinga tu madre, cabrones!*

Yet, I know that this debt, this neatly packaged product, will simply be sold off to another collection agency, one that can speak the language. The Miamians have gained maybe a week of time without the phone ringing one more time, a week without someone with a high-speed Internet link to a credit bureau calling to do their financial planning for them, a week without their safety net—however threadbare—being threatened, a week without having to walk the plank.

Chris and Bob will tell you not to blame *them*—they are simply the messengers. As Bob told me, "We—er, I mean, *our clients*—helped you out. Now, when it comes time, you better pay up." I can't argue with his logic, nor could I find anyone else who could, either. In all of the interviews I conducted, no one disputed that debts deserved to be repaid. After all, Sheila Bryan's dream was to repay her creditors. Ditto for Pamela Hood. Yet, everyone I spoke

---

*Another euphemism, I think.

with, from good ol' boy Dave Ramsey to the Harvard Law professor Elizabeth Warren, blamed the collections industry for forcing an unnecessarily high number of Americans into bankruptcy.* The problem isn't so much individual collectors like Chris and Bob. For all of their smarminess, they are simply capitalists who believe in a system that worked for a long time but that has been released from its tethers and has mutated into a relentlessly efficient and voracious machine. When Chris and Bob stop calling you, this system guarantees that someone else will pick up where they left off. And every time that debt is sold down the line, you can assume it ends up on the screen of someone more desperate, someone more willing to cross the line, someone more likely to push you off the plank.

Several days later I retrace the journey that was probably Yvonne Pavey's last: a ten-mile rural road that snakes through a dense forest bordering the Ohio River north of New Albany. Yvonne's family is now in the early stages of the collection cycle; still, they have already heard from too many collectors to count. There have been the kind ones, like the woman from Chase who apologized when she heard of the tragedy and promised that the account would be removed; and there have been the nasty ones, like the prick who told Yvonne's husband that since he was so "damned nosy" about the purpose of the collector's call, he should be able to find his wife. These are the folks with whom Yvonne spent the last months of her life, always clutching the cordless phone so she could appease them with something, anything, never knowing she was just buy-

---

*It's the same in the UK. The Credit Services Association, the "voice of the credit industry" in the UK, says that the amount of debt now passed to its members for recovery exceeds £5 billion.

ing *them* more time. MBNA is suing her husband for repayment on a NASCAR credit card he has never used.* Jon informs me that credit card companies are now inserting clauses into their cardmember agreements which make the cardholder liable for charges made by any member of their household, whether authorized to use the card or not. This is not yet the case in the UK, but as this scheme was pioneered by MBNA, a major issuer here, it may already be on its way. The case has gone into arbitration. In the UK in 2005, Richard Cullen, a bank worker from Wiltshire, committed suicide after what started out as a £4,000 loan grew into a £130,000 he felt he could never pay off. A month later, his wife Wendy reported that some credit card companies her husband had owed money to had written off the debts, for the sake of good public relations, but others hadn't and were still chasing her for repayments on the debts which, incidentally, she had know nothing about prior to her husband's suicide. It wasn't until several months later that Royal Bank of Scotland, which had loaned Mr Cullen more than £35,000 through four different brands, eventually agreed to write off his outstanding debt with them.

I arrive at the boat launch with only my cameraman. Yvonne's husband jackknifed the truck he drives for FedEx the week before and is recuperating at home, minus a job; Jon and Kathi are both at work, getting on with their lives. A shockingly fit park ranger greets us, right on time, but the launch is covered with thick mud from a recent rain, so he guides us a mile or so farther, where three other rangers join us and then we hop onto a converted Boston Whaler with special sonar equipment and the rangers begin their search for Yvonne's blue Mercury Tracer.

The river is calm, the surrounding forest thick and obscured by low fog, a little foreboding. I can see how this would have been an

---

*Jon informs me that credit card companies are now inserting clauses into their cardmember agreements that make the cardholder liable for charges made by any member of their household, whether authorized to use the card or not.

obvious place to do what Yvonne might have done. With the exception of a bunch of trailers huddled inland, there isn't a soul in sight. The search goes slowly as the Whaler cuts a distance roughly one hundred yards downstream of the launch into an infinite number of rows. The sonar screen is primitive: It can only sense when the river's bottom has become a little more shallow, it cannot tell you why. I ask one of the rangers if he's familiar with Yvonne's story and he says he knows it's a missing person's case, but that's about it. I guess he can figure it out. After several hours we have discovered only one possibility, maybe fifty yards from where Yvonne's car would have entered the water. But the rangers don't have the underwater vision equipment they need, so they will return the next week, without us.

Close to a year later I am sitting in my office in Los Angeles when I receive word that Yvonne's car has been found. The sonar blip the rangers noticed that day was a stolen pickup truck, but they returned on another search, and it was then that they discovered the blue Tracer obscured by a large tree branch. Yvonne's lower body was still strapped into the driver's seat and a local news crew managed to reach the scene in time to shoot the inside of the car, which it aired. But even with that money shot, there wasn't much of a story for television, only that a local missing woman had finally been located.

There has been a debate among the police as to the official cause of death. Jon tells me that his preference is not suicide, and I think it's not just because of the difficulties that this might present with insurance but because Jon doesn't believe it tells the whole story. After all, Yvonne was one of those special cases that Chris and Bob told me about: a client who didn't tell his or her spouse. How many of the debt pirates had figured that one out? I wonder. "There's no telling what was said to her," Jon says over the phone one day. "That they were going to publish her name in the paper, take her home, tell her friends." And she would have believed it all, no doubt. Though he doesn't explicitly say so, my guess is that Jon views Yvonne's death as a homicide.

Eerily, news of Yvonne being found coincides with a voicemail from Bob, who wants to know how the film is going. When I call him back, I learn that People First Recoveries has moved to a new building in order to facilitate a staff of forty-five collectors—forty-five Mr. Johnsons—a 900 percent growth rate in roughly a year's time. Bob has married his hot girlfriend, and, even better, as of 2006, they have a brand-new market. For the first time in its history, the Internal Revenue Service has decided to outsource its collections to private agencies like People First.

I congratulate them both. Their ambition and hard work have paid off. They are not ridiculous. They are on the big scoreboard now. They are living the American Dream.

Seven

"The fact is that banking is a branch of the information business."
– Walter Wriston, chairman of Citibank from 1970 to 1984

The town of Clearlake, Minnesota, is an hour's drive east of Bob and Chris's office, one of those places collectively referred to as the heartland of America. Clearlake is gently rolling hills and small family farms that smell of manure. It is the kind of place where you live because you have lived there all of your life or because you have grown tired of seeing your neighbors as competitors. It is the kind of place you move to because you are wary of having your every move recorded on a video camera and paying for your gas in advance. You move to a town like Clearlake to drive a pickup truck and raise some animals and look people in the eye and shake on a deal and when you go to the bank you are known and you don't have to show your driver's license. The people in a town like Clearlake know who you are and they know who the strangers are and you are never a stranger.

I have driven to a modest spread of maybe eighty acres to meet Doris Gohman, who may be one of the few Americans who does not suspect that something is wrong. Doris, who is in her midfifties

134

but has the rosy cheeks and innocent smile of a Cabbage Patch Doll, greets me in the driveway, where a huge pickup truck and an SUV hold court in front of the two-story home built by her husband. She has dressed up for the occasion in a light-gray skirtsuit and I can tell she's more than a little nervous as she gives me a tour of the place: the hogs her husband keeps for slaughtering, the roosters that squawk incessantly, the small cornfield, the chickens. We are escorted by a very enthusiastic black Lab who seems to think it's his duty to keep the other animals in line. Though farming is only a hobby for the Gohmans, it's obvious that Doris will be buried here, only a few miles from where she grew up. When she talks of the neighboring town and its new Super Target store, it is with a combination of amazement and horror. The traffic, she says, is just unbelievable now. The city world, with its endless supply of cement and video cameras, is getting a little too close for comfort.

We mosey inside, leaving the dog barking expletives outside the screen door, and settle at a table in her quaint, *Brady Bunch*–era kitchen. A few minutes later Doris's brother, Bud, rolls up in an old-ish pickup truck. He's a solid man, a little younger than she, with a gray beard and leathered face. A few years ago he gave Doris one of his kidneys. "We were always real close," Doris tells me. "Now I guess you could say we're a little closer."

Bud has joined us from his home a few miles away to help tell an extraordinary story: how, just over a year ago, Doris died.

At first, neither Doris nor Bud were aware of her passing. But one spring day, when she was preparing for her oldest daughter's wedding, a salesman at David's Bridal encouraged her to apply for a store credit card because charging it would save her 10 percent off the bridesmaids' dresses. Doris naturally obliged—I get the feeling that Doris is the sort of person who would see rejecting such a gift as a crime—and the salesman dutifully entered her Social Security number into his computer. *Declined.* So he entered it again. *Declined.* Then he verified the number with Doris. Declined again.

Doris left the bridal shop as angry as she probably gets—more disappointed than angry, really—and without the discount. As far as she knew, she had perfect credit. When she got home, she called the credit bureau and, after navigating several phone trees and being transferred to several different departments and writing down the special fax numbers and addresses to send correspondence to and so on and so forth, she finally reached a live human being who told her the reason for her credit denial: Doris was deceased. Upon further investigation, Doris learned that an employee at Wells Fargo, where she had cosigned a student loan for her younger daughter years earlier, had mistakenly entered *Doris* as deceased when her daughter committed suicide eleven months previous. Wells Fargo promptly corrected the error and Doris went on living. Problem solved.

A few months later Doris accompanied Bud to the local Ford dealership where she'd always bought her "vehicles," as they call them in the Midwest. Bud wanted a new pickup and Doris had offered to help him get it. So they picked out a shiny new F-150 and then the salesman led them both to a windowless room in the back. (They do this to give you privacy, Doris informs me with a straight face. How sweet of them, and of her, I think.) The salesman, who knew them both, was shocked to discover that the woman sitting in front of him, the same one whose own vehicle had been purchased at his dealership, was not, in fact, among the living. A short argument ensued. Doris and Bud insisted that she was, indeed, alive. The salesman pointed to the computer screen and said that, clearly, Doris Gohman was not alive. The argument ended with the salesman threatening to call the cops on the Doris impostor sitting in his office. So the Gohmans left, angry and scared.

Doris went back to the phones. No one seemed particularly interested in her problem, though she did learn that Wells Fargo had corrected the mistake on their computer; it was the credit bureaus that were refusing to accept the change. For Doris, the whole thing was incomprehensible. She felt uncomfortable making a fuss, but Bud wanted his truck and it just didn't feel right being a ghost, come to think of it. Eventually, after exhausting herself and making sure never to blame the good folks at Wells Fargo—they are very nice people, she assures me—Doris did something I'm certain she has never done before: She hired a lawyer. I think she still feels guilty about it. "Basically," she says, "I was just a real big typographical error."

There are three large credit bureaus: Experian, Equifax, and TransUnion. They are all private corporations and they are all in the business of gathering and selling as much personal information as possible. Although they like to claim that individuals like Doris are their customers, this is really not true in any meaningful sense. Selling individual credit reports and charging the "expedite" fees that people are forced to pay to have incorrect or expired items removed from their credit reports in a timely manner are not material to their profits. Ironically, since 2004, when the government insisted that they provide one credit report a year free of charge to consumers, people like Doris and you and me are probably seen as that much more of a nuisance. The major customers of credit bureaus are creditors and debt collectors. And these two customers have something in common: They prefer as much information as possible. Creditors like more information because the more information, the greater probability for *negative* information. And the more negative information, the more they can charge in interest and fees. The bureaus are not unaware of this bias. In fact, they send creditors reports showing how many of their negative items have been deleted from their customers' credit reports. These creditors do not like to see their negative items disappearing. It reduces their leverage.

Debt collectors like more information because it gives them more tools with which to work.

I learned much of this from a former insurance attorney at a corporate law firm in Shreveport, Louisiana, named David Szwak. Szwak has built a booming practice around suing credit bureaus on behalf of consumers like Doris. He tells me that cases like hers are not uncommon. In fact, he's argued several of them within the past year. Having depositioned dozens of credit bureau employees and attorneys, he's come to the conclusion that the system is fundamentally flawed because it is simply not in the bureaus' interest to correct mistakes. In order to protect their special relationship with creditors, the bureaus have effectively stolen the identities of their customers. In one chilling deposition, when asked about the accuracy of individual credit files, a credit bureau attorney guessed that roughly 90 percent contain errors. Yet, when the individual has the audacity to complain, to try to correct a falsehood that is being spread about themselves, they are faced with a stone wall disguised as indifference or incompetence. The industry closes ranks on them. "They beat you by attrition," Szwak, who looks a little exhausted himself, tells me. "That's their game. And they have your credit report. That's the ax to the neck of the consumer."

But Szwak has another, more sinister theory. He thinks that the vast information held by credit bureaus, which is broken down by Social Security number and processed into individual credit scores by another private corporation, a Minneapolis-based outfit called Fair Isaac Corporation, aka FICO, has the effect of discouraging consumers from utilizing their bankruptcy rights. FICO, as credit scores are now commonly known, is increasingly used to determine one's eligibility for utilities, jobs, homes, insurance, and a variety of other things that most of us find useful. One of the fastest and most enduring ways to destroy your FICO is to declare bankruptcy. Bankruptcy not only sends your credit score reeling south, but it remains on the credit report for ten years, three years longer than unpaid debts.* The message is clear: If you intend to work, or if you intend to rent or own a home, drive a car or enjoy the benefits of gas and electricity at a reasonable price, you should not plan on declaring bankruptcy—or argue with the credit bureaus. They are busy people and they have other, more profitable things to do with their time.

I shared Doris's story with Jon Ballew, a man who would feel right at home in Clearlake. He was not the least bit surprised. When his bank switched to the FICO system, Jon was no longer allowed to make any credit decisions. "If a John Smith walked in and you knew him, even if you knew it was *the* John Smith that you'd been dealing with for years," he tells me, "you couldn't approve him if the FICO score came back under a certain number or even if there were negative items on his credit report that clearly did not belong to him. All that mattered was what it said on the computer."

So we now require intelligent, experienced human beings to become mindless, indifferent robots as a condition of keeping their desks. All in the name of worshipping a uniform standard: the credit score.

And no single person is more responsible for making us aware of that score than Suze Orman, Oprah's financial guru and host of the aptly named *The Suze Orman Show* on MSNBC. From her televised pulpit, Suze implores us, *daily*, to learn our FICO score and then monitor it religiously. She calls FICO the key to our financial future. She tells us what to do and what not to do, lest we offend the folks at Fair Isaac Corporation. Interestingly, I have yet to hear Suze explain that FICO has nothing to do with the one thing that defines your ability to repay: your income. Nor have I

*In the UK, bankruptcy only stays on your credit file for six years—although there, too, it is likely it will have to be declared for some more years after if obtaining large loans, a mortgage, a job, or a flat, etc., etc.

heard her explain that there is actually more than one FICO. Indeed, FICO is just a nickname for any one of dozens of algorithms that Fair Isaac Corporation have developed for a variety of industries, e.g., insurers, utilities, credit card companies, mortgage lenders, and employers. In theory, these algorithms compute an individual's "risk"; I suspect, however, that, in practice, they are more effective at delineating which customers are the most profitable, i.e., the best at making minimum monthly payments and generating lots of fee income.*

Suze, who can tell you why you should never, never lower your credit card limits, even if they are ludicrously high, has recently been permitted by Fair Isaac Corporation to sell a FICO "kit" on her Web site for the bargain price of $99—a kit which tells us all exactly what we can do to please them and therefore get more credit. Please, please, if you do nothing else, she implores, order the kit, take care of your FICO score. It needs to be cultivated like a living thing. It cannot be left ignored to wither away. FICO is the oxygen that allows you to exist. It determines how much credit they give you and, trust me, you will need that credit sooner than you think.

Jon Ballew tells me that, shortly before she disappeared, his mother-in-law Yvonne had heard a similar appeal on the Dave Ramsey show. Call up the credit bureaus, Dave had told them, pay them each ten bucks so they'll let you know some of the information they've got on you. Do it today! Before it's too late! Before someone steals your identity!

---

*Coincidentally, the state with the highest FICO average is Minnesota, where Fair Isaac Corporation's alchemists reside.

Jon believes that the credit reports may have pushed Yvonne over the edge. After all, she must have realized that those reports contained all of her secrets; she must have appreciated the absurdity that all of these strangers who never stopped calling knew everything that the man she went to bed with didn't.

I recently read that the Internal Revenue Service is launching a pilot program whereby individual tax returns will be sold to the credit bureaus and collection agencies for a fee. This information hasn't been made public since 1934, under the notorious "pink sheet" law* that was aimed at shaming loophole-loving millionaires like J. P. Morgan into paying income taxes. That law was repealed in less than a year on privacy grounds. I wonder if the new scheme will stick. If nothing else, it's one way to pay down the federal debt.† And at least the information on our tax returns is information that we provide ourselves—even if we apparently don't own it—so the chance for errors, intentional or otherwise, should be well below what we've become accustomed to.

It is January 2006 and I am pondering the issue of privacy. This is not part of my regular routine. It has been thrust on me by reports that my president may be spying on me and that his nominee for the United States Supreme Court may think that's fine and also by two pieces of mail which I had previously ignored.

---

*So named because income tax filers were required to fill out a simplified "pink sheet" showing their income and taxes paid. This sheet was then made public.

†Though it may be quickly offset by another plan. On March 30, 2006, IRS commissioner Mark Everson "freely admitted" to Congress that the agency's plan to use private debt collection agencies would cost more than just hiring more employees. But, Everson said, the IRS would necessarily bow to "political" realities and pay for the collection agencies anyway.

One is a letter from my bank—the Bank of America—which begins as follows:

> Dear James Scurlock:
> The security of your information is a top priority at Bank of America. That's why we regret to inform you that we recently learned some of your customer information was on a Bank of America laptop computer that was stolen.
> Information on the laptop may have included your name, address, telephone number, Social Security number, e-mail address and the ID you use to access your account through Online Banking. (This does not include your passcode.) Access to the customer information on the laptop would require authentication or technical expertise and at this time, we have no evidence to indicate that your customer information has been accessed or reviewed by an unauthorized third-party. Nonetheless, we feel it is important to provide you with notice about this incident and reiterate our efforts to help safeguard your customer information.

The letter is signed by a senior vice president of something called "executive customer relations" and goes on to generously offer not one but two free "trials" of credit protection services with the credit bureaus, offers that are suspiciously familiar: As it turns out, I see them daily on my Yahoo! homepage. My mother recently signed up for one of these programs in order to protect herself from identity theft. What she learned is that the credit bureaus have decided that she and my father's second wife are, in fact, the same person. I have advised her not to bring the mistake, as grating as it must be, to the bureaus' attention for the simple reason that I do not like to see my mother cry. But I digress. This makes me question whether the bank really views me as an executive customer and whether this letter is being used as an opportunity to make a particularly insidious sales pitch for credit protection. In any case, I am hugely relieved to know that, one, those pricks didn't get my pass code (in which case they might have caught on to my quirky sense of humor), and two, using this information against me would require technical expertise. I pray that whoever stole this laptop mistook it for some lesser machine that they do understand how to use—a Game Boy, perhaps, or an abacus—and that they don't have any friends who work at the Apple store. Otherwise, apparently, I'm screwed.

I also wonder how exactly it came to pass that my most personal information would be stored on a laptop that some careless intern just happened to leave out on her table at Starbucks when she got up to pee. Once again, I wonder: Could this letter be nothing more than a clever ruse to sell me the credit protection I've been so indignantly avoiding, despite the good money they've been paying Yahoo! to reach my demographic? I am not Doris, after all. I no longer believe in the benevolence of large financial institutions. Wouldn't put it past them.

This really gets me thinking. Several months earlier a loss-prevention specialist at the Century City Robinsons-May department store—where I have never had the pleasure of spaving,* by the way—called to ask if I had just purchased $1,500 in gift certificates. When I told him I had not, he strongly suggested I call Bank of America's fraud department, which I dutifully did. They repeated the question, then informed me that someone had just presented

*The practice of simultaneously spending money and saving money.

my check card (which was still in my pocket), as well as a photo ID, and bought three $500 gift certificates, two of which had already been redeemed. Oddly enough, Bank of America had authorized the purchases and only afterward decided to verify their authenticity. That seemed like the wrong order of things to me, but then again, I don't claim to be an expert in loss prevention or fraud. I leave such matters to the authorities.

The next day Bank of America replaced the $1,500 and my account was placed on probation until they could determine whether the "real" James Scurlock is an investing dork with a hopelessly small and outdated wardrobe whose friends give him clothes out of sympathy, or a more whimsical creature who drops bank at Robinsons-May. As I minced my check card into sixteen little squares, I realized that I had only seen a therapist twice in my lifetime and that my memory is not the greatest and there's a good chance that, in a court of law, I would not be able to claim to know myself nearly as well as the Bank of America, which has monitored my activities for several years, or the credit bureaus, which have been doing the same for three decades.

I started to get a little paranoid, then curious. Had my identity been lifted from a laptop computer? Or was my identity theft, as I now suspected, the result of some tricky waiter with one of those reverse swiping machines I'd heard so much about on the local news? Or perhaps it had been one of those crafty Russian crime rings who work with telephoto lenses, snapping your card at a distance as you feed it into the ATM?

Or could it be that my personal information—my identity— was available to almost anyone for a few bucks?

A month later these questions are serendipitously addressed by a second piece of mail, this one from another bank whose credit card I carry. The envelope looks like a solicitation, except that in boldface letters it announces the following: Important Information Enclosed:

Privacy Policy; Arbitration Agreement; Changes to Your Account. Normally this would not strike me as a must-read, but as I open the envelope and unfold its many inserts, I realize that the contents may provide the necessary clues to discover who might have been in the position to steal my identity. In other words, if I am able to glean who the bank allows to violate my privacy, I may be closer to finding my man. Or woman . . .

But my hopes are soon dashed by unfolding the rather thin brochure entitled "Your PRIVACY POLICY." The question, it turns out, is not who does the bank share my information with but who do they *not* share it with? Here's an abridged version of the helpful Q & A inside:

Q. What information do you have about me?
A. To provide services and meet your needs, we collect information about you from various sources.
Q. Is information about me shared within your family of companies?
A. Yes.
Q. Is information about me shared with service providers and financial companies outside your family of companies?
A. Yes.
Q. Is information about me shared with non-financial companies outside your family of companies?
A. Yes.
Q. Is information about me shared in any other ways?
A. Yes.

The Q & A goes on to list two ways in which you can "opt out" of the information sharing process, ending with the following caveats:

- Even if you do tell us not to share, we may do so as required or permitted by law.
- Even if you do tell us not to share, we may share other types of information within our family.*

I am left no closer to finding the thief of my identity and a little spooked by all of this Mafia-esque talk of "family." I also realize that I'm a little hazy on the definition of "opt out." (By the way, the arbitration agreement states that I have waived my rights to take any disputes that might arise to a court of law, as the Constitution seems to guarantee, but I seem to recall Eason Mitchell giving me a heads-up on that already.)

So why do banks and credit bureaus like to share so much anyway? Because "sharing" is little more than a warm and cuddly euphemism for *selling*. Wriston's observation that banks are a branch of the information business has become a self-fulfilling prophecy. The more banks "share" with each other and with the credit bureaus, the more information the credit bureaus have to "share" with their clients, who then take that information and bounce it back to the credit bureaus, who then "share" it again with the banks. The sheer volume of such information generated and then recycled back into the system is probably beyond calculation at this point, but that's by design. Because information is money now.

Szwak, the attorney, tells me of a recent phone conversation with an in-house lawyer at a sheriff's office in the South. According to the lawyer, a representative of one of the credit bureaus had called on their office, offering to put a credit bureau terminal on everyone's desk, gratis. In exchange, they wanted the sheriff and his deputies to "share" information—any kind of information—on individuals who'd been detained or arrested or otherwise had business

---

*I learn that these things are equally true across the pond.

with them. The sheriff would gain access to a huge amount of personal information on virtually anyone he chose to investigate, for any reason. The credit bureau would gain a lot of information to "share" with its clients. Szwak advised the sheriff's lawyer to decline their generous offer on constitutional grounds.*

Not surprisingly, processing trillions of pieces of information has created some staggering technological challenges. The industry parlance for assigning information gathered from multiple sources to individual files is called "cross-referencing" and it has been, by most accounts, a massive failure. In order to match a piece of information—a car repossession, say, or a foreclosure—to a specific individual, the bureau may use an address, a name, a Social Security number, or any fraction thereof. So if you have a name that sounds like someone else's name and you happen to live in the same neighborhood, there's a good chance that you two "share" a lot in common, at least according to the credit bureaus and whomever they decide to "share" with. In some cases, like Mom's, you may even share an entire identity. In the UK, address is key, and sharing a house with someone who has bad credit will impact you too. So if your sister or brother has defaulted on a mobile phone, for example, but you don't know about it, you soon will if you go to buy your own mobile phone and suffer the embarrassment of being declined credit for it in front of a shop-full of people—all because someone else at your address has bad credit. So it goes.

The Department of Homeland Security has recently employed cross-referencing in its attempt to defend us all from terrorists. My friend Paul, a twentysomething Aryan who went to Middlebury and now makes his living gathering information for the telecom industry, found this out a while ago when he was mistaken for a former Iraqi dictator at Logan Airport. Turns out *Hughes* sounds

*The mere fact that the sheriff's counsel seriously considered the credit bureau's offer is more than a little chilling.

suspiciously like *Hussein* to the TSA's *Buck Rogers*–era voice recognition software. Like Doris, Paul has tried to inject some sanity into his situation (he is too fair-skinned to even think of having Saddam's fabulous tan, nor does he own a single AK-47 or RPG launcher), but, as of this writing, Mr. Hughes and his entire family remain on Homeland Security's terrorist watch list.

You might think that any industry with a 90-percent error rate would fail or at least reassess its business practices. In the case of information "sharing," you would be incorrect. Indeed, one of the trademarks of the industry has been rapid growth, facilitated by opening up brand-new markets for information. ChoicePoint, a spin-off of Equifax Inc., was hired to delete noneligible voters from the Florida rolls in the 2000 presidential contest. A couple of years later they thought they had discovered another new market, but ended up selling 160,000 credit files to a Nigerian drug cartel whose "qualification" for receiving such supposedly privileged information was a fax number at Kinko's and a working credit card. But, as it turns out, the Nigerian drug dealer market pales in comparison to the industry's real cash cow: the United States government.

It is impossible to say how many government agencies are buying personal information to "cross-reference" or simply to analyze for whatever purpose they deem necessary. It is impossible because, unless we ask, they won't tell us. And even then, the chance of getting a straight answer is rather low. Here's an exchange I recently witnessed between Senator Christopher Dodd (D-CT) and Edward Gramlich, a governor of the Federal Reserve Board:

> Gov. Gramlich: We have collected data on individuals and
> credit cards. What we do with that data, I can't really tell you.
> Sen. Dodd: Are you telling us you have the authority to
> collect this data? It's not a question of authority, then,
> getting the data that we're talking about . . .

148

Gov. Gramlich: We've purchased private data. Other than
that, I'm not sure I should—
Sen. Dodd: Where does this data come from?
Gov. Gramlich: It comes from a private company, and I'm
not sure if I should say that, or if I've already said more than
I should. Let me talk to our lawyers and I'll get back to you.

I can now picture a salesman from the credit bureaus knocking
on the doors of the various offices of our overly curious and apparently underinformed bureaucracies and pitching: *Remember that*
constitutional right to privacy that's been screwing you guys for so
long? Forget about it. All you have to do is buy information from
us and stop worrying already! Constitution, Schmonstitution! Our
computers can be as nosy and inaccurate as they want to be, until
someone gets a court order to restrain us, which is very unlikely
considering our legal resources and our connections, if you know
what I mean, and you guys get to share in the fruits of our labor.
The best part is, as long as you're not the ones gathering the infor-
mation, it's perfectly legal! Your hands stay totally clean! (Just
don't tell anybody, if you can avoid it, thanks, and feel free to
charge it on your government-issued MasterCard . . .)
So what information "sharing" ultimately amounts to is a
brilliant end run around the Constitution. And sometime very
soon, when the IRS starts handing over individuals' personal information to private collection agencies* and selling their tax returns to the credit bureaus, the circle will be complete, and then I
guess there really won't be any distinctions left between the government and large corporations and I'll have to join one of those
groups that hoard canned food and guns and live in communes in
Montana—the ones I've dismissed for so long as wackos. In the

---

*This went into effect in October 2006.

meantime, I just hope the IRS cuts a good deal for We, the People. The information industry needs them more than they need the information industry. Indeed, once our right to privacy is formally abolished, the credit bureaus' business plan is toast. They'll have to dig up the Nigerians' cell phone number, or maybe learn Russian.*

But for now, the credit bureaus reign supreme. Is there any other monopoly in the history of our democracy that has been allowed to hold so much power over the heads of so many?

As I write these words, Doris Gohman remains deceased. Several months after having the audacity to insist that she was a living, breathing human being, the credit bureaus sent a team of eight attorneys to Minneapolis to grill her for two days. The proceedings were videotaped and recorded by a stenographer. This was all meant, of course, to intimidate Doris, to break her down, and she finally did cry on the second day after a barrage of questions to the effect of "Is your daughter really dead?" The credit bureaus are not trying to prove that her daughter faked it, of course, or that Doris is dead, for that matter. They are simply protecting their monopoly. I'm sure the attorneys didn't actually *enjoy* beating down this sweet, humble midwestern woman for politely pointing out that their client had made a mistake. God, I hope not.

My last conversation with Doris suggests that she has finally turned a corner. After some pleasantries about her new granddaughter, she asks me how the film is going and wonders, ever so humbly, if I might include something about the credit bureaus. It just seems to her that maybe something isn't quite right.

*Note to credit bureaus: I hear that Russians are notoriously cheap, so talk to the Nigerians first.

Eight

"Only in America do people save to go bankrupt."
– Elizabeth Warren, author of *The Two-Income Trap*

Elizabeth Warren is no Doris Gohman. One of the only female tenured professors in the history of the Harvard Law School, Warren speaks with barely a hint of the twang she must have owned as a girl growing up on a farm in Oklahoma. Pretty and sharp, she evokes that rare combination of common sense and passion possessed by every great teacher. She can get worked up talking about charts and graphs and statistics because she knows that there are living, breathing people behind them. Warren is one of the only people I expect to meet who will call bankruptcy law "fascinating."*

Had I studied under professors like Warren at Wharton, I probably would have stayed the course. Then again, my knowledge of washing dishes and skewering raw chickens would be much the worse for it.

We are sitting in Warren's spacious office in a brick Colonial building next to the frozen Charles River and she is patiently

---

*Another is her husband, Bruce H. Mann, who wrote a truly fascinating book called *Republic of Debtors*.

explaining the history of bankruptcy law. The founders of our country, she tells me, were debtors themselves. That's why they took such care to reserve bankruptcy rights under federal law.* And as our society has evolved, that right has become more important, not less. Bankruptcy is what allows the individual to take risks without threat of imprisonment or utter ruin. Bankruptcy is the bargain struck between the society and the individual: If things turn out badly, one will forfeit nearly everything to one's creditors, but then the slate is wiped clean. Bankruptcy is the threshold beneath which we have agreed not to let our fellow citizens wallow. If Eason Mitchell is right and societies are defined by how the most unfortunate among us live, then bankruptcy sets the bar for all of us.

Most Americans could not name the last piece of legislation to cross the desk of William Jefferson Clinton in January 2000, but that piece of legislation was the Bankruptcy Reform Act. Despite having lent the bill a great deal of support early on, Clinton's last official act as president was a veto. And the reason for the veto was Professor Elizabeth Warren.

Six years earlier, a fellow Oklahoman, Mike Synar, had asked her a simple question: Why were so many Americans going broke? Synar had just been appointed chairman of the National Bankruptcy Review Commission by President Clinton and he wanted to know why, in such prosperous times, the bankruptcy rate had risen higher than during the Great Depression. The financial industry was pushing their bankruptcy "reform" bill as the remedy, but Synar, who had recently lost his seat in Congress, found their solution—making it harder for Americans to get out from under and easier for the industry to lend them even more money—more than a little suspect. He wanted hard data to justify his vote, wanted to know what was really going on out there. As Warren explains, he wooed her by saying he

*Article 1, Section 8, if you're looking.

would never run for office again and was done carrying water for the financial industry. Specifically, he wanted Warren to gather the industry's amortization tables: the calculations of how long it was taking their customers to pay off their balances. In other words, he wanted to know exactly what kind of trap the industry was setting.

Warren tells me she hemmed and hawed, even though she'd been studying the issues around bankruptcy for close to a decade.* She didn't want to get her hands dirty in partisan politics. But the congressman appealed to her sense of civic duty, and Warren ultimately relented. She was, however, far from an objective observer. "I had my finger sharpened," she laughs. "I was prepared to point it at Americans for being irresponsible, for spending too much money on Prada shoes."

Shortly after accepting her commission, the credit card companies refused to hand over the data. So Warren turned her attention to the bigger picture, consumer behavior, and it was there that she hit the jackpot. The federal government had been tracking household spending for decades and the records were gathering dust in an archive, just waiting to be mined by someone like her, someone with an analytical mind and a passion for turning raw data into sharply honed statistics. Here was the definitive historical record of how the American middle class had survived for generations, through the best and worst of times. With the help of a government employee, Warren spent months sifting through the data, carefully adjusting for inflation and matching expenditures by category: clothes, electronics, food, etc. And what she found was shocking. The most reliable predictor of whether someone would declare bankruptcy wasn't the number of credit cards or pairs of shoes in the closet, it was whether or not they were female.† And then

---

*She had published her first book, *As We Forgive Our Debtors,* in 1989.

†This is also true in the UK, where more than 50 percent of debts being sought by debt collection agencies are held by women.

whether or not that woman had a child. Children were making families go broke! She delved deeper into the statistics and discovered that bankruptcy was not, as many assumed, a tool used by people to escape their debts but an epidemic among middle-class families whose incomes hadn't kept up with basic costs: health care, education, and housing. How could you blame someone for wanting a roof over their heads or medical care for their kids?

Warren discovered something else that surprised her conservative sensibilities. Americans were not rushing to bankruptcy court or being seduced by predatory attorneys. They were avoiding it like the plague. She personally interviewed dozens of people. Their stories still bring tears to her pale blue eyes. There was the mother who had finally admitted her family's plight to a neighbor and then asked if she might run a garden hose from the neighbor's house through the kitchen window in order to have some water to cook with and flush the toilets. There was the Gulf War veteran who'd killed without wincing but who, once in bankruptcy court, became so inconsolable he had to be carried out by the bailiffs. When asked to name the defining moments of their lives, a majority of those she talked to mentioned bankruptcy rather than weddings, graduations, or even the births of their children. Families, she realized, were suffering in silence.

Warren had gathered incontrovertible proof that bankruptcy reform, now a slam dunk for passage, would make matters much worse for middle-class Americans, particularly for the most vulnerable: women who depended on child support. These women had always held a privileged position in line for their ex-husbands' money. If the new bill were to become law, the credit card companies could claim a greater share of the pie and thanks to the bill's arbitrary formulas, interest charges and late fees could crowd out child support and basic living expenses. But even as Warren toiled, the financial industry's top lobbyists were keeping a close watch on

Synar's committee. As the members prepared their report, the financial industry's mercenaries made it known what that report should say. According to Warren, they were even generous enough to offer writing the report themselves, just as they'd written the Bankruptcy Reform Act itself. And without Synar,* the dedicated truth-seeker, the financial industry easily prevailed.

Warren, however, didn't go away. She testified before Congress more than once, against the bill, but her statistics fell on disinterested eyes and deaf ears. I guess Janne could have told her they don't listen to the families, they listen to the money. The Bankruptcy Reform Act would ultimately pass the House of Representatives and then the Senate. But Warren was now on a crusade that transcended a single piece of legislation. As Congress waited for the president to sign bankruptcy reform into law, she published a second book called *The Fragile Middle Class,* based on her findings and it started to get noticed. And, as it turned out, the book gave her a last chance, at the proverbial eleventh hour, to shift the terms of the debate and snatch victory from the jaws of the financial industry's lobbyists.

Hillary Clinton was coming to Boston and she wanted to meet the female tenured Harvard Law professor. Warren was summoned to a conference on women's rights where she listened to the First Lady speak and then was ushered into a side room for a private audience with the then most powerful woman in the world. Warren had come prepared, as I imagine she always does, with her charts and graphs. She deconstructed the new law in firm, concise sentences bolstered by mountains of data, showing how bankruptcy reform would hurt middle-class Americans in general and single mothers in particular. Hillary Clinton, who Warren calls "the greatest student I've ever had," flew back to the White House that afternoon and told her

*Synar was diagnosed with a malignant brain tumor shortly after appointing Warren to the commission and died within the year.

husband he'd changed his mind. Staffers told her it happened so fast there were skid marks all over the West Wing.

In retrospect, it's amazing that no one in the Clinton administration had thought this one through. After all, they were supposed to be a bunch of idealistic, liberal policy wonks who cared very much about the welfare of women and children. I suspect the word *bankruptcy* freaked them out. It carries that stigma, that instant feeling of shame. Most of us don't even like to say the word. Yet, had the Clintonites known the history of their own party, they would not have rushed to judgment. They would have been aware of the deal struck late in the Carter administration—a deal that indirectly led to the dusty statistics Warren had uncovered.

In 1979, America was suffering the scourge of "stagflation": an economy that was simultaneously experiencing contraction and inflation. According to classical economic theory, this situation is not supposed to exist. In any case, Jimmy Carter didn't seem to know what to do about it other than admonish Americans for being too materialistic and consuming too much. After two weeks at Camp David meditating on the state of the American soul, Carter returned to the White House and delivered his famous "malaise" speech in which he warned his fellow citizens that their material ambitions were not only irresponsible and immoral but that they threatened democracy itself. We didn't have a crisis of credit, he admonished, we had a crisis of *confidence.* I can imagine Dave Ramsey telling his listeners the same thing today.

While Carter was giving Oval Office sermons, a crusty six-foot-nine pragmatist named Paul Volcker was taking over at the Federal Reserve. Volcker's mandate was simple: lower inflation. And Volcker did—not by moralizing or encouraging people to cut up their credit cards (Carter had already tried that, with some success) but by jacking interest rates into the high double digits (which reduced the ability of individuals and corporations to borrow) and, more important, keeping a lid on workers' wages. Volcker became convinced that inflation could never be tamed so long as incomes rose, so he declared war on wages. It seemed to work.

When Reagan fired the air traffic controllers a few years later, he was taking a cue from Volcker. The controllers weren't just threatening the airline industry, their union was threatening the entire economy by standing up for higher pay, ergo higher inflation. The effect of Reagan's bold stroke rippled through the economy and sent a chilling message to workers everywhere. But Reagan was really just acknowledging a new reality: America was fast becoming a consumer society. The majority of our gross national product, even then, was a result of spending, not production, which requires investment and saving. As long as we became bigger and bigger spenders, the economy would continue to thrive without savings. Production, i.e., manufacturing jobs, could be outsourced to China or India or Mexico, where it was more efficient, i.e., cheaper. An economist might have asked the obvious question: Wouldn't sacrificing all of those highly paid union jobs eventually depress the country's spending power? Not if Americans had access to an unlimited pool of credit, it wouldn't.*

When Alan Greenspan retired recently, much was said about the Greenspan era of high growth and low inflation: Stagflation had inverted itself to endow us with the best of both worlds. Not only that, Greenspan had kept it going for two decades! How had this miracle come to pass? Productivity was the obvious answer. Thanks to technology, American workers had become more productive, so we could grow the economy at a steady clip without a corresponding increase in the cost of labor, ergo low inflation. But this situation—an economy that is

*The consumer economy has now been replaced by a financial economy, in which debt creates the growth. Consider GM, GE, and most other large American industrials, which make far more money financing their goods than producing them. Even Target, a discount retailer, now makes more than a third of its profit from its credit card division.

expanding without a corresponding rise in prices—is also an anomaly, at least according to economic theory. Moreover, the low inflation/high productivity theory turns out to mostly be a myth, an accounting trick. Over the past generation, the real increase in the cost of housing has jumped 70 percent. Ditto for health care. The cost of an education is up about 100 percent. Sure, you can still find cheap burritos at Taco Bell, but the basics cost much, much more. Worse, wages have remained stagnant, increasing by roughly 1 percent over the same period of time.*

How have Americans bridged this rather large gap? As Warren tells me, they've added another worker to the household, they've stopped saving,† and they've taken on more and more debt. In other words, we have not only outsourced producing, we've outsourced saving.

In 2003, Warren published a book called *The Two-Income Trap*, which explains why Americans are not only living on the edge but why an ever increasing number of us continue to fall *over* the edge: divorce, medical emergencies, and job loss were cited as the primary reasons in nearly all personal bankruptcy filings. She wrote the book because in the midst of testifying before Congress she suddenly got Janne's religion. Warren realized that she, the tenured Harvard professor, was being ignored! Why? Because her clients, American families, had no political action committee, no lobbyists, no advocates, even.§ They were too busy to speak for themselves or too politically unaware to know how. If their voices were never

---

*It's happening just the same across the water. In the UK, wages are still rising at a fairly good rate—3–4 percent. But house prices are rising at around 7 percent a year.

†In 2005 the national savings rate was *negative* 0.5 percent.

§True, there are organizations that represent consumers, such as ACORN (Association of Community Organizations for Reform Now), but, some of these rely on funding from the financial industry.

heard, they would slowly, inevitably, continue their downward spiral into poverty. The statistics were that stark.

Warren and her charts have occasionally attracted the attention of the industry. Several years ago a vice president of Citigroup invited her to speak on how to limit losses from "charge-offs," customers who have stopped paying their credit card bills. So Warren spent two days in Manhattan belaboring a rather obvious point: If Citigroup would stop lending to people who clearly couldn't afford to repay them, they would instantly cut their charge-off losses by more than half. But then, at the end of her doubtlessly brilliant and thorough arguments, a short man she'd barely noticed stood up in the back of the room and called out her name. Everyone froze.

"It was that classic moment," she remembers, "when you realize *that's* the guy who has all the power here."

The short man gave Warren a concise lesson in the economics of modern banking I doubt she'll ever forget. "If we cut out those people," he told her, "we're cutting out the heart of our profits. That's where we make all of our money."

And with that, Warren remembers, the Citigroup meeting was over.

Warren has also reached out to the masses. I recently caught her on an episode of *Dr. Phil,* alongside a woman whose tap dancing addiction had gotten her tens of thousands of dollars in debt (the shoes are very expensive, apparently); and an admitted shopaholic whose behavior represented (according to Dr. Phil) issues relating to her distant husband, who was duly dragged onto the stage to stew next to her. It was classic Dr. Phil and it was Suze Orman and Dave Ramsey all over again: *You can be rich and thin if you just learn to behave yourself!* What it wasn't was true—at least true in the sense that it represented why most Americans can't get out of debt. I half expected Warren to give Dr. Phil a lecture on the thesis of her book, pull out her charts and graphs, but she minded her southern manners and graciously gave the other guests some budgeting advice.

As disappointing as the Dr. Phil and Citigroup experiences must have been, nothing could have prepared Dr. Warren for 2005. President George W. Bush, whose first election was due at least partly to the work of ChoicePoint, and whose number-one campaign contributor was MBNA, made passing bankruptcy reform a top priority of his second term. In the Republican-controlled Congress, the legislation's sponsors indulged him with a brilliant new angle: Because irresponsible people "game" the system, responsible folks like you and me are forced to pay higher rates, while the poorest among us are denied the credit we/they deserve! This must have been news to CitiFinancial, whose agents were still dragging $5,000 checks through the trailer parks of southern Mississippi.

Once again Warren testified before a hostile Congress, bringing her charts and graphs. She found an ally in Senator Charles Schumer (D=NY), who had delayed bankruptcy reform for several years by attaching an amendment that prevented abortion protesters from using bankruptcy to shield their assets from clinics they'd bombed—a deal breaker for many conservatives. But the financial industry created new friends across the aisle. MBNA, for example, gave James P. Moran, a six-term Democratic congressman from Virginia who'd recently fallen on hard times and was near bankruptcy himself, a $447,500 low-interest loan to bail him out.* He subsequently became a sponsor of the bill. Even Hillary Clinton, now the junior senator representing Wall Street, had a change of heart and suggested that she would vote in favor. (Ultimately, Clinton was the only senator not to vote on the bill, which came to the floor the day of her husband's triple-bypass surgery.)

---

*MBNA asserts that the loan was made at market rates and that it would have been made available to anyone with Moran's credit. And Moran says he didn't know that MBNA was a backer of the bill. Okay.

I imagine that Warren has known all along that the odds were not with her. Still, I think she must have felt genuinely betrayed when the United States Senate made passing the bill their highest legislative priority of 2005.* I hope she has at least congratulated herself for stopping it the first time around, protecting the rights of her beloved middle-class families for five years or so. During that time, close to nine million American households filed for bankruptcy protection.

"How could any democratically elected body," she asks me, still angry, "support a bill that denies millions of Americans their constitutional rights in order to protect the profits of a few companies? I just don't get it." She pauses—a bit of theatrics she's learned on the talk-show circuit perhaps. "I *do* get it. It's about campaign finance, it's about who wields power in Washington and it sure isn't American families." But it's also about a Senate composed of millionaires and a Congress made up of people who are themselves protected by six-figure salaries, who can always depend on the kindness of lobbyists, who must find it difficult to imagine how anyone could not dig themselves out, if they truly wanted to.

Ultimately, bankruptcy reform is a power grab—the Congress assuming powers traditionally reserved for the judiciary. The new law is, in fact, a brilliant one-two punch. First, it establishes a uniform means test for those who wish to discharge their debts, a test that orders a judge to assume that over half of applicants are criminals; then it forces those still contemplating bankruptcy into credit counseling before filing.

Previously, the means test was determined on a case-by-case basis by a bankruptcy judge who could, at his or her discretion, reject the application if it was determined to be abusive or fraudulent. Now any applicant making at least the mean income in his or her state is

---

*According to polls, Americans were far more concerned about Iraq and the skyrocketing deficit that year. But whatever.

assumed to be defrauding their creditors, no matter the circumstances. The purpose is clear enough: Shut out half the middle class from discharging any debt. But it exposes a basic misunderstanding of the purpose of bankruptcy itself. As Warren explained to me, bankruptcy law has never been about the poor, who have traditionally been unable to accumulate much debt or take financial risks in the first place. Its fundamental purpose is to provide a safety net for the middle class. So we have regressed back to the eighteenth century, when legislatures—not judges—decided whether or not a debtor should receive a fresh start or be imprisoned* for the remainder of their days.

And whereas Chapter 13 bankruptcy trustees—public servants—have traditionally counseled debtors and helped them to structure repayment plans, they are now glorified data-entry clerks who must abide by a counseling agency's preliminary assessment. This does not seem particularly wise or especially practical, either, given that people who are using their neighbors' garden hose to flush the toilet probably don't need counseling sessions to know that they're broke, or given that the nation's largest credit counseling agency, AmeriDebt, recently filed for bankruptcy after disclosing it had funneled its clients' money to companies owned by its CEO rather than paying its clients' creditors. But AmeriDebt is hardly alone. In 2006, the Internal Revenue Service revoked the tax-exempt status of 40 percent of the nation's credit counselors because of fraudulent behavior. There are so many scams out there that prey on the debtor's conscience by promising to avert bankruptcy—offers to clean up bad credit; systems that are supposed to wipe out debt by sending magic letters to the banks and credit card companies; "secured" cards that charge fees in excess of the card's credit limit or that can only be used to buy vastly overpriced

---

*In those days, *prison* was a literal term: now it is largely metaphorical, but just as real. In England up until the nineteenth century, bankruptcy was a capital offense, punishable by execution.

goods—that it's impossible for the government to keep track of who's reputable and who's not. One thing is certain: The further bankruptcy rights are placed out of reach, the more people will be forced into the hands of the con artists.

The irony, Warren tells me, is that "gamers" who declare bankruptcy have become some of the industry's most valued customers. Immediately after filing, they are inundated with offers to "rebuild" their credit and "restore" their lives. (These firms also operate in the UK.) They are sent "personal" letters from bank executives who empathize with them, who understand what it's like to make mistakes and the importance of a fresh start. After all, isn't getting a second chance a uniquely American privilege? The bad cop/good cop routine that Congress and the financial industry have perfected must be confusing to the uninitiated who fall on hard times. Congressmen scold them for being irresponsible bad apples, while the credit card companies shower them with easy credit and forgiveness. At the end of the day the credit card issuers win customers who can't declare bankruptcy for another seven years and who have already demonstrated a voracious appetite for credit. But who's zooming who here? How many letters and invitations of credit will it take for the good apples, the silent majority we now know to be victims of circumstances beyond their control, to become the gamers the Congress has made them out to be?

F. Scott Fitzgerald, who introduced us to the ultimate gamer, Gatsby, once defined *intelligence* as the ability to hold two mutually opposing points of view without going insane. If this is true, then the financial industry must be the most intelligent collection of individuals ever assembled on this earth.

I want to know more about these people, but where to begin? Citibank is advertising a new credit card whose major selling point is the privilege of talking to a real live human being, but I suspect pursuing this route would lead to a rather unfulfilling conversation with a Bangalorean. Banks in the UK are courting customers with the same tactic. Some offer customers the chance to deal with "UK-only" call center staff, and NatWest also offer the chance to deal with staff in the branch. Now there's a thing. Suze has warned me that applying for a credit card will automatically hurt my FICO.* On the other hand, an intensely friendly gentleman has been calling me lately. He says he is responding to an "opt in" e-mail I never sent and he offers me terrific terms on which to refinance a home I do not own. Alas, his voice is a recording, and what he has to say really isn't all that enlightening. Of course, like everyone else, I receive countless e-mails from financial industry professionals—as well as from an astonishing number of penis-enlargement specialists and naughty girls who want to pleasure me in a terrifying assortment of ways—but frankly, I'm worried that if I ever had to disclose that I'd met my source over the Internet, my reputation would be harmed, to say the least.

So it is that I set up an appointment with the vice president of media relations of the American Financial Services Association, the credit industry's chief lobbying arm, at their pleasant offices in Washington, D.C. The meeting turns out to be amiable, the vice president a presentable woman in a designer wool suit whose head is no doubt full of interesting facts and insights that might clear up some of the confusion I've been feeling of late. But she doesn't say much. In fact, I get the feeling that she's just sizing me up, and when I ask for a second, on-the-record interview, she declines via e-mail. An acquaintance promises to set up a meeting with the vice

---

*This is another anomaly of the credit scoring system: Any signal that you might need or want credit is used to increase the cost of that credit.

president of media relations at Experian, but he turns out to be unavailable.

My final chance is a company called Bankers Training & Consulting Company. Bankers Training sells industry training videotapes. Titles include *Teller Sales: Setting the Stage for Selling* and *Predatory Lending vs. Sub-Prime Lending.* The synopsis of *Predatory Lending vs. Sub-Prime Lending* includes the following heads-up: "Unfortunately, it is all too easy to take unfair advantage of customers." I order all three tapes (on VHS), and am invoiced close to $1,000. When they arrive, I am sorely disappointed. The dialogue is expository and the acting sucks. But then I realize that the Bankers Training Consulting Company has brilliantly captured the essence of every teller interaction I've suffered in the past five years: fembots dutifully regurgitating lines written by cross-marketing experts.* So, are the tellers at my bank "acting" as well? I wonder, or just mimicking the phony videos? I return the tapes without paying for them. This is getting a little creepy, a little too *Matrix*, if you know what I mean.

I do, of course, have one final option and that is talking to Jon Ballew, the banker from Indiana. I send him a rough cut of the film and he is quick to respond. He tells me that we've treated his mother-in-law's story with due respect (a huge relief) and that, for the most part, we've done a pretty good job of capturing the business. Except for one area: bankruptcy. We should, he says, acknowledge those who are cheating the system, using the courts as a way to shirk their responsibilities.

I revisit my video of the House debate on bankruptcy reform. This is not as tedious as it might sound, because the Republican ma-

*By far the worst lines are those written to seem spontaneous, e.g., "I notice that you don't currently have a credit card with us," "You know, we've got some terrific rate deals right now," etc., etc. I must admit to becoming totally flustered in these scenarios. Perhaps I should write my own talking points the next time I visit the teller window in order to respond more naturally.

jority graciously limited the debate to one half hour on either side. Only James Sensenbrenner, the Wisconsin representative who was probably the bill's most effective champion, is willing to guesstimate the percentage of evildoers: 5 to 10 percent of the total number of Americans who go bankrupt. *Five to 10 percent?* These guys are willing to shut out at least half of the middle class to punish 5 to 10 percent? I wonder if Sensenbrenner owns a calculator.

So begins my quest to find a "gamer," well aware that "5 to 10 percent" does not constitute great odds. I quickly decide to limit my search to particularly intelligent men and women. These gamers, after all, have systematically fooled federal bankruptcy judges, who are themselves pretty clever folks.

I talk to maybe a dozen people who have declared or are presently considering bankruptcy. None are obvious gamers with the exception of a 20-year-old drag queen who goes by the name of Visa D'Kline. Visa, aka A.J., has just had his car repo'd and he's maxed out two credit cards on gowns and wigs. He has no intention of paying anything back because, like a number of those I've met, Visa is saving his money to file for bankruptcy. I realize that bankruptcy attorneys are doing a terrific job of holding down filings by demanding to be paid in cash.

I return to Nashville and its endless highways dotted with yellow and brown Waffle House restaurants. My producer has discovered a population that is now going bankrupt at more than twice the national rate. They are not gamers, though they are not necessarily prisoners of circumstance, either. They have all made the same fatal mistake: trusting the United States government.

* * *

Brandie and Will are playing with their newborn son under an American flag when I arrive. There are two SUVs parked in the driveway of the tiny brick house, which belongs to Brandie's parents. Will has just returned from Baghdad, where he's serving as an MP. He has pictures, but isn't sure he wants to show them. He's got a lot of memories and doesn't want to share those, either.

I'm guessing you have to be pretty angry to talk to a documentary filmmaker when you're active duty, but Brandie and Will seem more flustered than bitter. Sharing an old purple couch in the tiny living room, they are still just kids living with their parents, trying to make sense of the world together. Brandie is only 19. Will is four years older.

Twenty-three months ago Will was called up for duty. He was then working for a local police department, earning close to $20,000 a year. He was making payments on a trailer and he had a lot of credit card debt. When the police department didn't make up the difference between his regular pay and the small stipend he received from the National Guard, he was doomed. The trailer payments stopped. The credit cards were allowed to lapse. Brandie dealt with the collectors but finally came to grips with the mathematical reality: They couldn't make the interest payments *and* buy groceries. So she called up Will's commanding officer and begged him to let her husband come home for two weeks so he could declare bankruptcy. At first, the Army said no. When Brandie threatened to come to Iraq and get him, they relented.

Will says he was prepared for six months of duty, which is what the government told him to be prepared for. But somehow six months of duty became a total of twenty-three months of nation-building his commander in chief had promised not to engage in in the first place (Remember when the military was for "fighting and winning war"? That was *so* 2000) and it has left Will tired and bitter. When I ask him who he is most angry at, he thinks for a moment and says, "The military for not paying us more." One of the most humiliating things he's had to endure in his short life was receiving his initial 179-day tour of duty—exactly one day shy of the number that would have qualified him for health care. Not that that necessarily matters: Many soldiers are now receiving calls from collection agencies demanding repayment for medical services provided by the armed forces as a result of battlefield injuries.*

Brandie doesn't think it's fair to suffer while Will is risking his life to give freedom to millions of people in debt-free Iraq. She finds it "confusing" that they have been treated this way by their own government, but there are more immediate annoyances. Conseco keeps demanding trailer payments, even though the trailer was discharged in Will's bankruptcy. Six years ago Conseco purchased Greentree Financial, a sub-prime lender that originated the loan, but then Conseco went bankrupt and the whole thing has become a gigantic mess. The poor trailer has been left to rot in a field in northern Georgia. There's no money in it. For now, Brandie is trying to stay focused on raising her child, finishing medical tech school, and taking care of her blind father. It seems like an overwhelming burden for a 19-year-old with an absent husband, but she's holding it together in this tiny house.

Having met his son for the first time, Will is headed back to Iraq in a few months, back to fight a war that is costing the Chinese and the Arabs $120 billion a year and that will cost us much more than that: maybe our future. When it came time in the United States Congress to spare citizen-soldiers like Will the restrictions of bankruptcy reform, Congress said there wasn't time. And when, a year later, Hurricane Katrina ravages millions of lives, Congress will decline to make exceptions for these unfortunate Americans, either. As Warren has learned, Congress does not believe in precedent or even statistics, maybe not even facts. In their ignorance they have set the bar so low

---

*The government blames its computers and has promised to look into it.

as to be practically meaningless. When a society forces men who fight for their country to lose everything and denies the most basic protections to those who have already lost everything, you have to wonder what the full faith and guarantee of that society is really worth. You have to wonder if the society itself is not already bankrupt.

For all of his moralizing, even Dave Ramsey told me he opposed the bankruptcy reform bill and its bizarrely cruel restrictions. When I spoke to Dave's bankruptcy attorney, Edgar Rothchild, who I half expected to tell me he was closing shop, he just shot me a knowing grin. "Where do they think the money is going to come from?" he asked.* Rothchild thinks that bankruptcy reform will ultimately push more of those who file Chapter 13—the ones trying to pay their bills—into Chapter 7, or else they will just stop answering the phone and opening the mail. Disappear. What else can they do? Rothchild says that the counseling industry will be overwhelmed when the filings don't stop as Congress hopes and that the federal government will eventually be forced to pay attorneys like him for counseling, and attorneys like him do not come cheap.

Warren shares some of Rothchild's resignation. The notion that we can reverse a tidal wave of systemic problems by making it illegal for Americans to go broke is just too ludicrous. "It's as if we decided to stop hospital admissions because too many people were getting sick," she says. But she still has not given up. Warren recently sent Alan Greenspan a letter demanding to know how we can keep surfing the massive federal debt on the backs of the maxed-out. The sage has not written her back, but I hear he's busy conjuring up the

---

*A 2006 study showed that 97 percent of bankrupts have no money to pay back their debts, i.e., they're broke.

biggest book deal of all time—so big, perhaps, that maybe he'll have to answer the big questions. When Warren runs into a politician nowadays, she asks the same question—*What's the master plan here?*—but all she gets in return are blank half smiles.

It's sad that someone like Warren, someone who's done the math, is ignored. She could tell them that the $120 billion a year we're borrowing to fight a war on the cheap amounts to $300 billion per year, once you include interest, payable over the next thirty years. She could tell them that two years from now they will be unable to steal the Social Security surplus—the difference between what working men and women pay into the system and what it pays out to their parents and grandparents—because there will no longer be a surplus to steal and they will have to start digging under the cushions in the House Chamber for spare change. She could tell them that consumers cannot continue supporting the economy much longer with no savings and that the financial industry's solution—flood their customers' mailboxes with more debt—amounts to little more than "baling wire and chewing gum." She could tell them that if interest rates return to the levels they were a generation ago, every penny of our tax dollars will go toward paying interest on old debts. She could remind them that we can't save an economy by outlawing broke people and that sometime, maybe sometime soon, this house of cards is going to collapse. The United States of America will then have to declare bankruptcy or Greenspan's successor will have to print money at such a feverish pace as to make it worthless. But the men and women of the United States Congress don't get it. And it is not because they are not very intelligent people—they are. They simply do not care to be bothered by all of those charts and graphs and statistics of hers, nor by the obvious questions they imply.

They are busy building bridges to nowhere.

Nine

"Can you believe this is happening? Can you believe that
this is happening in, not only the richest country in the world,
but the richest country in the history of the world?"

**– Joe Scarborough, four days after
Hurricane Katrina hit New Orleans**

When I arrive at Lynn Stavert's charming Cape Cod home at five
a.m., she has already been up for an hour—not because she has
trouble sleeping (she does) but because she has learned that her
children will not help. They will sleep in and allow their 60-year-old
mother to do all the work.

Lynn is struggling with a box that is bigger and heavier than
she is, trying to coax and drag it out of the three-car garage and into
the driveway. Transferring her family's excess stuff, like this never-
used hot-water heater, from the garage outside has become a
weekly ritual. As soon as she wrestles the box in place and sets up
the folding tables, she'll slide the GARAGE SALE sign onto the spare
tire of her van, which is parked on the sidewalk. Then she'll take a
chair from the living room, sit down, and knit a lime-green scarf for
her boss's new daughter. She hates her boss.

Lynn has been holding her weekly garage sale for several
months now, but she's still got plenty of stuff to sell: her daughter's
old collection of stuffed frogs, dozens of paperback books, an electric

171

shoe polisher, and, above all, her extensive collection of Franklin Mint decorative plates. Lynn must be The Franklin Mint's best customer. Inside her spacious four-bedroom house, the walls are bordered with hundreds of them. Something is instantly familiar about these eight-inch round glazed objets d'art, each commemorating a bit of American history. I have probably seen every one of them advertised in *Parade* magazine over the years, which is why I do not have to be told that each is a limited edition of "hand-painted" original artwork. It does not surprise me to learn that The Franklin Mint is now generous enough to grant you credit so there is no excuse *not* to buy, no reason for your collection to lack a single glossy testament to America's goodness.

Lynn walks inside the house and chooses two plates for today's sale. These are the "teasers": If customers bite, she will take them inside and show them more. So far, Lynn has managed to rid herself of maybe two dozen plates. Where they once proudly hung there are now only disconnected lines of nailheads. She has struggled with this glaring imperfection, these tiny reminders of the desperate situation in which she finds herself. For months Lynn has waited for the foreclosure papers to arrive. She has not paid her mortgage for nearly half a year and even she knows that The Franklin Mint plates are not going to fetch the $25,000 required to keep the house, not to mention the $50,000 in credit card bills and the car loan, and insurance, and so on.

Lynn rests in her rocking chair, knitting the scarf, trying to focus on getting the knots just right. Trying not to think about what she will do when she has no house, what those lazy kids who are still asleep will do then. Maybe someone will finally buy the hot-water heater—Mexicans, probably, they are good customers, though they don't like to spend a lot—or maybe she'll just sell a lot of paperback romance novels for fifty cents apiece and then at least she'll have some gas money. The other day Lynn found a hundred-dollar bill and it seemed like a gift from God, but then she thought about it and the fact that she was taking someone else's money, even though fair and square, that was humiliating. She spent it on groceries.

An old man from the neighborhood stops by and flirts with her, then magnanimously announces he's buying some more paperback novels for his wife. Their exchange is pleasant, familiar, neighborly. Does he understand Lynn's plight? Is that why he stops and buys *something* every week? Is he trying to communicate that he gets it, that she's not alone? Does he sense the geyser of tears that Lynn's wrinkled skin is always holding back, but just barely? Is he trying to say, *You are not alone?*

I am the first person to whom Lynn has confessed. Even her kids don't know the extent of her problems. Not that they are so unusual: Husband dies, wife inherits debts, mortgage, and a business (trucking) that is not as successful as everyone thought—not profitable at all, actually; the woefully unprepared widow left behind to pick up the pieces. In her determination to stave off bankruptcy, Lynn fell for an Internet con that promised to wipe out her credit card debt, which she'd been using to pay the mortgage, by selling her magical form letters. Lynn was to copy the letters, fill in the blanks with her name and her account numbers, then send them to the credit card companies. The letters contested the legality of the credit card agreements she'd signed and they were supposed to take advantage of a little-known loophole in the law, exempting her from having to pay what she knew, in her heart, she owed, but all these letters did was piss off some attorney at Wells Fargo who responded with a nasty rebuttal. Evidently, the bank's legal department had seen these magical letters before. In the end the con artists billed Lynn $8,000 to her Citibank Visa—money which they said she wouldn't have to pay back anyway, once she sent those letters.

Next she pursued the obvious solution: She called up a broker to refi the house. Everyone knew that rates were at historic lows and Lynn's home had probably doubled in value over the past several years. Her last appraisal had come in just south of $800K. Why not unleash the hidden value of the home to save it? she thought. But at the end of the day Lynn got the same bait and switch as the poor souls whom Mike Hudson interviewed in Mississippi. When it finally came time to sign, at the precise moment when Lynn could wait not a day longer, the historic lows had vanished for whatever reason and the new payments were even more than the old payments. Lynn learned an important lesson that has somehow been forgotten in the great real estate boom of the 2000s: If you can't afford the house, you still can't afford it when it appreciates.

Lynn is saving up for bankruptcy and she's stopped answering her phone. She's terrified of what the neighbors will think when they find out. I tell her that many of those neighbors are having the same issues, but she finds this very hard to believe. After all, the homes in this master-planned community of Discovery Bay (nautical theme) are so spacious and expensive, the lawns so manicured, and the man-made lake so idyllic.

"There's a lot of shame when it comes to financial problems," Dave Ramsey had told me several months before. "Everybody thinks the other couple's got it together: Everybody else has the perfect marriage, everybody else has the ideal situation. Well, you know what? I've met Ken and Barbie and they're broke."

But Lynn doesn't listen to Dave's radio show and she can't see past the quaint facades of Discovery Bay. If she could put on a pair of X-ray glasses and study her neighbors' credit card statements or magically overhear their arguments about money, maybe it would make her feel better, less alone, a bona fide member of the debt culture who's paid her dues in spades. Maybe if she looked up the local Debtors Anonymous and went to a meeting, she'd believe that you're only as sick as your secrets and maybe that would give her the courage to tell her children the awful truth. But other peoples' money problems are *their* problems, and they only boil to the surface occasionally as meaningless statistics in the newspaper. Until someone has had enough of suffering in silence and does something so extraordinary, it pierces the tranquility of the neighborhood and shatters all of those facades forever.

11616 McGee Road in Collegedale, Tennessee, is a stately, five-bedroom colonial that bears more than a little resemblance to the Ballews' place in Indiana. The home sits on three acres of Kentucky bluegrass, a polite distance from the neighbors and just a mile or so from the train tracks. At night you can hear the grinding of steel wheels and sometimes a whistle. When the Billingtons lived here, the driveway was variously filled with the parents' two SUVs, the daughter's tiny pickup truck, and the son's brand-new Mustang.

The family kept to themselves and not that much was known about them. They had come from England by way of California, where Nigel, the father, had held an executive position at a textile manufacturer, which subsequently laid him off. He moved to Tennessee for another job with a sock manufacturer whose major client was Wal-Mart, and his Italian wife, Gerardina, took a job at the local Coca-Cola bottling headquarters in Chattanooga to help pay for the house and the SUVs. Relatives in England and Italy received frequent letters and photographs of the house, evidence that the Billingtons had conquered America.

Their daughter Amanda, 21, the youngest, had finished college and was studying for a master's in psychology. Their son Peter, three years older, had bounced around universities and finally

settled down at the local branch of the University of Tennessee—
the first university to sign a major "co-branding" deal with First
USA, Chris and Luke's sponsor. He, too, was studying psychology:
he wanted to work with children someday. To pay for the Mustang
and his girlfriend, he got a job working nights as a baker at Panera
Bread Company, a fast-growing franchise whose owners had
founded a hugely successful chain in the northeast called Au Bon
Pain. In addition, Peter took a job at the Boys & Girls Club in Chattanooga. One summer he worked for his dad's employer, designing
baby socks for Wal-Mart, but then the company decided it couldn't
compete with the Chinese at eighty cents a day for labor. So the
owners, real estate billionaires from Chicago, shut it down. It just
wasn't worth their trouble.

Nigel couldn't find another job in the textile business and he
started floundering. His last job was at a car dealership, selling financing plans, but he was too proud or too kind to screw people, and
he was soon fired. In the meantime, Peter was falling behind on his
debts and took out a Capital One card in his sister's name on the
sly. Before too long, everyone in the family was maxed out and
British tempers and Italian passions couldn't coexist peacefully,
even on three acres. Arguments were constant and always about
money. Peter claimed he was helping his parents out, while they accused him of dragging them down. Before long they were all underwater. His mother demanded to be put on his checking account,
forcing him to repay his sister, whose credit he'd already ruined,
and pay *them* back for all the money they'd invested in their son
over the years. Peter said he would but, between school and two
jobs, he just never got around to it.

On the morning of May 20, 2002, Peter entered 11616 McGee
Road from the back door (always surprising how light it felt, how
cheaply made) and found himself headlong into another argument.
He had just come from a night of baking, hadn't slept for two days,

and was in no mood for more conflict, not at eight a.m. at any rate, but his parents wouldn't stop. They accused him of wasting their hard-earned money on his girlfriend and on Internet pornography. His mother kept yelling, "You're going to bankrupt us!" She told him she wanted to search the Mustang, "find out what you've been spending your money on." Peter refused to hand over the keys. Didn't matter, she shot back, they had another set. This was too much. Peter's deep, dark eyes betrayed a whole new level of rage. He ran upstairs, returning with his dad's nine-millimeter pistol. As his mother continued to taunt him, Peter claims the gun just went off, killing her instantly. His sister freaked out. His father screamed at him, out of control. Peter shot his dad twice, then walked up to his sister and shot her in the head, point-blank. Writhing on the floor, crying now, his father vowed that if he lived he'd "get you, boy." Peter pointed the gun at him and pulled the trigger but nothing happened. So he ran back upstairs, reloaded, and within a minute his dad was finished off.

For the next hour Peter drove around Collegedale and Chattanooga in the Mustang, stopping only to take a piss at the local mall and get rid of the gun in an old field near the railroad tracks. By the time he returned to McGee Road, he'd hatched a plan. He parked the Mustang in the garage and opened the door to the kitchen, just enough to see the bodies of his late family spread around the tiled floor. Then Peter ran a hundred yards to the next door neighbor's house and pleaded with the old woman to let him borrow the phone. Somehow the neighbor knew not to open the door, she dialed 911 herself. When the Collegedale Police arrived, they had to call the sheriff because they'd never encountered a murder scene, much less a triple homicide. They did have the sense to cuff Peter and lock him in the back of a patrol car, where he practiced his story: He'd just returned home from a friend's graduation and found them there. But he could never get past being cool, could never work up the necessary emotion. It didn't take long for two Chattanooga detectives to coax the truth out of Peter Billington, triple murderer. The local news blamed the credit card debt. The sheriff was at a loss, observing that everyone has problems. He said there must be another reason than a little 'ol credit card, but what that reason was, he couldn't say.

I meet Peter in a small consultation room at the Rocky Mountain Correctional Facility, a drab compound located in the highlands of the Cherokee National Forest, just miles from the Biltmore Estate, which is still the largest private residence ever built in this country, a relic of the robber-baron age commissioned by George Vanderbilt, one of history's great spenders. A reminder of how excess and poverty can peacefully coexist, though it's probably wise to hide the excesses behind a bit of forest, as Bill Gates has also learned.

By now Peter has retracted his confession, hoping that the British consulate in Atlanta will pull some strings and somehow get him back "home," where they treat murderers with greater leniency. He can't talk about the crimes. But Peter is affable nonetheless and more than willing to discuss what he calls the "bear trap": the cycle of maxing out card after card, loan after loan, until you're in so deep you can't possibly escape. He talks of himself as a young man heroically trying to save his family by working long hours but who ultimately could not protect them from their own mistakes and misfortunes. He mentions that his mother had formulated her own escape plan: She'd decided to leave Tennessee and return to Italy, where her relatives would welcome her and where credit is not the center of everyone's universe. Peter is angry at the media for painting him as a monster, as a terrible person, when he knows he's just a victim. He speaks of better days ahead working with children (yes, that's creepy) when he gets out. With three life sentences left to serve, those days seem unlikely to come.

Earlier I had met with Peter's attorney, Lee Davis, a pleasant yuppie who wears pink polo shirts and works out of an old Victorian in Chattanooga's tiny arts district. He had generously shared the records from Peter's case, now housed in a decaying garage next to the office, and talked extensively about this young man who had committed this unthinkable act. Lee will not conjecture a motive, but he can say that, of all of the murderers he's represented—and we are talking hundreds, apparently—Peter remains the only one for whom there was no indication of violence in his past. He was a good kid, made good grades, behaved, didn't get into more fights than the other boys, didn't torture animals or whatever else young monsters do to sharpen their teeth. Peter is also, Lee told me, an extremely intelligent guy, one of the smartest young men he's ever met. How someone like that could fall into the bear trap so easily, well, there's a real mystery for the sheriff.

Lynn's husband called his company All Points Express, or APE for short. The logo is a cartoon ape who looks like he's in a hurry. Her son, Keith, is the company's only driver now. He leases a brand-new twenty-six-foot Ford Diesel that's already having problems keeping the tailpipe on. The insurance company thinks that Lynn drives the truck, because, after several accidents, Keith is uninsurable. Good-looking and tall but already sporting the sunken frame common among truck drivers, Keith gets most of his business from hauling ice cream freezers from Nestlé's warehouse in Oakland to convenience stores around the Bay Area for the local distributor. They used to pay him forty-two bucks a freezer, but some dot-com millionaire just bought the business and this lucky ducky has cut Keith's take by more than half, to a clean twenty. If it's a replacement freezer, Keith gets nothing. So he's maxed out two American Express cards, an MBNA card, a First USA card, plus a couple of gas cards just to stay on the road. His mom pays for insurance and is supposed to do the accounting, but I doubt there's all that much for her to do. When I accompany Keith on his daily route, we spend most of our time waiting on other people, and the back of the truck is mostly stale air. By the end of the day we've moved maybe six ice cream freezers and spent over a hundred bucks on gas. I can do the math in my head. As we pull into APE headquarters—a tiny ramshackle warehouse filled with the carcasses of discarded ice cream freezers that is costing Keith and his mom $2,500 a month—Keith tells me they held his father's wake here and I realize that the sky blue Nestlé freezers resemble nothing if not miniature coffins.

How his dad managed to keep APE afloat for more than a decade is a fair question, and Keith doesn't know the answer. Has he thought about it? The bear trap was Keith's inheritance and therefore he probably can't even see it. He just assumes that the business generates profits that pay his mother's huge mortgage. He assumes that they will always get by, as they did when Dad was alive.

I visit Keith a few months later, when the cracks have become more pronounced. Lynn has let him in on the fact that she's losing the house, though she hasn't told him that she now thinks of suicide often and as soon as she figures out a way to make it look like an accident she'll be outta here, finally sprung from the trap. The endless well of credit has dried up, become nothing more than a stain on the pavement, so today, instead of chasing ice cream freezers, Keith and I set out for the local CCCS* office, where he's booked an appointment with a credit counselor. CCCS is the largest network of credit counseling agencies in the country and among the most reputable.

*Consumer Credit Counseling Service.

The CCCS method is simple: First make the client cut up all of their credit cards, even if they're already maxed out, which they usually are, then generate a personal income statement listing their income versus all of their monthly expenses, down to the daily latte at Starbucks. This not only induces a reality check for the client, it gives CCCS a good idea of which bills can still be paid as agreed and which will have to be folded into the payment plan it will negotiate with the clients' creditors. CCCS then collects a single check from the client every month and disburses the funds to his or her creditors. The goal is to force the client to live on a cash basis while using the income statement as leverage with creditors. In the past few years, however, creditors, who have traditionally financed the counseling industry, have become less and less accommodating. They have cut back their financial support to counseling agencies and are negotiating less. When bankruptcy reform goes into effect, there will be little reason for them to negotiate at all, since debtors will have a much harder time discharging their credit card debts. In the UK, the method is slightly different. Those in debt tend instead to cut a deal directly with the lender to cut up the card and start paying back the loan in installments, but the principle is the same.

Keith is silently nervous—as he should be. His suspicion that "something is not quite right" is about to be validated by simple mathematics, and for a brief moment in the reception area I think he considers leaving. But then the counselor, an exhausted-looking woman with long gray hair pulled back in a ponytail, appears, shakes his hand, and leads him to her little office in the back to play the financial equivalent of *This Is Your Life.*

The meeting starts with the normal pleasantries and, of course, a small fee, $80, which Keith puts on his check card. Keith mentions that his mother is also in a great deal of trouble but she has refused to join him today because no one has been able to help her, which is putting it mildly. The counselor says she should come in anyway, that CCCS is different, that they can always help. Then she leads Keith through the card-cutting ritual. Pieces of Keith's platinum and gold cards are soon dripping out of his sweaty fingers into a fishbowl, swimming with the others under imaginary water. The counselor makes a joke about having everything but that new "Elvis" credit card in her collection and she's sure that someday someone will come in and give her one. Even the King can't protect his fans from themselves.

The counselor presses a button and a spreadsheet appears on her computer screen. It takes some time to list Keith's creditors and the monthly payments required to keep them from hounding him. He hasn't paid American Express for months, ditto for MBNA, though he has managed to make the payment on the big truck as well as his newish F-150. Together, the vehicles in his life eat up more than $3,000 a month. All told, Keith's racked up over $60,000 in unsecured debt, not including the trucks, and he needs about six thousand bucks every month to live. His income is $1,100 a month, a salary that has probably been funded by cash advances off of Lynn's credit cards. So he's five thousand in the hole every month and he can't *not* pay because paying is what keeps him in the truck that is his job, not to mention the one thing that keeps the memory of his father alive.

The counselor suggests that Keith pursue "the legal option," never once mentioning the word *bankruptcy*, as though this has suddenly become a polite conversation, impersonal. Or maybe she's had bad luck using that word in the past. What's clear to them both now is that Keith is knee-deep in the bear trap. He leaves without saying a word, clutching this laser-printed portrait of his future, re-alizing that there is no hope for him because the place that can help anyone has told him as much and the numbers in his hand don't lie. There's no way he's capable of bridging the gap. Thank God his mother didn't come with him! Would've been too much for her frayed nerves. So Keith lifts himself back into the truck with the funny ape logo and drives off to pick up another ice cream freezer for twenty bucks.

When I last talked to Keith he was, like millions of Americans, trying to beat the deadline before bankruptcy reform went into effect. He didn't have any time to writhe in the bear trap while being told the obvious over and over again. At 24, he is the same age as Peter when he killed his family.

Suze Orman is now trying to reach Keith and Peter's demographic. She's got a new bestseller called *The Money Book for the Young, Fabulous and Broke* that retails for $26.95. The back cover promises that this book is different from the other financial how-to books; it's got none of the financial mumbo jumbo, none of what kids today don't want to read, none of her past books' unrealistic mandates—like saving, for example. This time, Suze-Dogg is keeping it real, yo. She's even shortened the sentences and broken up the paragraphs with lots of oranges and lime greens that grab the eye. She's tossed in something called an "interactive planner"—no extra charge! The resourceful Suze has even invented a new contraption called "quick playback," a bite-size recap of every chapter for Gen ADD. Being of that persuasion, I'm tempted to buy the book myself, but I've become exhausted just reading *about* it and, to be brutally honest, I find the front cover a little, well, *gross*. In order to "relate" to America's maxed-out youth, "Hey, girlfriend!" Suze has decided to become one of them. She's dyed her hair Breck blond and bought a new leather jacket that looks very expensive.

I have no doubt that *Young, Fabulous and Broke* is full of some very interesting factoids for some very fabulous people, if not for Peter and Keith. First of all, they couldn't afford it. Second, I imagine that they know more about their situations than she does. At least they know that Dee Hock's vision has finally been realized. The financial companies *have* magically created a new currency, credit, with one glaring caveat. As Walter Wriston once observed, a currency's only value lies in its scarcity. Yes, I suspect that Peter and Keith have learned this one pretty well.

Which reminds me: Beth's new house is surely finished by now. I call her cell phone and leave a message, but she never calls back. Perhaps she is busy selling more multimillion-dollar spec homes, but real estate sales are finally starting to cool off and the nation's largest homebuilder has just dramatically lowered its sales estimates. Talk of a bursting bubble is getting louder, closer. The bankers are holding trillions in bloated real estate loans and refis, which they will, of course, want to trade in for harder currency at some point. Nationwide, foreclosures are up 38 percent over last year.

Does Beth understand that the only value of all of this credit that has fueled her career and that has built her home ultimately lies in its scarcity and not in its abundance? Does she realize how quickly a 10,000-square-foot mansion can become a bear trap or how many Peter Billingtons may live among the cul-de-sacs of her perfectly manicured master plan?

Maybe she should pick up a copy of *Young, Fabulous and Broke*, girlfriend.

Ten

"People are really hurting out there. We need a change."

– Brian Lurie, owner, Yuppie Pawn Shop

There is a bumper sticker that reads, *I wasn't born in Texas but I got here as fast as I could.* Invert that sentiment and you've got my dad. An early bloomer from Houston who became everything he was supposed to become—a football hero, most important—Dad couldn't wait to leave. He'd heard the *n* word too many times, listened to too much small-minded talk around the dining room table that offended his remarkably gentle sensibility. When confronted with needless suffering or any kind of social injustice, the corners of Dad's mouth retreat inward to withhold a deep rage and you don't know whether he's going to cry or explode. The melancholy of a solo cello, however, rarely fails to summon a few tears. Dad was in Dallas the day JFK was shot—it happened on his birthday—and my grandmother tells me he was weeping when she called him.

Dad was only 19 when Kennedy died, but I imagine he'd already made up his mind to leave the Lone Star State. He held out another six years because Rice University (Houston) was offering a free education to white males at the time, and Southwestern

185

Medical School (Dallas) was something like $2,000 a year. Still, he didn't have it easy. To make ends meet, Dad literally sold his shit to a researcher who was investigating the effects of an all-Mexican food diet.

Dad arrived in Seattle by way of Massachusetts, where he served his Vietnam sentence as an Army doctor, getting married to my mother along the way. A Navy brat who'd lived in plenty of places, she fell in love with the Northwest the moment she entered its lush rain forests, reminiscent of the Scottish Highlands. Seattle held a particular allure for both of them—for her, the promise of freedom from the strictures of military life, and for him, a solitude they'd never let him experience in Texas, where everybody was always in everybody else's business. When we moved to Seattle in 1979, one of the first things Dad did was turn our spacious basement into a refuge where he read books, tinkered with the first IBM PC, and spent hours practicing the cello. He wore thick glasses and grew a beard. Traded in the cowboy boots for Birkenstocks. Made friends with attorneys and doctors with Scandinavian accents and Ivy League degrees. When his mother came to visit with her big hair and her fur coats, she loudly complained about the rain, but it kept her from coming more than once a year. Like most Seattleites, my Dad has an odd affinity for rain.

I remember Seattle before it changed. I remember when Seafirst Bank wasn't the Bank of America; when Nordstrom was the local store you went to twice a year, during the sales; when people drove old Volvos rather than new Range Rovers; when Starbucks was a place you patronized on special occasions rather than a cattle call with stale pastries (they've upped the prices a lot since those days, by the way). And I remember when it changed: when stock options replaced the weather as the main topic of conversation and then again when talk of stock options was replaced by real estate chatter. I remember coming home from school and watching Bill

Gates's $150 million mansion take shape across Lake Washington, most of it built behind dense evergreen trees or underground, like a bunker, because he didn't want it to look pretentious.

My parents remained defiant as the big small town they'd retreated to was annexed by the larger forces of the culture, as the dreaded Californians moved north, fleeing expensive real estate prices and bringing their frozen-yogurt franchises and their tanning salons and their tacky strip malls with them, but worst of all pushing home prices (and property taxes) north. Then came the grunge acolytes, thanks to Kurt Cobain. They came from out of nowhere, like crows in their black overcoats, instantly making Seattle the teenage homeless capital of the universe. Mom and Dad planned to brave it out in their sanctuary—our modest cedar house at the bottom of the hill in the middle of a rain forest—but one day, as Dad drove home across the floating bridge, he started doing the math in his head. The comfortable five-figure salary he was making as a staff anesthesiologist at the Virginia Mason Clinic wasn't going to cover two kids in private school plus music lessons, not to mention expensive colleges at some point (even Rice was no longer free). So he called up a colleague he knew was making big bucks in private practice at Valley General, the massive complex that treats most of the employees at Boeing. They didn't have a job for him, but, as Bob Johnson observed, fear is a terrific motivator and I'm sure Dad was terrified of either impending financial ruin or, worse, of having to rely on the Texans to bridge the gap, so he refused to take no for an answer. A week later Dad was in private practice at Valley.

Even as his income crawled into the mid–six figures, and even as his peers upgraded to Mercedes and BMWs, Dad kept driving the old sky-blue Chevy wagon, which was really more at home in the patients' lot, and Mom refused to give up the rust-colored Datsun that never failed to embarrass when it delivered me to school or tennis lessons. Whenever I asked Dad why we couldn't have a Mercedes like everyone else, he reminded me that most of those other people didn't *own* their cars: they leased them from the bank. Of course he was right, though the fact that we *owned* our pieces of crap never made me feel any better.

Dad only gave me two nuggets of financial wisdom that I can remember: One, if wishes were horses, then beggars would ride; and two, everything is for sale for the right price. It was Mom, her roots in Scotland, who taught me to balance a checkbook in fifth grade, but even then I never really understood how money worked because I'd never known life without it. As deprived as I felt sometimes, I never doubted that there was always more. The fact that my parents lived like hippies, at least relative to my friends' parents, was by choice. The possibility that other people were compelled to live with far less never occurred to me. So it was only during the dark days that I discovered what is euphemistically referred to as the universe of "alternative" banking. In other words, I went to a pawnshop.

I was less than a year out of Wharton and several months from receiving the final payment from Boston Chicken, Inc., that would put me back in the black: In other words, I was young, dumb, and cash-poor, one of the most attractive demographics for the merchants of instant loans. I can still remember the Dallas heat burning through the windshield as I pulled into the parking lot, clutching the brushed-steel TAG Heuer diving watch my dad had given me not two years before. While I'm sure the humiliation of the moment dawned on me at some point, I was far more concerned with how much I could get for the watch. I'd bounced several checks at the local Albertsons, and didn't have the gall to ask my sister for another quick loan. So there I was.

The guy behind the counter was relatively young, all business. He took the watch and my driver's license. So now I had assumed the guise of potential criminal—there was a wake-up call I never expected! After polishing the face a little with a small cloth, he asked me if I still had the spare links, which I'd barely remembered touching when I'd opened it a couple of years before. I had to rush home, adrenaline and shame conflating into a bizarre sense of stress I've never felt again as I dug through every drawer and box in my apartment, everything else I possessed tossed around the floor like garbage. Ultimately, I emerged victorious and returned to the pawnshop, links in hand. I can't remember what he paid me for the watch, other than it was enough to stay out of jail and far less than the watch was worth. But I never went back to reclaim it, even though I should have. I never wanted to set foot in a pawnshop again.

The Yuppie Pawn Shop takes up half of a generic strip shopping center in Kirkland, Washington, which is midway between Bill Gates's mansion and Microsoft headquarters in Redmond. The name was chosen to make people like me feel comfortable, but it also reflects the ironic sensibility of its owner, Brian Lurie, a bald, stocky man with a salt-and-pepper goatee. I'm guessing Brian's in his midforties but he acts much younger. Brian accentuates nearly everything he says with a sophomoric laugh and an easy smile. But he never takes his eyes off of you, either.

Brian started the business twelve years ago with $1,000 in cash and a Sears catalog. It must have seemed like a particularly bad time to be in the pawn business. The tech craze was roaring toward its crescendo, the stock market was booming, the mini-recession of 1992 had been long forgotten. But Brian noticed something very interesting: The better the economy got, the more people needed his quick cash. Business grew at a steady clip and the 1,000-square-foot shop blossomed into a 5,000-square-foot showroom staffed by two middle-aged women—"the girls" as he calls them—as well as a harmless Labrador named Dot. In the UK, glorified pawn shops— they are more like stores really—are also sprouting up in numbers, particularly in the poorer areas, such as the run-down inner-city towns around Birmingham and other parts of the Midlands. They don't call themselves pawn shops of course. Place such as "cash converters" brand themselves as purveyors of secondhand goods, when really they are selling on the things that people couldn't afford to buy back when the deadline passed—pawn broking.

Brian gives me the tour, starting with the long line of motorbikes parked in the front window. Every one has a story. There's the Coast Guard sailor, "delightful," who guards the homeland with his M16 but can't afford the $150 per month the Japanese crotch rocket's costing him in insurance; there's the mechanic, "really nice guy," who always has at least one Harley in the shop, swapping them as needed for cash to buy parts to keep his business running; there's the jeweler, "really interesting," who started hanging with celebrities and maxed himself out on two powerboats and has lost everything, including this nice little Ducati, but he's really much happier now, more philosophical; and finally, there's the tiny Asian woman, "adorable," who brought in this vintage Indian motorbike the other day, completely out of the blue, and swears she's coming back for it. Hinted it was gambling related. There's a lot of women like her who drive to the Tulalip reservation on their off days, feeding all of their cash into the slots while the husband assumes they're at home baking cakes or something.

Dozens of expensive-looking mountain bikes are suspended above us. The walls are decorated with art of the Thomas Kincade variety. The market's been flooded with them ever since Kincade started franchising and Brian knows they're terrible investments but he buys them anyway. "You should see my house," he dead-pans. Then there are the display cases full of watches and wedding bands. Trillions of them, he says, a slight exaggeration. "People see these"—he points at the gold rings—"and they say, 'that's so sad.' No it's not! Thank God they got rid of the jerk and managed to get some cash out of the deal." He smirks. There's no ring on his finger. We move on.

Apparently, yuppies love porn. There are several shelves de-voted to DVDs of the adult persuasion that Brian tells me we don't need to film—this is a respectable establishment, after all, this *al-ternative* bank—not realizing that my cameraman considers such remarks an invitation. Brian relents after realizing his mistake. "We have guys come in here," he trills, "and look for half an hour. I'm, like, 'What are you looking for? A different *plot*?' " He cackles. Mov-ing on to the non-adult DVDs, which he can't sell but he can't not buy them, either, because if you're bringing in something that's only worth a buck you've got to be desperate. "If a blonde in a miniskirt walks in," Brian says, "the girls won't let me near her." He has his weaknesses. Otherwise he always beats up the newbies a little. One of the tricks of the trade is to never buy the first item someone brings in. You make them go back home and fetch the good stuff: the gold jewelry, the diamonds, the Rolex watch—Rolex watches are the best and you'd be amazed by how many there are out there. DVD players and televisions are *not* the good stuff. Ditto for computers, fax machines, and clothes. Clothes are death. Worse than garage sale shit. Brian won't insure your stuff—otherwise he claims there'd be a fire every week—and if you try to negotiate too much, he'll tell you to leave. On the other hand, if he senses you're desperate, he'll quietly hand you a five or a ten or maybe a twenty from his wallet. "If the girls had any idea of how much money I've just given away, they'd never allow me near the cash register." He grins.

Moving on again, Brian comes across an item from my recent past: a gold-rimmed Franklin Mint collectible plate featuring a pleasing arrangement of blossoming red roses. "Nobody buys plates," Brian complains. "It's amazing how Franklin Mint survived making them all these years. It's bizarre. Typically it's people who don't have a large income who think that these are going to appreciate in value; they're attracted by the fact that you can buy one from Franklin Mint with a little bit down and a little monthly payment. And people come in and want to sell them because there's nowhere else to sell them. It's like the Beanie Babies. Remember the Beanie Babies?"

As it turns out, Brian's industry is facing some big challenges. There's too much easy credit out there, too many places to get quick cash. Plus everyone from Costco to Home Depot is suddenly offering instant credit. Why buy a used tool set for $500 cash when you can buy it brand new for twenty bucks a month? "And frankly, I shouldn't say this"—he beams—"but new is nice." In the past few years the nation's fourth-largest bank, Wells Fargo, has staked a giant claim on the frontiers of alternative banking. They've quietly funded the country's largest check-cashing chain and the largest pawnshop chain, so now Brian's mom-and-pop is competing with the big boys. Brian knows he's got to adjust his strategy, *evolve*, think outside of the box. He's having a lot of success on eBay, the online auction site. People buy everything on eBay, even Franklin Mint plates.

Selling abandoned items is the most profitable part of the pawn business—he typically pays about one-fifth of an item's value—but Brian prefers that his customers keep their stuff. Selling is a one-off, not the way to build a business, not the future. What keeps Yuppie Pawn going are the regulars—a fact I find somewhat shocking, considering my brief foray into the pawn world. But there are now between twenty and forty million Americans without a bank account: not because they don't have any money, but because they don't have *enough* money to avoid the new fees and traps. For example, many banks authorize debit cards over their limit, then slap insufficient-funds fees when the transactions put the customer's account into the red.* And their computers are programmed to clear the largest checks first, so if an account is overdrawn, it is overdrawn multiple times rather than only once. This, of course, means multiple fees, which have risen from $10– $15 to $30–$45 over the past decade.† Though it seems hard to believe, pawnshops are more heavily regulated than the banks—and often cheaper. Pawns have to charge a uniform, capped interest rate with no special penalties. The rate schedule must be printed in full view of customers and there are no additional fees. Banks used to be bound by the same kinds of laws that now protect "alternative" customers, but now they can charge whatever interest rates they determine necessary and whatever fees they consider fair—these remarkable and unprecedented freedoms courtesy of the United States Supreme Court.

"We are their bank," Brian says of his regulars, and some of them have kept their possessions with him on and off since he opened, selling them when they lose a job or have an emergency and then repurchasing them whenever they can afford to. "I've got one customer"—he winces—"super guy. He and his family have been coming here for over ten years, and now he's three months behind on his payments, so the girls are having to put his stuff up for sale. How do you do that to someone?"

Lucky for me, it turns out that Brian is not only a talker and eminently likable but also a very curious guy. Like a neighborhood banker of the old school, he develops a rapport with most of his customers, asks them what's going on. The answers are the same,

*Overlimit fees may also apply. See "Cardmember agreement."
†In the UK, the figures are the same but you can put a pound sign instead of a dollar sign in front of them.

almost verbatim, as those you will find in Warren's study: job loss, medical emergency, family emergency—the immediate concerns of the just-getting-by who have no health insurance, no car insurance, no money to repair the car, no money for Dad's funeral, no Dave Ramsey– or Suze Orman–approved cash emergency fund and no open balances left, only an old television or a gold bracelet or Grandma's diamond ring. Recently, Brian's been meeting a lot of military parents who've been forced to buy body armor for their sons and daughters in Iraq because the Pentagon has yet to make good on its promise to equip them. But, as the Secretary of Defense says, you go to war with what you have and not what you wish you had. This really pisses Brian off and I notice the edges of his mouth suddenly receding inward, Dad-like, and I don't know if he's going to cry or punch his fist through the wall.

Brian takes a deep breath, looks around at his vast collection of orphaned Rolexes and lesser nonessentials, his cemetery. "There are so many reasons," he finally sighs. "People are having a hell of a time."

Brian's decided to get political in middle age. The other day he went to a rally for Senator John Kerry, the billionaire's husband, who stated what Brian, on the front lines of the economy, knows is a rather belated BGO:* *something isn't quite right.* All of the government's statistics are looking better than ever—the GNP is rising steadily while inflation remains tame—yet 70 percent of Americans now believe that the country is headed in the wrong direction. The number of millionaires hit an all-time high in 2005, even as foreclosures and defaults keep on rising. Bank profits and credit card company profits are exploding while their customers' savings disappear.

So the president has been pushing a new idea he calls "the ownership society." He wants all Americans to own their own home, to

*Blinding glimpse of the obvious.

own their own slice of Social Security, to own their own medical savings accounts, to own their own businesses, even. Yet, the country's most successful investor, Warren Buffett, the chairman of Berkshire Hathaway and otherwise known as the sage of Omaha, is dissing the ownership society as a red herring. What we're creating, Buffett has observed in his latest sermon, is a society of sharecroppers, not owners. At least Buffett has put his money where his mouth is: He is by far the largest shareholder of Wells Fargo.

Brian has formulated an interesting theory to explain these contradictions: The owners are voting in their own self-interest but the sharecroppers aren't. So the "invisible hand" of the free market has morphed into a biased government contraption that favors a few lucky duckies while the many watch from a distance, hoping their turn comes soon. I've read that three-quarters of Americans consider themselves middle-class, that roughly the same percentage think they're doing better than their neighbors, and that close to half are planning on winning the lottery before they retire. They will all be rich some day. As the comedian Louis CK jokes, rich people may not know what it's like to be poor, but every poor person knows exactly what it's like to be rich. And when they move into their 10,000-square-foot palace with the elevator and the dual washers/dryers, they don't want to pay higher taxes.

Needless to say, neither the mind-set nor the statistics inspire much hope that the disparities in wealth created over the past generation—the greatest since the 1930s—will get better before they get worse.

Brian tells me about a machinists' convention he attended a while back, where he ended up in conversation with a bunch of laid-off union guys. When Brian ventured that things had to change, that maybe we should start to treat each other a little better, he might as well have been from France as far as these guys' guys were concerned. *They* weren't paying higher taxes to cover people who couldn't afford health insurance. They weren't subsidizing the welfare queens and the bankruptcy gamers. These guys were dyed-in-the-wool, flannel-wearing members of the American middle class. Why should they pay for people who'd gotten themselves into trouble? Reeks of socialism, un-American.

"I told them, 'That's you guys,' " Brian recalls, eyes wide now, smile nervous. " 'That is *you*.' " He pauses, shakes his head. "But they don't get it. *They just don't get it.*"

This observation takes me back to a long drive around inner-city Lancaster, Pennsylvania—a picture-perfect example of urban blight, the kind of place where pawnshops and check-cashing joints are the only banks. My guide was Mike Sprunger, the director of a small nonprofit community center called Tabor. Tabor began in the 1950s as an advocacy organization for blacks who were then having the frustrating experience of responding to FOR RENT advertisements, only to find the apartment had mysteriously been taken off the market. As time went by, Tabor evolved into a full-service credit counseling agency for the poor. Now it's evolved again, to serve the newly poor, aka the formerly middle class. Mike was using the tour of his 'hood to show me why you cannot automatically accuse a person of acting against their own self-interest just because they went to a check-cashing joint that charges them a ridiculous fee or a pawnshop that gives them one-fifth of the value of their stuff. These people, he told me as we meandered through a maze of dilapidated row houses, are experts in their own survival. They know that by paying that fee at the check-cashing place, they are avoiding the possibility of a $39.00 bounced-check fee. They know that having savings disqualifies their children and themselves from most government aid. They've learned not to trust the big institutions. They know that the system does not favor people like them.

I thought back to my experience at the pawnshop and, of course, Mike was absolutely right. On the face of it, there had been no reason for me to avoid a pawnshop but shame, ego. Had I gone there in the first place, I would have avoided well over $100 in fees (both Albertsons and Bank of America charged NSF* fees). So now I know why a lot of folks prefer to wait in line at the post office to buy their money order for fifty-nine cents and then stew in the even longer line at the electric company payment window, all for the privilege of bypassing the banking system.

But there's another, more primal reason than math or even self-interest. This reason not only defines our relationship with credit but explains a curious phenomenon of the Greenspan era that has baffled social economists: Why do a large percentage of wealthy people who could easily pay off their credit card balances every month choose *not* to? Why, even when credit seems unnecessary, do so many of us *choose* to pay high interest rates and fees anyway? The answer is fear.

Mike explains by way of a homeless man he used to counsel. This guy was friendly and intelligent, resourceful even, fine with a job. He just couldn't hold on to a buck for more than a day. If he came into any money at all, it was gone immediately. So he'd come to Tabor and asked Mike if he could give him whatever money he earned on a daily basis and would Mike then pay his bills for him? Mike was used to structuring payouts like the ones CCCS arranges for debtors, but he'd never just held someone else's money for them because they didn't trust themselves. The homeless guy pleaded. He just couldn't handle his own money! Mike relented and, over time, he learned what was really going on. At a very young age spent on the wrong side of the tracks, the man had been beaten up and robbed every time he had money. So he'd learned to get rid of it fast—before someone else took it from him. Now in his midthirties, every time he cashed his check or someone gave

*Nonsufficient funds.

197

him a dime, he regressed into the 5-year-old and got rid of it as quickly as he could.

This story puts my journey into a much sharper focus. I realize that all of the people I've met—Beth, Fergie, Katherine Brown, Sheila, Lynn, and Keith—acted in their own self-interest. They were all well aware that if they didn't take the credit that was offered them, it might not be there tomorrow. Credit implies the threat of denial, works on our fears. So the rational thing to do is *act now* before someone takes it away: Build the McMansion; get the suite at the Four Seasons; refi the house and create more credit, double down; send in the Providian application; charge the Escalade if they'll give it to you; pay the mortgage and the car payments with a cash advance. Build the chicken restaurants and hope for the best. Take the money from the Arabs and the Chinese while they still want to give it to you. *Do it while you can, before the money vanishes as magically as it appeared!* You play with the hand you're dealt, after all, not the hand you wish you'd been dealt. If someone offers you more chips, you play them. You don't argue over terms or look too closely at the fine print or think too much about the future. At the end of the day, the more chips you have, the longer you can stay in the game.

For the past twenty years Dad's been warning himself that he won't make nearly as much money as last year. The government and the insurance companies are tightening the noose around the medical profession, treating doctors like costs that have to be minimized. Health care, he assures me, is going to be nationalized. No question. Give it ten years, max.

Doctors, Dad insists, are destined to become civil servants, i.e., poor. Yet, every year, his income climbs further and further into the six figures. And these days he finds himself doubly fortunate. Albeit through no fault of his own (my father routinely votes against his own financial interests by supporting the Democratic candidate, as do most of my wealthy neighbors), Dad has found himself on the receiving end of George Bush's tax "relief" in a major way. He's seen his income tax bracket fall to the lowest rate in memory, but the real kicker is the dividend and capital gains tax cuts. Bush wants to get rid of them altogether, along with the so-called death tax. Guys with a lot of passive income like Dad are making out like bandits while the union guys assembling the airplanes at Boeing, whose incomes derive from their labor alone, haven't been so lucky. It's one of the philosophical tenets of this administration that I just don't get: If you *didn't* earn the money, you shouldn't be taxed on it, and vice versa. So working Americans are now carrying a greater share of the tax burden than ever, which means that workers are paying off a greater share of the national debt they didn't incur, and when Alan Greenspan says that payroll taxes will have to rise in order to save Social Security, you know what that really means: that the sharecroppers are going to have to work harder and harder to pay off older and older debts, that their "productivity" is going to have to keep on rising indefinitely. Why? The owner can now move his or her assets to safe havens around the world in nanoseconds, but the sharecropper is tied to the mortgaged soil.*

The financial industry has just unveiled its solution to the quandary that, with health care costs soaring and employers unwill-

*Things are a bit better in Britain, it seems. The highest earnings marginal tax rate is 40 percent and begins to operate after around £32,000. Any additional income (rents, dividends and interest) is added to wages and is therefore taxed at the highest marginal tax rate. The capital gains tax is also 40 percent once you make above £32,000, but all this assumes that the household is not sophisticated enough to open an offshore account in Jersey to protect its income from the taxman.

ing or unable to absorb the difference, many of the lucky duckies, i.e., the insured, can no longer afford their co-pays or deductibles. The solution, of course, is another credit card. Dubbed the "medical-only" credit card, it has a fixed rate of 8 percent—unless the patient is ever late or if the patient is unable to pay off the balance within a year, in which case the interest rate triples. So the industry has thrown its customers another "cement life raft," as Warren likes to call them. Meanwhile, Dad has been forced to *invent* ways to spend his ownership windfall—something he's gotten very good at. The cedar house at the bottom of the rain forest he and Mom bought for $120,000 was sold long ago and, despite giving her half of his net worth (she now lives in a modern townhome that was just appraised at $420K, nearly three times what she paid), Dad and his new wife own two expensive homes: a charming Cape Cod on a corner lot in tony Madison Park, up the hill from the Boeing estate, and an eleven-acre spread on a private island in the San Juan Islands that was recently featured in one of those ubiquitous home style mags.

In the years after the divorce, Dad developed the middle-aged man's appetite for Ferraris and purchased two. Then he set his sights on racing sailboats, which are considerably more expensive (and beautiful) toys. Dad's also built up a fairly serious wine cellar. The other day he informed me, with a little shrug, that it contains more bottles than he could ever hope to drink. On a recent visit to Seattle, I notice that he charges our Starbucks lattes to his Bank of America Alaska Airlines Visa card—"for the miles," he says, kind of sheepishly. A friend tells me that the private high school my sister and I attended, the one that is indirectly responsible for Dad's present income, now costs upward of $20,000 a year—plus books and laptop computer. M.I.T., my sister's alma mater, now costs more than twice that. So, in a way, Dad got off easy. But I wonder if it hadn't been for us expensive kids, would he have stayed at the old hospital with the five-figure salary? Would he have owned Ferraris and racing sailboats and the island home? Would he have remained content in the Seattle he fell in love with?

Dad and his partners just won a contract to do the anesthesia at a state-of-the-art bariatric clinic—where severely overweight people go to have their stomachs reduced with a scalpel or a rubber band, depending on whether or not they want to keep their options open, I guess. Bariatric is all the rage now, and Dad calls me on his cell phone to share how *gorgeous* the building is, says it feels like a Ritz-Carlton more than a surgery center. *Fabulous!* The future of health care. He betrays a passing concern over the size of the mortgage these surgeons must have taken out to build their medical palace, but then again, they're too young to get many referrals, and Dad figures the polished wood and the thick-cushioned chairs will help them build—what? Cachet? A reputation? A customer base? After all, if you look like you make money, eventually you will.

It won't hurt that bariatric surgery is basically an all-cash business. This is not the clinic's fault, by the way. The insurance companies don't want to foot the bill for an epidemic that they, like Dave Ramsey, see as a behavioral issue. So the clinic is accepting credit cards and they will even help patients arrange a loan from a finance company. I doubt that the "no-insurance" policy has slowed their business: After all, fifty million Americans may not have insurance, but they will always have credit.

Eleven

"The rich are getting richer. That ain't gonna change
and that ain't gonna stop."
– Robin Leach

SONA is not the kind of place I'd normally choose to go for dinner. Nestled in a one-story home on the edge of Beverly Hills, the restaurant is far too chic for my wardrobe and far too expensive for my budget. The sad truth is that I have never been able to appreciate French food or the sort of austere circus that these über-hip restaurants create with their *je ne sais quoi*. Nor can I pull off the foodie thing with my limited command of the language, so I tend to spare the waitstaff the aggravation of translating the menu for me by just not showing up. But tonight I have made an exception. I have been invited to enjoy a five-course French meal with wine pairings* and cocktails for the bargain-basement price of fifty bucks. For, as it turns out, I am a member of an exclusive club. I am a Visa "signature" cardholder. And though I'm not sure what this really means, I've been told that my reward is this under-priced meal at SONA.

---

*A huge plus, since I find wine lists extraordinarily intimidating and am inevitably convinced moments later that I've made the wrong selection.

My friend, the mortgage broker, has jumped at the chance to accompany me. By sheer coincidence, he also happens to be a "signature" cardholder—a factoid I received several weeks before with a hint of annoyance and even betrayal, I'll admit. But what the hell? It isn't every day you get to dine at one of the most expensive restaurants in Los Angeles, by invitation (okay, they placed an ad in the newspaper and I just happened to call right away) *and* as an acknowledged VIP.

When the appointed hour arrives, the friend and I find ourselves among forty or so well-dressed older folks mingling with cocktail or mineral water in hand—one of whom tells us that this event sold out immediately. After spending a half hour thus contemplating our good fortune with our fellow signature members, we are seated across a small table from a middle-aged couple: a former investment banker who is now speculating in residential real estate; and his wife, a Japanese woman who works for a property management firm. Despite three-quarters of us being in the same industry, there turns out to be surprisingly little for us all to talk about, so it's a relief when the chef-owner appears and describes the menu in painstaking detail. He is followed by the sommelier, a rather introverted and very tall man whose knowledge of obscure European vineyards turns out to be mind-boggling. Around the room, young and hip Visa International employees—Dee Hock's progeny—perch like hawks, neither eating nor drinking. Just *watching.* I am not sure what could possibly be so intriguing about a bunch of cheap old people with great FICOs, but I feel a strange sensation of guilt come on, as though I am eating at their expense or else my fancy restaurant manners are sufficiently rusty to warrant their disapproval.

The food is fantastic, though a little complicated. The only real disappointment is the dessert, a paper-thin apple strudel with no middle. As everyone begins digging for their valet tickets, one of the

Visa people—a rail-thin woman in a business ensemble—foils our collective departure with a canned speech about how she hopes we've enjoyed ourselves and that Visa is happy to provide these wonderful rewards for us and so on. And then the kicker: Her minions blanket the room with surveys for us to fill out. *So that's it!* I realize too late. They've subsidized our expensive meal in return for more information. They want to know if we're really worth rewarding after all; if we're ready to dump our American Express cards for the quasi-prestige of the "signature" Visa; if we're ready to become revolvers; if we're corruptible. Firms are trying similar tricks in the UK, although some of them leave a lot to be desired. For example, attend a soccer match on a Saturday and the attractive but scantily-clad woman in the street outside the ground will give you a free hat, as long as you sign up your interest in taking out a credit card which has likely been endorsed by that same soccer team. Go team!

The guilt dissipates. I've hoodwinked myself—spent fifty bucks I would not have otherwise spent; gone to a restaurant I would otherwise not have patronized. All in the name of "spaving": getting something for nothing. I have the urge to disguise my humiliation as protest, maybe storm out of SONA, tearing up their survey on the way and tossing the pieces around the sparse yet elegant decor like angry snowflakes. But instead I follow the lead of my fellow signature cardholders and meekly ask to borrow a pencil from one of the Visa reps. Then I thoughtfully complete each question.

I return home to learn that the Greenspan era is officially over. The eleven o'clock news leads with outtakes from the House Banking Committee Hearings. Greenspan's familiar, nebbishy, corpse-like countenance has been replaced by a slightly younger, nebbishy, bearded countenance. The new chairman of the Federal Reserve Bank is named Ben S. Bernanke. The honorable members of the House Banking Committee, however, don't seem to notice the change. They treat him to the same routine as his predecessor.

Democrats try to make him admit that the economy is in crisis, while Republicans try to bully him into gushing that the U.S.A. is still number one, everything's fine, the national debt no big deal because those nice foreign folks wouldn't lend us the dough if we couldn't afford to pay it back, don't look a gift horse in the mouth— even a socialist country like China or a terrorism den like Saudi Arabia. Bernanke hedges more bluntly than his predecessor. He talks about not ruling things out but not ruling them in, either. Will interest rates continue to rise, Mr. Chairman? Maybe, maybe not. By a quarter point or half a point? That is difficult to say. We will have to analyze the data, Bernanke concludes time and again, *we must wait and see*. In the papers tomorrow he will be lauded as a brilliant man. One pundit will go so far as to give his performance an "A-plus." The Wall Streeters will be unanimous: Bernanke did what he needed to do. He calmed the Street.

I am not calm. Despite Suze Orman's books promising to put an end to my worrying, and Ms. Carter Franke* sending me "courtesy checks" every month (to help me "relax," she says), my journey around the country has made me more concerned than ever. In fact, I am having a hard time sleeping, which is disconcerting because sleeping is one of my favorite pastimes. At my office I now work beneath both the words and the visage of Senator Connie Mack, courtesy of the *New York Times*. His expression never wavers from the blank half smile, no doubt intended to convey a kind of confidence that is, unfortunately, less than infectious.

I am having my own "crisis of confidence"—the term Jimmy Carter used a generation ago to describe what he'd learned about the state of the union during his two weeks meditating on the mountaintop. I do not understand how we can hope to escape our dark days if we do not first acknowledge that we are living in them.

*Senior vice president of marketing for JPMorgan Chase.

I don't know how the middle class intends to save itself when it lacks the funds to be heard. I wonder how the president intends to keep his pledge to cut the deficit in half by jacking it up to record highs and by pretending that the $500 billion spent on the war in Iraq should not be considered part of the budget.

Yet, this is not a political crisis, at least not entirely, and what causes me the most concern is the behavior of my fellow citizens. Last year a majority of Californians voted to borrow $20 billion to make ends meet, a year after electing a governor who promised to solve the Golden State's fiscal crisis by making "tough choices." All over the country, we are voting to put ourselves deeper into debt in order to have trophy-like skyscrapers and sports stadiums that will be owned by billionaires who didn't pay for them. Colleges and universities are cutting deals with credit card companies and still forcing students to mortgage their futures in order to boast of winning football teams and gourmet food services. Tax breaks for SUVs and special financing programs are propping up the sales of Hummer H2s while guys like Will schlep around Iraq in unarmored dinosaurs. But these are relatively minor grievances compared to what the papers are calling the biggest theft of public goods in the history of our country: $65 billion of publicly owned natural gas and oil to be donated to the energy industry, royalty-free, by the federal government. Most of this oil and gas is located just off the coast of New Orleans, where, six months after Hurricane Katrina hit, dozens of bodies are still rotting, facedown in mud-swamped homes, because FEMA has closed shop and the local emergency services don't have enough money to retrieve them.

Last year Osama bin Laden sent one of his creepy video letters to the sheriff who, four short years ago, promised to bring him in, "dead or alive," and revealed that the true intention of 9/11 was to bankrupt the United States as he'd bankrupted the Soviet Union: by instigating an endless war impossible for the superpower to win. The

International Monetary Fund jumped on Osama's bandwagon, warning that the sheriff's profligate spending was not only destabilizing the world economy but pissing everybody off. Now when our trade representatives complain that China is not playing fair— mainly because we don't think they spend enough on Buicks—their premier treats us to a lecture on fiscal responsibility or else a euphemism wrapped in a fortune cookie that, translated, comes out as "Don't bite the hand that feeds you." They have a great sense of humor, those Chinese. They know we're knee-deep in the bear trap. They have ten times as much cash in the bank as we do and they consume less than half the energy. Theirs is a real productivity miracle, one built on sacrifice and saving.

But nothing is so nerve-racking as the quasi-folksy platitudes that Citigroup is painting on most of the billboards in my hometown of Los Angeles, e.g., "Tell Your Mother You're Marrying Artsy," "You are not silver, gold or platinum, you are you," "The best blue chips are the ones you dip in salsa," etc., etc. Call me paranoid, but whenever I see one, I can't escape the nagging subtext that these adverts are telling me: "Don't worry that you have no money left. It was never yours to begin with." But at least I know where my Citi MasterCard annual fee is going. The same cannot be said of my tax dollars. In my state, as in many others, what I thought I was paying for seems to be slowly disappearing. Libraries are closing, public parks are cutting their hours, public universities are increasing their fees ten times faster than the rate of inflation, and public broadcasting has started airing bona fide commercials. When I call 911, I receive a busy signal or am put on hold. Ten miles west of my apartment, Santa Monica is experiencing an explosion of homeless men and women who, a recent study confirmed, are not—as a lot of people suspected—a bunch of Okies hoping for a glimpse of Jane Fonda; nope, they are our former neighbors minus the roof over their heads. The city council's response was to outlaw sleeping in empty doorways at night. I imagine the mere sight of these folks was depressing property values, a terrifying threat in the age of refi.*

It has occurred to me that all of the elements for a revolution are now in place though I hesitate to use the *r* word because it seems so third-world. I like what Senator Christopher Dodd told the credit card executives at the banking committee hearing a few months ago: "I've been around long enough to know that the pendulum swings both ways," he lectured. "And the pendulum has swung very far to one side now and eventually it's going to swing back just as hard in the other direction." Was this a veiled threat? I wonder, a coded call to arms for la Résistance and the hordes of angry customers who have been waiting for their excuse to revolt? Or was it simply a statement of fact, that you can't squeeze people this hard without provoking a reaction of similar force? Eventually they notice the hand around their neck and some of them, at least, will start to yell and scream and bite and get everybody else riled up, and pretty soon you've got a real problem on your hands.

Midtown Manhattan is surprisingly pleasant at four a.m., as though the city has finally hit a manageable stride. The light of the street lamps bounces off the concrete, forming a pleasant glow. Empty taxis and limousines pass on their way to the airports without honking. A newspaper vendor throws bundles of the *Wall Street Journal*—now a little smaller to save on rising paper costs, I hear—onto the pavement in front of a closed convenience store. Next to

*The UK is the same. The "official" number of homeless families now exceeds the 100,000 mark, which some charities are taking to mean half a million people, a figure that's up 7 percent on the same time last year.

me, Jon, my cameraman, is obsessively guarding his line of vision from the occasional passerby. The camera is pointed at the side of a skyscraper across the street where workers are rushing to install a huge electronic sign before dawn, when their permit expires. The sign, known to many New Yorkers as the National Debt Clock, was built in 1988, at the height of President Reagan's record budget deficits. It was taken down in 1997, when deficits briefly turned into surpluses. The sign is the brainchild of Seymour M. Durst, an eccentric real estate mogul who died in 1995.

I had met Helena, Durst's granddaughter, the day before at Durst's favorite restaurant, a generic diner across the street. Helena had ordered her grandfather's favorite lunch—an egg sandwich and mint tea—and showed me an album of photographs. Durst was a tiny man with white hair at the temples, long fingers, and thin lips. There is a photograph of him flipping a giant light switch at the unveiling ceremony in 1988. He is wearing a nondescript rain jacket and looks more like a little kid with a new toy than a billionaire who's fought his way to the top of a tough industry in a tough city.

Helena, a fellow college dropout and self-described child of privilege (she is a lifelong equestrian and knows her Prada) is trying to carry on her father's legacy. She explains how the whole thing started—how Seymour would send letters to congressmen that read "This is the national debt. Have a nice day," or something like that, and he paid for countless banners on the front page of the *New York Times*. Instead of advertisements, he'd pen folksy sayings which might inspire people to live better, more frugal lives, e.g., "Beware the Four-Letter Word—Debt" and "Borrow, Borrow; Enjoy Tomorrow Today. Tomorrow will be Terrible." Durst singlehandedly revived this once-seedy stretch of Sixth Avenue, renamed it Avenue of the Americas, and built gleaming skyscrapers of glass and steel over the flophouses' rubble. Helena worships her grandfather, misses him terribly. She will never feel closer to him than when his beloved Debt Clock is resurrected onto one of the family's buildings, directly across the street from her office.

As the street lamps extinguish themselves and the street is filled with the sun's early glow, the workers nervously flip a switch and the hundreds of orange bulbs burst to life. There are no cheers, just hurried nods. The workers load their tools and themselves back into three trucks and hightail it to the warehouse in Queens. Jon and I pack up the tripod and the camera. He reminds me that Helena will be able to see her grandfather every day now.

Seymour Durst reminds me of Marriner Eccles, the Federal Reserve chairman who warned that the economy had become a lopsided poker game. Like Eccles, Durst built his empire on debt, but he was not a gambler like his peers. He was unfashionable, a traitor to his class—no Donald Trump, that's for sure. Durst understood that credit had to be rationed. He knew that debt is a lever capable of turning small differences in wealth into huge disparities over time. He knew that this should be avoided.

Durst also understood that the federal debt amounts to nothing less than a massive theft—not only of the wealth of future generations, who will have to pay for it, but more important a theft of confidence. Is it just a coincidence that—at the same time we are borrowing 95 percent of our debts from foreigners—Microsoft and Yahoo! are helping the Chinese government suppress dissidents, eliminating the word *democracy* from their vocabularies? Is it by chance that our largest corporations are "parking" billions of dollars in foreign nations at a time when the Social Security Trust Fund is short $1.5 trillion? Isn't it a bit strange that, as the numbers of millionaires increase, a growing majority of us feel that something just isn't quite right with the American Dream?

While most people with Durst's kind of money could have cared less that China was paying for their tax cuts or that the Social Security Trust Fund was being robbed to pay for wars and corporate subsidies (you don't get rich waiting around for a payoff down the road; you get rich by taking the money up front), Durst understood the broader implications. Perhaps because he could still remember the Great Depression, when long lines of middle-aged men in suits and hats had snaked around Manhattan to get a bowl of soup and a lot of Americans had felt that maybe the Russians had got it right with communism, Durst had an unusual sensitivity to the plight of the ignored and the invisible. He started a newspaper that the homeless still publish and sell for a dollar on the streets. He helped out countless people quietly, without giving a speech about it or listing every bit of charity on his income tax return, demanding a deduction. He saw himself not as a billionaire but as a member of the working class. He ate egg sandwiches in their delis, wore their clothes, walked to work. When Durst designed the National Debt Clock, he created a special window counting up his and their family's share of the debt, revealing, to the dollar, what is being stolen from all of us.

Helena shares her grandfather's sense of compassion. She has seen too many friends drowning in student loans and credit card debts, their lives mortgaged before they've landed their first entry-level job. When I wonder if a child of such privilege can truly relate, she reminds me that the Durst Organization, like most real estate developers, remains heavily in debt, that the banks own a greater share of these skyscrapers than they do. They are just sharecroppers, she is saying, like everyone else. But the Dursts are far luckier than most. Helena is not being shipped back to the Middle East in fatigues, like Will. She did not inherit a bear trap, like Keith, or fall into one, like Peter. She works in a glass tower and mingles with boldfaced names at art galleries. For all of her allusions to poverty, Helena is still a lucky ducky.

In February 2006 the government brought back the thirty-year bond and the demand was overwhelming. Investors around the globe reaffirmed their insatiable appetite for the United States' debt. The investment bankers on Wall Street breathed a collective sigh of relief, as though they had just dodged an atomic bomb. The great crisis had been averted, once again, thanks to cash-rich hedge funds and the kindness of foreigners. I wish I could call up Seymour for a truism, but then I realize I don't have to. His thoughts are reflected in the orange glow of his clock's incomprehensible sum, now a trillion dollars higher than when I began the film. Seymour is still doing our math for us.

In the late 1980s the comedienne Carol Burnett was looking for a place to shoot her white-trash send-up of the prime-time soap operas *Dallas* and *Dynasty*. What she needed to find was the most unglamorous city imaginable. A sense of decay was essential. The show was all about people who thought they were still wealthy but who had fallen from riches long ago—people obliviously living beyond their means and past their primes. The city Burnett eventually chose was Fresno, the once solidly white, middle-class farming community in California's central valley. Fresno had clearly seen its best days already. Burnett was simply pointing out the obvious. Whether or not she knew that the city she'd chosen was also the birthplace of the credit card, I'll never know, but I'm sure she'd appreciate the irony.*

I visit Fresno just two years from the fiftieth anniversary of Bank of America's inaugural BankAmericard direct-mail campaign. Previous anniversaries of "the drop," as it is known, have been com-

---

*The show was, aptly enough, called *Fresno*. Incidentally, home prices in Fresno rose at an average rate of 21 percent per year from 1999 to 2004: not bad for one of the most undesirable real estate markets in the country.

memorated in Bank of America ad campaigns, but I doubt that
number 50 will be one of them. Downtown Fresno reminds me of a
bigger version of downtown Macon, Mississippi, nearly deserted.
Drive a few miles in any direction and the streets are littered with
neglected buildings, though the fast-food chains have stuck around,
for now. Stopping in a few retail establishments, I don't hear English as much as Spanish. Migrant workers from the south have replaced the upwardly mobile whites of yesteryear.

Fresno is a roadside attraction, a brief stop on my way to Bakersfield, an hour or so to the southeast. Bakersfield is an old oil
town. Like Fresno, it has seen better days. My destination is just
south of the city limits, in a neighborhood of chain-link fences and
overgrown yards. The small shotgun shack that matches the address
on my MapQuest printout is the home of Janis Williams and her
parents. Janis, I have decided, may just be a revolutionary.

I arrive shortly after the conclusion of the family's weekly
garage sale. Janis's mother, a large, pleasant woman who looks
chronically frantic, greets me with a quick handshake and a smile,
then continues hauling the trash that didn't sell back inside. Her father, an endearing lumberjack of a man in worn overalls, rants
about the president and tells me there's no one on earth who could
possibly hate this godforsaken state as much as he does. Then he
jumps on his John Deere and drives around the lawn for the next
hour, dreaming of an imminent move to the Midwest.

Janis arrives late, having stepped out to the drugstore for some
medicine. She reminds me of her parents. She shares their dimensions, though, at 50, Janis is still pretty and her sensibility more tol-
erant, more resigned to the way things are. She leads me into the
tiny living room where her mother, an incurable pack rat,
has stuffed every space with what appears to be all of the stuff
that didn't move at Lynn's garage sale. As a counterpoint to
Lynn's Franklin Mint plates, Janis's mother has hung an impressive

collection of porcelain clocks in the shape of cuddly animals along the walls.

Janis clears the clutter off a large comfy chair and sits down. She has spent the last twenty years working as a professional caregiver, most recently at a nursing home, and she's had three children, been married and divorced without ever sticking her head too far out of the woodwork. When she was diagnosed with rectal cancer a year ago, Janis's first thought was that she wouldn't have to deal with all of the bullshit she's quietly suffered over the past five decades. But then she had a change of heart. She decided she wanted to see all of the historical places in America; she wanted to make a quilt and ride a horse; she wanted to see the leaves change in Vermont and sleep under a blanket of stars in Oklahoma; she wanted to be part of a powwow because there's a little Indian in her blood. In other words, Janis decided to live.

But staying alive turned out to be much more complicated than she anticipated. Janis's health insurance was canceled two weeks after she lost her job, so she called up the welfare office, but they said she was too old for Medicaid and too young for Medicare, though they could send her some food stamps. In the UK, of course, to many the idea of being refused medical care because you can't afford it is absurd due to the fact that people pay national insurance contributions during their working lives to cover them for sickness when they are older. Then again, we Americans always assumed the same of social security and medicare, but now, after paying in, are told that the benefits were never a promise to begin with. So Janis moved back into her parents' place and then she swallowed her pride and drove herself to the county hospital, while she reminded herself that her youngest son had been serving his country in Iraq for the past fourteen months so she had more than every right to cash in on that debt. Her country could serve her for once. The sign over the hospital door promised *No one is to be turned away even if they cannot pay.* This proved to be an exaggeration. The county hospital was out of funds. They couldn't help her.

"You've got to be kidding me," Janis, who has a sharp tongue sometimes, told them. "You'd better take down that sign, then."

Janis rubs her tanned forehead as she recalls falling through the cracks, suddenly realizing that "something is definitely wrong in this country," knowing that if she wanted to live she'd have to fight. She told herself there was no use crying about it because crying wasn't going to help and there was only one thing left in her to fight with: her breath. So she called a local news station and told them her story. "As long as someone will hear me"—Janis smiles— "I'll keep talking and yelling, because I'm not going to give up. I'm a fighter."

Janis teamed up with a local television reporter named Alexia and they started asking the big questions, out loud for once: *Is this the kind of America we really want? Is this really where we want to set the bar now? Telling the mother of a soldier to just go off and die? Are we a third-world country or are we a civilized nation? Is something not quite right here?* Less than a week later the county hospital's administrator claimed they'd made a mistake and Janis would receive treatment after all. But in his apparent haste to make the cameras go away, he forgot to inform Janis, or anyone at the hospital for that matter. She got the news from Alexia two weeks later.

There's a hint of pride in Janis's voice, though I can tell what she mostly feels is exhaustion. The fight has given her strength but the cancer has made her tired. She pulls down the neck of her pink T-shirt to reveal a small device pumping chemotherapy drugs beneath her skin—a device that may save her life or may not. The machine was reserved for a paying customer but Janis shamed them into giving it to her instead. Now, according to her doctors, she's got a fifty-fifty chance of making it, of facing all of the "bullshit" she

might have avoided: the kids and grandkids who are constantly calling, never getting their lives in order, struggling on soldiers' pay;
the aging parents, the ranting dad; etc., etc. "If it's not one damned
thing, it's another," she sighs, but she's glad to be here for the
dance, as she calls it. She's become a team captain of a billiards
league down at the Hitchin' Rail Tavern, a local biker bar, and her
friends there have become her family. They've taught her not to
take anything too seriously, not to try to make sense of things, like
why the government would spend millions of dollars studying how
frogs reproduce when they've been getting along fine for millions
of years. Janis laughs. If she had a PhD next to her name, they'd
give her a million bucks to watch flies mate or some other stupid
thing, but a nobody like her has to fight like hell for that little bag
of chemo.

Still, Janis isn't bitter or scared. She tells me she loves a challenge. The more they tell her to go away, the harder she fights. It occurs to me that she's lucky to have somewhere to fight. In New
Orleans, most of the hospitals don't plan to reopen. They are pri-
vately owned, for-profit ventures, not public goods anymore. Market
forces, not needs, will determine whether or not they should exist.
There is no money to build the kind of levees that are needed to prevent another such catastrophe, much less rebuild old institutions
that serve welfare cases who are, as the president's mother famously
observed, really much better off huddled in sports stadiums and
cheap hotels in strange cities. This is the new definition of "fresh
start."

At an extraordinary press conference shortly before the hurricane, the president himself had explained why the soaring national
debt is actually "tremendously positive news": by running up
record deficits, the administration is forcing Congress to be responsible, to finally end the welfare state once and for all. Mr. Bush
called what he's created the "fiscal straitjacket," claimed it was great

news for the taxpayers. So now we can make ourselves responsible by being irresponsible. By the absurd logic of the perpetual debtor, maxing out forces us to live within our means.

A little later in the press conference, Bush, more than a little exasperated with all of the budget questions, finally admitted that "there's not as much money in Washington as there used to be." I imagine this came as news to Connie Mack, but then he probably just called Prince Bandar or Premier Li to confirm that the president had misspoken. Of course there was more money than ever. There *had* to be because we needed more money. And sure enough, less than a year after the press conference, the president submitted the largest budget in the history of the Union. And a few months after that, he would say he needed another $140 billion extra for Iraq, off-budget of course. He also asked for $4 billion to help the citizens who'd remained in New Orleans, but only after Louisiana's governor, a feisty Cajun named Kathleen Babineaux Blanco, threatened to fight the theft of her people's precious oil and gas reserves. Like Janis, Blanco's learned that they're not just going to give it to you.

I've tried to reach Janis in the months since our interview, without success. It's amazing how easily people can disappear in this day and age, when so much is known about them. I suppose I could call up Chris and Bob, have them run a skip trace, but I'm a little nervous. I hope we didn't make Janis wait too long for the chemo bag. I want to believe that she made it to Vermont or Oklahoma or the Grand Canyon, that right now she's feeling what it means to be an American: to be free.

I realize now that Janis and Seymour are my heroes. They stood up to a system that most of us accept as preordained, inevitable. And they said no. Something isn't right at all. They held up a mirror to our culture of debt and to all of the choices we've made and continue to make. And once confronted with our own reflection, I wonder if we won't make very different decisions. I wonder if we will finally decide to treat one another with compassion, to help the unfortunate and the desperate rather than prey on them, to set the bar at a level where we can truly call ourselves a civilization, where we can look into the mirror and be proud of this great nation whose highest ideal will always be liberty.

Twelve

"I think it's all about money.
Whether or not you've got enough money to save your life."
– Janis Williams

Elizabeth Warren, the Harvard Law professor, often says that debt has infected the American family. A more accurate statement would be that debt is infecting most of the globe. Britons have now surpassed Americans as the world's most profligate borrowers; the South Koreans' economic miracle has been followed by a spending binge unmatched by any other country; in Australia, the government is handing out American Express cards to poor Aborigines; the Thai government has dictated that all public employees are to make purchases with credit cards (to be more efficient); in Japan, traditionally a cash society, cell phones can now be used to buy Big Macs on credit; in Germany, a major city, Dresden, has sold all of its public housing to an American investment bank to pay off crushing debts; Europeans are terrified that American-style debting is headed their way, that easy credit will prove as irresistible as Madonna and Frappaccinos; the governments of the EU are chronically unable or unwilling to stick to the debt limits their charter imposes. The sovereign nation now holds no right so dear as the right to borrow as freely as it chooses.

The problems surfacing around the world sound eerily familiar. In England, the government is hiking tuitions at public universities, once seen as the most inviolable of public goods—the key to ending centuries of classism. The country that used to punish debtors with execution now has its own Janis Williams. Her name is Ann Marie Rogers and, like Janis, she is middle-aged, she has cancer, and the public health system refuses to treat her because the cost of the prescription drugs she needs is, as they put it, "excessive." Ann Marie sued, but the High Court denied she had a claim. So now she's taking her case to the media, asking the public to decide whether she should live or disappear.

In South Korea, the country's largest credit card issuer had to be rescued by the government after defaults soared to over 10 percent of balances—this, despite a booming economy and a raging stock market. The Japanese have witnessed a sixfold rise in personal bankruptcies over the past decade, even as unemployment has remained enviably low and per capita income relatively high. Millions of Japanese are still recovering from their own real estate bubble, which burst in the late eighties and has left them owing more on their condos than they are worth. In Scotland, the government is considering slapping health warnings onto credit cards, and Fergie's former mother-in-law, the Queen, recently warned of the dangers of predatory lending in her speech opening Parliament. The Australians are considering price controls on housing because the real estate boom there has made it next to impossible for middle-class families to live anywhere close to the cities where they work. In Taiwan, American Express stopped issuing new cards for two months because defaults are skyrocketing. Citigroup, never one to miss an opportunity, will buy over half a billion dollars' worth of bad debt from a mainland Chinese bank, proving that even the thriftiest people on earth are not immune to the temptations—or the traps—of easy credit. Meanwhile, the United States, obliviously beating its chest as the "locomotive of the world's economy," loudly chides the rest of the world to follow its example to the bitter end and spend, spend, spend—as though American-style retail therapy would solve the problems.

I recall my conversation with Peter Billington—the picture he painted of himself as a victim, a clueless young naïf in a strange land where everything was inverted, where credit was good, not bad, where in order to save you had to first borrow, where in order to be rich you had to look rich. I didn't buy Peter as hapless victim, partly because his crimes are so horrific, so unthinkable. Yet, the long list of catch-22s that formed Peter's American experience demand the question: Why is it that the wealthiest countries and the wealthiest people have the hardest time saving? And, conversely, why do the poorest countries with the poorest people, e.g., India, save the most?

Answering these questions requires a look back at Elizabeth Warren's study.* The wealthier a society becomes, the more expensive the basics like housing and health care. In the beginning, credit can be used to bridge this gap, and the members of the middle class continue to have what we expect them to have. But if there is no reasonable limit to the amount of debt that a household is allowed to use, then, as more people compete for intrinsically scarce goods—the five-bedroom house in the good school district, the high-quality medical care, the college education, the designer clothes, etc.—credit becomes a lever that pushes up the prices of these goods exponentially. Whoever is willing to take on the most credit wins the most goods. Take the Home Depot cashier as an example: If she opts for an interest-only, negative amortization, adjustable-rate mortgage, she can easily outbid a family with twice the income, as long as that family has chosen a traditional, thirty-year fixed-rate mortgage. If, as

---

*I highly recommend her book *The Two-Income Trap*, which discusses her findings in a succinct and surprisingly engaging narrative.

Dave Ramsey strongly recommends, the family opts for a fifteen-year mortgage, they could have three times the money to spend on their home and still lose.* It's easy to see how those who are unwilling to leverage their credit to its fullest, i.e., who refuse to be irresponsible, quickly fall out of the middle class and begin to look and act suspiciously like the poor.

But there is another answer. Perhaps the past five decades have been an anomaly. Perhaps the notion of a middle class was simply an experiment and there have always been only two classes of people: owners and renters. Perhaps Senator Dodd is right about the pendulum but he's wrong about where we are on the cycle: Perhaps the pendulum has only now begun to swing back to the owners' favor. Perhaps our conception of wealth and poverty is nothing more than marketing fantasy. Perhaps the wealthy are simply those who own, regardless of the amount, and the poor are those who borrow their capital and their goods, no matter how impressive those goods may look parked in front of a big house that is also, in fact, rented. Perhaps *ownership* has become a cynical euphemism, a ruse dreamed up by Madison Avenue and rubber-stamped by politicians. Is it not Fannie Mae—the government-chartered corporation that has sold Americans nearly $7 trillion in debt over the past generation—whose slogan is "We fuel the American Dream"?

Perhaps it is time to take another look at how the owners and the renters in our country have come to coexist, possessing contrary yet complementary values, sometimes under the same roof.

* * *

---

*For a sobering look at how this works, I suggest visiting any of the mortgage calculator sites. A few not only crunch the numbers but graph the different mortgage options with their required monthly payments, side by side.

Yolanda Garcia grew up in the market town of Tlacolula, Mexico, which is located just off of the Pan-American Highway in the southern state of Oaxaca. The youngest of five, Yolanda was a chubby girl who was always called upon to help with her mother's chores and later work at her father's little *tienda de abarottes*.* Yolanda can remember siphoning gas with her mouth from large barrels into smaller cans for resale, and waking up at five a.m. to fetch bread from the bakery so that her father could sell sandwiches to the girls who passed by on their way to school. When Yolanda's brothers were sent off to college, her father made it clear that she would not be following them. She was needed at home.

Yolanda was 25 when her mother fell over at the market, dead instantly of a thrombosis in her brain. Her father quickly found a Zapotecan woman who sold tamales from a basket, and when he bought her home, Yolanda was told that she was no longer needed—or wanted—around the house. So Yolanda sold her possessions and flew to Tijuana, where she paid a *coyote* $300 to cross the border. They walked at night, chased by border patrol agents. Out of thirty who began the trip Yolanda was one of five who made it and the only woman. Her *compadres* called her their lucky charm. They spent the next week together in a small safe house, without food, waiting for another *coyote* to take them north from San Diego to Los Angeles.

When that day came, Yolanda was given some water and placed in the trunk so that the car would not look overly full, suspicious. Yolanda had no money so the *coyote* took her home and gave her a job as a maid. Later Yolanda found permanent work at the Paper Mate pen factory in nearby Santa Monica, where she worked for several years until an INS raid at the height of the Carter/Reagan recession left her jobless. By then she was married with two children and

---

*Essentially a convenience store.

another "in the oven," as she puts it. Without health benefits, Yolanda had to travel back to Mexico in order to have her third son at a public hospital, then walk back north the same way she came, baby Angel in her arms.

When her husband lost his job washing dishes at a beach hotel, she pounded the pavement, landing the usual jobs at restaurants and hotels, quickly realizing that these jobs would not support her family. When business was slow, they told you not to show up and they didn't pay you. Yolanda needed something steady and she was willing to do anything for her children. She was determined that they would have the education denied her, that they would be something better than she could ever have imagined: members of the American middle class.

It was during one of her walks that Yolanda encountered a fellow immigrant woman scrounging cans and bottles from a Dumpster. They struck up a conversation and, by the time it was over, Yolanda had found herself a new job: collecting recyclables. For the past twenty years she and her husband have woken up at midnight, pushed their bicycles down the deserted sidewalks of Venice Beach, and trolled the Dumpsters and garbage cans for empty cans, bottles, and old newspapers, which they save in their tiny apartment until the end of the week, when everything is hauled into their cramped pickup truck and driven to the recycling center in Inglewood, where the good Reverend Doctor G. Landry-Humphery and her small army of ex-cons sort through it all, weigh it, and pay them their salary in cash. The work is dangerous, the stench often unbearable, the humiliation worse at times, but it is regular work and the Garcias can never be fired or have their hours cut. They've averaged about $20,000 a year Dumpster-diving, and though they are both U.S. citizens now, they've never accepted any kind of government assistance. Still, Yolanda and her husband have managed to send one son to M.I.T. (mostly on scholarship), a daughter to the University of California at Riverside, and another son to San Jose State. Several years ago the Garcias bought a three-bedroom house, in which they have accumulated roughly $200,000 in equity, while sending thousands of dollars home to Yolanda's father, who complains that the neighbors in Tlacolula know that Yolanda makes her living from the trash.

I had read about Yolanda in the *Los Angeles Times*. Later I learned that she had also been featured in *People* magazine, *People en Español*, appeared on the local news, and even been flown to Miami to do *Sábado Gigante*—the most popular Spanish-speaking show on television. Several years ago Yolanda landed a small role in an independent film called *Floundering*, in which she played herself, opposite the sultry James LeGros. *Floundering* is the tale of a brooding young white man who aimlessly wanders the streets of "post-riot" Los Angeles, pausing only to ponder the meaning of poverty with fellow angst-ridden hipsters and once entering a bakery to meditate on whether or not a kaiser roll is indeed "the staff of life." I don't recommend it, but they paid her $150.00.

Yolanda's life is one of those rare stories that plays equally well in both the red and blue states. Conservatives like pointing to her as an allegory (the American Dream borne of hard work and rugged individualism); liberals hold her up as a cautionary tale—a heart wrenching failure of unbridled capitalism (a mother of three forced to dig through shit in a crime-infested neighborhood just to put food on the table). In the end, all of the publicity Yolanda has garnered, including a recent stint on *20/20*, has solved only one of her problems: the police who thought she was a drug dealer and the drug dealers who thought she was a narc are both finally satisfied that Yolanda is nothing but a very determined mother.

I started filming Yolanda and her husband a few months before her eldest son graduated from M.I.T., for a documentary titled *Parents of the Year.* By then, the skin on Yolanda's face had formed a dark leather from all of those hours in the sun, and her legs were shot from walking fourteen hours a day, but she was kind enough to rehash her story for me, day after day, as we sat on the steps of the Cadillac Hotel, just a few blocks north of Muscle Beach. A friendship developed quickly as the American Dream story evaporated into the marine layer. Yes, Yolanda was excited to see her son graduate from such a prestigious university—she wore an M.I.T. sweatshirt most days—but her daughter, Adrianne, was making her life a living nightmare. The girl had maxed out a credit card; she had bought a new Mustang for which the parents were paying $350 per month, plus insurance; her cell phone bills—which Yolanda dutifully paid, for fear of ruining her credit rating—often ran into the hundreds of dollars; and still Adrianne always needed money from her mother. Adrianne's love of credit caused Yolanda's tears to flow onto the steps more than once. I would put my arms around her and say, *"Your daughter is an American, and that's how American girls are taught to behave,"* like a mantra, and she would either begin to laugh or insist that, no, Adrianne was a Mexican. She had been raised as her mother's daughter, after all.

I filmed her son's graduation in Boston, never knowing that something was terribly wrong, interpreting Yolanda's silence as awe for the massive columns of Building 7 and the legions of academics in their colored robes and festive hats. Like the *Boston Globe* reporter who met us at the airport and all of the journalists before and after him, I wanted to witness the American Dream realized. But within two days Yolanda was back digging through Dumpsters, trying hard not to stick herself with the occasional hypodermic needle—impossible to see in the dark—tolerating the clueless well-wishers who'd read the news and peppered her with hopeful lies:

that Yolanda would stop working, that her son would take care of her from now on, that the American Dream had finally kicked in after all this time and pretty soon she'd be driven around in a limousine.

Her son moved home a few weeks later. He'd taken a job at Raytheon, one of the world's largest defense contractors, working in the lab that designs optical systems for "smart" weapons. On one occasion I remember him sitting at the dinner table with his mother, trying to describe how the lasers and the mirrors had to be carefully calibrated, bragging that "America always wins." I thought I noticed Yolanda give me a look that said she finally realized that her son really was an American now, and that was trouble.

Not long after that, he made his first purchase: a $40,000 Lexus. Then he bought a new couch for the house, on credit, and they sent the bill to Yolanda. The relatively light conversations on the steps of the Cadillac took a dark turn. How could her son do this to her? Yolanda demanded, the tears streaming down like raindrops on glass. How could *he* betray his own mother? Once again I tried to explain to Yolanda that her son was an American, and in America, this sort of behavior is to be expected. Hell, it's *encouraged*. Didn't she see the billboards all around, telling us that an SUV equaled freedom, or that an expensive watch was an investment? Didn't she ever watch television? Didn't she know that you had to spend to save money, that buying on credit was the smart thing to do? That denying yourself amounts to a moral failure in this country? What more perfect symbol of achieving the American Dream, of having climbed the heights of the middle class, was there than a brand-new Lexus? It was her son's monument—not only to himself but to her struggle.

Yolanda's health, already bad, got much worse. She had developed bleeding ulcers and arthritis and her blood pressure was touching the stratosphere. The drugs they gave her at the family clinic weren't working, and she couldn't really afford them anyway. Nor would she let me pay for them—not with a son who was doing so well. And though her son did help out with the mortgage, she was doing his laundry and cooking his meals, too. Yolanda was cracking under the pressure, but everyone assumed she was still the rock she'd always been. Since her American doctors seemed incapable of doing anything but prescribing medication she could not afford, I convinced her to let me take us both to Tlacolula so she could see her family's longtime doctor, Salvador.

Yolanda's father met us at Salvador's tiny clinic in the middle of downtown Tlacolula, which is a series of one-story clay buildings painted in vibrant primary colors. The old man started the conversation by wondering why the staff could not fetch him a cup of coffee and complaining about his own health. Then, as we waited for Dr. Salvador, he laid into his daughter about her "job" and the neighbors' talking, how hard it all was on him, and so on. His eyes shifting from her to me and back every second, Papi's jaw didn't stop for fifteen minutes. It was only after we were told the doctor would see us that I noticed a sign even I could translate: *Clinico Psychológico*. Dr. Salvador was, among other things, a psychiatrist.

Dr. Salvador spent the next hour doing what good doctors do: he listened. Yolanda finally unloaded her true feelings from Boston that day, watching the commencement speaker—the honorable chairman of the World Bank—admonish the nation's young elite not to forget the dispossessed, the poor, the forgotten, and then seeing her son—one of *them*, now—walk up on the stage and collect his diploma as his name was announced over the speakers. What she'd felt was indifference. Salvador nodded his head, asked her if she cried a lot. All the time, she said. Then he took her blood pressure and told her she'd have to stay in Mexico for a few weeks, relax, or she would surely drop dead of stress as her mother had in the marketplace down the street thirty years earlier.

Of course she couldn't stay. We left Oaxaca the next morning so Yolanda could get back to work. When I'd tell acquaintances that Yolanda was back on the street, the reaction was mixed. Women wanted to kill the son; men didn't seem too fazed. I guess we expect our mothers to sacrifice everything for us because we know we hold their dreams. Still, the more I thought about it, the more I sided with the women.

I saw Yolanda the other day. She has a new job cleaning the homeless people's feces from the children's playground on Santa Monica Beach. Her hopes and dreams have passed on to her youngest son, a pudgy freshman at San Jose State. She told me they want $4,000 a year to feed him up there, an essential not covered by scholarships. I imagine she can feed her entire family on tortillas and *ropa vieja** for a very small fraction of that. Adrianne is still living at home, still running up bills that she expects her parents to pay. She's got one of those hip new phones that Verizon comes out with every year, the ones they generously make available for just $199, provided you commit yourself to paying them whatever they tell you to over the next twenty-four months or so. Yolanda's oldest son still works at Raytheon, though they've been cutting his hours and making him work at night. Even with the war on full throttle, the company is outsourcing what it can. Rogelio Jr. is considering going back to graduate school at Stanford or M.I.T. This will probably cost north of a hundred thousand, but there are loans available at great rates and he can even fold his living expenses into those loans, so it sounds like a terrific deal.

Yolanda has never had a credit card in her life, though she could easily get one. The only debt she and her husband have ever allowed themselves is the mortgage, which she pays religiously. She does not buy Suze Orman's books or listen to Dave Ramsey's radio show. If

---

*Literally, "old clothes." A dish of eggs and inexpensive meat.

you told her that she could save money by spending, she would laugh at you. If you tried to convince her that a new Cadillac was an investment or that a Chevrolet pickup truck meant freedom, she would know you were one of the crazies. Yolanda knows what her children and what many of us do not know: that dreams are built upon sacrifice. They cannot be purchased on credit or with any softer currency.

Last year I moved to Hollywood. I don't get to see Yolanda very often, but I think of her every time I hear the phrase *American Dream* tossed about by a journalist or an advertiser. I see her, at the end of her long day, sitting on the tear-stained steps of the Cadillac Hotel, watching the young Americans with their new mountain bikes charged on platinum Visa cards glide past without direction, while the bohemian yuppies slither around the side streets in their leased BMWs and Lexus sedans, hip and forever lost. I'm sure they barely notice the pudgy Mexican woman with the leathery face wearing the M.I.T. sweatshirt, if at all. But I know that she notices them. It has taken nearly fifty years, but she knows their secret now. Their dream is a mirage.

Solutions

"The issue which has swept down the centuries and which will have
to be fought sooner or later is the people versus the banks."

– Lord Acton

Maxed Out was shot over the course of a year. After we wrapped, a number of images stayed with me, like Christopher Dodd's pendulum swinging in an unknown direction, but also the image of Dodd and his fellow senators watching that pendulum, their faces frozen in blank half smiles, as though hapless observers. The myths lingered as well, none more so than the notion of endless debt surfing. Every one of the people I interviewed, from Lynn to Sheila to Peter, used credit as a means to buy time, to get by to the next month, not realizing that they were only falling further and further behind, the bear trap closing tighter around their ankles. I recently have heard both Dick Cheney and John Snow, the treasury secretary, repeat this myth with a new twist. They claim that the nation's chronic deficits are no problem as long as they remain under a certain percentage of GNP (excluding the costs of the Iraq war and future entitlements, naturally) and that current levels are historically sustainable. What they fail to mention, of course, is that the national *debt* is cumulative. When you have to keep borrowing to pay

231

James D. Scurlock

off old debts, the wave gets bigger and more treacherous. The law of compounding works against you, not for you. You are not borrowing time but losing options.*

The notion of a "fiscal straitjacket" appeals to a lot of conservatives because it seems like an easy way to reduce the size of government. But if our leaders are really trying to "starve the beast," as one prominent thinker calls it, they should have the decency to keep their hands off Social Security and Medicare—programs that are funded by workers and promised to them. If we can keep the cost of war off-budget, surely we can keep these "trust funds" protected from politicians, as their creators intended.

Another whopper is that the foreigners who continue to support our debt habit are expressing confidence in the strength of the United States economy. This is certainly one interpretation. Another is that we are desperate. Japan's treasury pays about one-fifth the interest rate that we do on their national debt. So perhaps in the global scheme of things we have simply become the planet's most profitable sub-prime borrower, its "preferred customer.' The longer we surf, of course, the higher the premiums they will fetch from us.

But the global economy remains a distant intangible to most of us, myself included. What stays with me are the stories I've listened to, the faces of the people I've met, and even the images of those I never knew, like the resignation in Yvonne Pavey's face as she drives her blue Mercury Tracer down the boat ramp, into the Ohio River. She was not only a grandmother; she and her husband were raising her disabled daughter's son, Aaron. In Jon's last e-mail, he apologized for not being able to attend the film's premiere because Aaron had required some medical attention due to the stress he's been through and taking care of his family is a higher priority than seeing himself on the silver screen. I worry about Jon and Kathi.

*Cheney and Snow should remember that the federal government now pays more in interest than for education, health care, and homeland security combined.

They've been through two traumas now—Kathi's sister passed away a month or so before Yvonne's car was found—and with Kathi's father out of work, things aren't looking up. Jon still ends each e-mail with a hopeful bit of scripture. They put their faith in God, but I've seen how the bear trap works and I know that he and Kathi will need to be vigilant to stay out of it.

So who killed Yvonne? That's the question I keep asking myself. True, she signed up for the credit cards, but if someone sent you free samples of cigarettes every day of the week, would you start smoking at some point? I sympathize with Jon; I don't think that *suicide* tells the whole story. Something besides an inner torment is driving those in financial trouble to commit suicide at an alarming rate. I learned early on that if I met anyone with at least one ankle in the bear trap, they had considered suicide seriously enough to know how they'd do it. My own uncle killed himself when I was in my early teens, and though I cannot be certain this was debt-related, I know he died broke and living with his parents. Unlike Trisha's daughter, however, my uncle did not spread his credit card bills out on the bed before doing the deed, so I'll never know for sure.

So, was Yvonne's death really the work of a vast financial conspiracy? There is plenty of evidence to that effect and there is no lack of individuals and institutions to implicate, but any conclusion is irrelevant so long as she remains dead and the system that entrapped her remains in place. My concern is the millions of Americans I never met. The silent ones who, like Lynn, believe they are alone, who have become convinced of the greatest myth—that their problems represent a personal, moral failing and that the world is better off without them. If we believe that these lives are worth saving, then we must consider Yvonne's death in a broader context and we must learn from it.

I can't remember who first told me that credit ratings had nothing to do with income, but it remains one of the most shocking elements of how the modern credit industry sets us up for failure. If there is any simple solution for the ills I've written about, it is fixing this loophole. Had Yvonne been limited by her minimum-wage income, she never could have received one credit card, much less six or seven. Ditto for Janne's son and Trisha's daughter. The issue isn't that credit card companies are allowed to market their wares on campus or anywhere else for that matter—the issue is giving credit to people who have no ability to repay it. If an unemployed student or housewife walked into a bank and applied for a personal loan at a reasonable interest rate, the bankers would quickly show them the door. Yet, that same student or housewife can get a high-interest credit card loan in the six figures without even asking for it. This has not only ensnared millions of Americans in the bear trap, it has made life prohibitively expensive for those of us who have resisted using credit.

What the current credit scoring system *does* take into account, of course, is how well an individual has managed to make payments in the past. There are a number of obvious flaws in this system. One, the debtor could be scrounging from friends and relatives to cough up the minimum payment every month, disguising their true ability to pay. Two, they could be "surfing"—paying off their bills with more, high-interest credit. And three, their financial situation could change dramatically within a short period of time. When I went from being an investor to being a documentary filmmaker, my income plummeted, yet the credit lines on my Citibank MasterCard and my Delta Skymiles American Express card more than doubled. Fair Isaac Corporation needs to change its algorithms* and banks need to maintain their accounts with the same vigilance that insurance companies monitor their drivers. In other words, no more liar's loans.

---

*The three major credit agencies have rolled out a replacement for FICO called the Vantagescore, but it will probably be no better. As a vice president of Experian told the *New York Times*, "I wouldn't say that consumers don't matter, but getting lender adoption [of Vantagescore] is the sharp end of the spear."

Will the financial industry reform the credit rating system on their own? I doubt it, though I agree with the bankruptcy attorney Edgar Rothchild: When the banks and credit card companies realize that outlawing bankruptcy isn't going to stop people from going broke, they're going to have to rethink their strategy. What *is* certain is that Congress probably won't compel them to do anything, which borders on criminal negligence. When Yvonne fell on hard times, there was no generous campaign contributor to bail her out with a low-interest loan, nor could she expect to have her credit file cleaned up before it reached her husband's desk. The two-tiered system we've tolerated for too long has shielded our representatives in Congress from appreciating both the magnitude and the urgency of the problem facing middle-class Americans. Janis suggested that congressmen should be forced to live on the minimum wage and that Dick Cheney should have to go to the county hospital for treatment. While I don't see these ideas being put to the test, it's easy to appreciate the sentiment. Why should Elizabeth Warren be the only lobbyist for American families on important issues like bankruptcy reform? And why should the financial industry be allowed to treat those in power any differently than ordinary Americans?

Should corporations, which were originally chartered to have the same rights as individuals, be allowed to keep those rights, e.g., bankruptcy, while living, breathing citizens are stripped of them?* If Congress doesn't want families to have the option of getting out from under, corporations like Enron and WorldCom shouldn't enjoy that privilege, either. Executives who have the foresight to pay themselves millions of dollars before their companies tank shouldn't be the only ones allowed a fresh start.

In the end, Yvonne was threatened and harassed by an army of faceless voices who were allowed to share everything they knew

*A recent study in the US provides one answer. The majority of Americans under 40 don't think that it is possible to regulate the financial industry.

about her, including her address, her phone number, the names of her relatives and neighbors, as well as her entire financial history. If consumers are to have a fair chance, the practice of information-sharing needs to be curtailed, not expanded, and consumers must have a bona fide right to opt out. The current system only allows consumers to opt out of receiving solicitations; it does nothing to guarantee an individual's constitutional right to privacy or protect them from being forced to walk the plank by inexperienced collectors. Needless to say, the government should respect the spirit of the law and not join in the game by purchasing private information from the credit bureaus. Nor should agencies like the Internal Revenue Service be allowed to share personal information with credit bureaus or debt collectors.

Rather than guaranteeing the profits of private banks through student loan and mortgage guarantees, the federal government should make a commitment to providing public goods without setting its citizens up to fail. Yvonne's gambling addiction was fed, in part, by the county's need for additional tax revenue, which led to the approval of Caesars Palace. In theory, casinos are a win-win for communities, increasing tax revenues without raising taxes. But it's time to admit the reality: that those additional tax revenues are offset by social costs that are either picked up by local communities or else allowed to fester unchecked. My grandfather used to say that if something sounds too good to be true, it probably is. Building more casinos is no more the answer to poverty than building more pawnshops, which, by the way, tend to sprout up around casinos.

That being said, we have a lot to gain by regulating banks in the same way that casinos and pawnshops are now regulated. If the interest rates and fees on Yvonne's credit cards had been capped the same way a casino's odds are set or a pawnbroker's rates are limited, Yvonne's $12,000 in debt would never have ballooned to $50,000 in a few years; in fact, the credit card companies probably would have thought twice about sending her all of those generous offers in the first place.

It's unfortunate that, over the last generation, regulation has been equated with socialism and deregulation has been mistaken for freedom. The truth is that all of the checks and balances that have disappeared over the past thirty years—from usury laws to limits on interstate banking—were created as a result of banking disasters; they were not the cause of them. The same is true of the uniform bankruptcy code, which resulted from the financial panic of the late eighteenth century and was designed primarily to protect merchants and, by default, the economy as a whole. The government has a long history of recognizing the uniqueness of credit and attaching reasonable limits to the ease with which creditors can take advantage of their customers, as the Bankers Training video observed. This is not because every Congress previous to the past ten has been a bunch of bleeding-heart commies. It's because we've learned that very bad things happen when powerful corporations are allowed to have their way, unchecked, with the rest of us. Is it a coincidence that the American people lack faith* in a Congress that has been asleep at the wheel for three decades, that has allowed the industry to set down the rules of the game, that has bought the myth that what's good for banking profits is always good for the people?

To resolve our crisis of confidence, faith must be restored in our government. We cannot continue to rob Social Security and Medicare and pretend that we're not. We cannot decide that hundreds of billions of dollars in war costs simply don't exist. We cannot believe the big lie: that as long as we can get credit tomorrow, we are buying time, when exactly the opposite is true.

But we must also have an honest dialogue about where to set

---

*As of this writing, Congress's approval rating is hovering around 28 percent.

the bar in this country. Every time a president brags about the increases in home ownership and college attendance, we should balance those statistics with the corresponding increases in foreclosures and student loan defaults. And it is time to create a new metric in order to judge how many middle-class Americans are joining the ranks of the poor. The poverty line is an absurd invention of the 1960s, based solely on the price of food.* If we are to honestly measure how the middle class is holding up, we must add increasingly costly essentials like housing, insurance, and health care to the mix. Once a family slips below the existing poverty line, it is already much too late.

It is impossible for anyone to say when the pendulum will reverse direction, bring us back to a place of greater equilibrium between the right of the individual to enjoy life, liberty, and the pursuit of happiness and the right of the banking industry to sell money for profit. Until then, I'm convinced we will see many more Yvonne Paveys. As the ever-philosophical Dee Hock observes in his memoirs, "If we choose to engage in . . . economic violence, social violence, spiritual violence and psychic violence, how can we expect to live free of physical violence?"

---

*The poverty line is defined as three times the cost of feeding a family of four. The UK poverty line is defined as less than 60 percent of contemporary median net disposable income.

Resources

The following organizations provide free, confidential, independent and impartial financial advice:

Payplan
Payplan is one of the UK's leading debt advice agencies and provides free debt management plans with on-line payment tracking. Individual voluntary arrangements are available with no up-front fees as well as free, impartial, confidential advice on all debt-related issues.

Call 0800 917 7823 or visit www.payplan.com

National Debtline

National Debtline provides free, independent, confidential and impartial advice by telephone in England, Wales and Scotland. It gives expert advice on dealing with debts and provides a free self-help pack.

Call 0808 808 4000 or visit www.nationaldebtline.co.uk

Citizens Advice Bureau

The Citizens Advice Bureau (CAB) service is an independent charity which provides free, confidential and impartial advice on a wide range of problems. There are over 2,800 outlets throughout the United Kingdom.

To find your nearest CAB, look in your local phone book or visit www.citizensadvice.org.uk.

AdviceUK

AdviceUK is a trade association for over 1000 information and advice centres. About 300 centres provide debt advice.

To find your nearest advice centre call AdviceUK on 020 7407 4070, visit www.adviceuk.org.uk or look in the Yellow Pages under 'Counselling and advice'.

For agencies in Northern Ireland contact AdviceNI on 028 9054 5919 or visit www.adviceni.net

Consumer Credit Counselling Service (CCCS)

The CCCS is a charity funded by the financial services industry providing free, independent support.

Call 0800 138 1111 or visit www.cccs.co.uk

The Institute of Money Advisers (IMA)

The IMA gives details of your nearest adviser for people in England and Wales.

Call 0845 094 2384.

Those in Scotland can contact Money Advice Scotland on 0141 572 0237 or visit www.moneyadvicescotland.org.uk

Community Legal Service (CLS)

Community Legal Service Direct provides free quality legal help and information. You can find a solicitor or legal adviser in your area, link to the right place on the best advice sites in the UK, see if you are eligible for legal aid or view legal information leaflets. Information is available in English, Welsh, Arabic, Bengali, Chinese, Gujarati, Hindi, Punjabi, Turkish and Urdu.

Visit www.clsdirect.org.uk